baby's
first year

the
netmums

guide to being a new mum

with Hollie Smith

headline

The right of Netmums Limited to be identified as the Author of
the Work has been asserted by them in accordance with the
Copyright, Designs and Patents Act 1988.

First published in 2009 by
HEADLINE PUBLISHING GROUP

1

Cataloguing in Publication Data is available from the British Library

Trade paperback ISBN 978 0 7553 1801 8

Typeset in Clearface Regular by Palimpsest Book Production Limited,
Grangemouth, Stirlingshire

Printed and bound in Great Britain by
Clays Ltd, St Ives plc

HEADLINE PUBLISHING GROUP
An Hachette UK Company
338 Euston Road
London NW1 3BH

www.headline.co.uk
www.hachette.co.uk

Contents

Introduction

What a year this will be for you! By the time it's over your beautiful, tiny, vulnerable baby might be able to climb the stairs, eat finger foods, scribble with a crayon, laugh along with you when you play games together and maybe even say 'Mummy'. There is no other year in a human being's life in which so many enormous developments take place.

This year will be the most amazing, enormous, terrifying, exhausting, earth-shattering, shocking, wonderful, magical year of your life. And those words are not just my words, they are words used by many, many Netmums members to describe the journey you have just embarked on. The incredible part is that it can actually be all of those things *at the same time!*

And you will grow from being a new mum to being an experienced mum. You will face situations, dilemmas and decisions you have never faced before. You will have times when you think being a mum is the most amazing thing you have ever done and you will have times when you wish you could have your old life back. There will be times when it all seems so hard you wonder if you can cope at all. But you will. You won't be the perfect mum because that just isn't possible, as many of us have learned the hard way. The first thing to learn is that your baby doesn't need perfection from you. Your baby just wants you – the real you – just the way you are.

I am delighted to be able to bring you this book to guide you through every stage of this special year. You'll find it's full of useful information gleaned from the experts but, most importantly, it also has many wonderful contributions from mums who have been through this first year and are pleased to pass on a few of the things they learned along the way.

This book, like Netmums itself, is not going to tell you what you should do or shouldn't do with your baby. Instead, it's about giving you the background knowledge and emotional support you need to help you believe in yourself and to trust your own instinct. And it's about giving you a whole bookful of mum friends who will share the ups and downs with you and let you know that you are never alone. And, if you ever find you need a friend to talk about your experiences of motherhood with, do come along to the Netmums website where you will find us, along with lots of other mums, sharing the ups and downs of our lives. You're guaranteed a warm and friendly welcome.

Siobhan Freegard
Founder, Netmums

Meet the Team

Hollie Smith
Hollie Smith is a journalist and mum of two young daughters. She has written about family, health and women's issues for magazines such as *Woman*, *Best* and *Red*, and for newspapers such as the *Daily Mail*, the *Daily Mirror*, the *Express* and *The Times*. When not writing and being a mum, she finds cycling, singing and the odd glass of red wine give her some release from the stress of those two things! A member of Netmums for the past five years, she is a firm believer in the importance of friendship, support and solidarity among mums.

Louise Cremonesini
Louise Cremonesini qualified as an adult nurse in 1993 and worked for five years in adult intensive care before training as a specialist children's nurse and spending seven years in paediatric intensive care at Great Ormond Street and the Royal Brompton hospitals. She then undertook a BA (hons) degree in public health and embarked on a career as a health visitor for Ealing Primary Care Trust. In September 2009 she will begin studying for an MSc in child protection.

David Cremonesini
David Cremonesini studied medicine at Oxford University and St George's Hospital Medical School in London, and has been working in paediatrics since

1997. He spent two years at the John Radcliffe Hospital in Oxford where he developed an interest in respiratory paediatrics and allergy. He is now a general paediatric and neonates consultant at a hospital in the West Midlands.

Louise and David are married and have a two-year-old daughter, Amelia.

Getting Started

What your newborn needs

Aim to get the essentials lined up in good time for your baby's arrival. Bear in mind that you need the basics in place before the birth, but everything else is optional – you can pick them up as and when you decide you need them. Opinions vary wildly among parents about what's useful and what's useless, so if you're planning to splash out on one of the larger pieces of equipment, ask around first to see if it's really worth it or not.

You can't do without . . .

Nappies: New babies get through a surprising number – up to ten or even more each day is not unusual at first – so have a good supply ready, whether disposable or the more eco-friendly, washable sort, which come in several different designs. For these, you'll need a nappy bucket and liners. You'll also want a job lot of cotton wool or wipes, and a barrier and/or nappy-rash cream. (For more on the pros and cons of each sort of nappy, see p. 35.)

Some clothing: Your nursery drawers may be overflowing with beautiful newborn-baby outfits bought as gifts, but the truth is that for small babies, stretchy, washable cotton sleepsuits with front-fastening poppers are the most comfortable and practical option, day and night (you'll be amazed how often they get dirty and need changing). Vests provide an important extra layer when the weather's chilly and, if hot, can be worn on their own. You'll need six to 12 of each. Newborns' poo is usually runny and often leaks, and milky vomiting is common, so it's not unusual to get through several changes in a day – and you may not get the chance to keep on top of the laundry. If you've got an average baby, go for 0–3 month sizes, rather than 'newborn' – they may look a bit baggy and long in the arm and leg for a while, but she'll grow into them before you know it. Babies need to be kept warm, so have a couple of soft cardigans. Socks won't be necessary if she's living in sleepsuits, which are generally enclosed at the feet. Otherwise, you'll need them to keep her toes warm outside, or under trousers. They also make effective scratch mitts, which can help if your baby has a habit of scratching her face. Some appropriate outdoor wear, depending on the time of year, will also be essential. If there's anything resembling a chill in the air, she'll need a lightweight but warm hat, a coat or all-in-one suit, and mittens (although these do tend to fall off). In warm weather, or whenever the sun's out, she'll need a wide-brimmed hat and/or a suitable parasol or shade for the buggy to keep her well protected from the sun. Bootees, though cute, are generally a nuisance because they tend to fall off and get lost all the time. Rigid-soled shoes are not a good idea until she is walking because a baby's feet are extremely delicate and vulnerable to damage. If you do put your baby in any type of footwear, make sure the shoes are made from a very flexible material, such as wool or ultra-soft leather, and that they're the right size – even fabric shoes can quickly become too tight for a growing baby's feet.

A car seat (if you intend to take her anywhere in a car): Hospital staff won't let you leave without one of these if you're driving, and the law states that you must use one when transporting your baby in a car. Safety experts advise against ever buying one from an unknown second-hand source, just in case it has been damaged in an accident. It's also important to buy a seat that's appropriate for your car. You may find it worthwhile to practise installing the seat in your car, and taking it out, before the birth.

Something for her to sleep in: It's perfectly OK to put your baby in a cot from birth, but something smaller, such as a Moses basket or crib, is a popular option for the first few months, mainly because a smaller unit is more portable than a cot, and provides a cosier sleeping environment. If you're planning to have more than one baby, one of these alternatives may be a worthwhile purchase – or you may prefer to borrow one. You could use a carrycot in the first few months, if one comes with your travel system, although you may need to buy a firmer mattress than the one provided – always check the manufacturer's instructions. If your cot, crib or basket is second-hand, it's recommended that you buy a new mattress for safety reasons. (There's more about this on p. 32.)

Some bedding: You'll need several cotton sheets and a couple of lightweight cellular blankets. Alternatively, you may prefer to try a baby sleeping bag, which many parents swear by. A sleeping bag can be used safely from birth, as long as you've got the right size. They're not suitable for premature babies.

A method of transportation: You won't get far without some means of taking your baby with you! Baby carriers come in a huge range of types and designs, from simple lightweight buggies to three-in-one travel systems. One parent's needs vary greatly from another's, but when you're choosing, bear in mind how comfortable the buggy is to push (is it the right height and weight?), how transportable and/or collapsible (for when you need to fold it to put in the car or take on public transport) and how much space it's going to take up at home – you should probably take measurements to make sure you will be able to get it in and out of your front door, especially if you're investing in a double buggy. Make sure it comes with a weather-proof cover, which is essential. Do consider looking for the sort of pram that offers an inward view of the world rather than an outward one (and many designs these days can be adapted to do either). It's more comforting for a very young baby to see your face rather than a confusing bombardment of images from the fast-moving outside world! You may prefer to venture out with your baby settled in a front carrier or sling. These are suitable for the first couple of months, and are a lovely way of keeping her close to you. They're also a good way for Dad to get a nice cuddle. Bear in mind that when transporting a baby in a sling, you'll have nowhere to put her down if you're planning to stay anywhere for a while.

Something to change her on: A lightweight, wipe-clean changing mat is really all you need at home for when she needs a nappy change, although you can get by with nothing more than a towel. Changing units can make an attractive and practical addition to a nursery, but are by no means essential. If you can't afford one or don't have the space, you won't be missing out.

A bag and a portable changing mat: You'll need something big enough to take the many bits and pieces that you now can't possibly leave home without – but you don't need to splash out on a specially marketed bag for new mums. An ordinary rucksack or roomy tote will do. A small, portable, wipe-clean changing mat is useful, although, again, a towel will suffice.

Some soft towels: You don't need a special baby towel to wrap her up in and dry her after a wash or bath – although the ones with the little hoods do look cute, and are good for keeping her head warm – but if your family towels are a bit rough, you might want to invest in some nice, soft, new ones.

Bottles, bottlebrushes and a sterilising unit: You'll need these only if you're going to bottle feed, or attempt to express your breast milk a bit later on, in which case you might want to buy a manual or electric breast pump. Some mums like to have these things at home from the start in case of problems, even if they plan to breastfeed, but be warned – doing so may affect your motivation to breastfeed exclusively for as long as possible!

Breastpads: To spare your blushes when your boobs leak!

A basic medical kit: Containing infant paracetamol and/or infant ibuprofen (see the section on antipyretics in the Health A–Z at the back of the book for more information on these), and a thermometer.

You might decide to get . . .

A baby listening device: These aren't strictly essential because most mums and dads develop finely tuned hearing when it comes to hearing their new baby cry – unless you have a very big house, or you're likely to be staying in one. But they do offer huge reassurance, especially to first-timers, and allow you to relax more after bedtime.

A baby bath: These tend to be bulky and are useful for a couple of months only, after which you can wash your baby very well in the family bath – you'll need a non-slip mat or a baby bath seat to help you keep her steady. Meanwhile, the basin (cover the taps with a towel) or a large washing-up bowl are good alternatives. In the early weeks, she won't really need a bath at all and you can 'top and tail' her (see p. 36). Although they're available, you certainly don't need a special bowl for the cotton wool – any clean plastic one will do fine.

Something to absorb spills: A bib will take up the worst of the excess milk, dribble and vomit, but multipacks of muslins are generally considered a better buy for the early months. As well as protecting clothes (yours as well as hers) during feeds, muslins can aid discreet public breastfeeding, act as makeshift sun protectors and be used to mop up a multitude of messes.

Baby nail scissors: It's important to keep her finger and toenails trimmed (otherwise she can scratch herself) but many parents find this a tricky task, and prefer to use their own fingers or even teeth rather than scissors, after first softening her nails in the bath.

A room thermometer: It's vital to keep your baby at roughly the right temperature (16–20°C is recommended). Overheating is one of the risk factors linked to cot death. Room thermometers are often included free of charge with cots and bedding by the manufacturers, or given away by baby magazines. Otherwise, you can order one from the Foundation for the Study of Infant Deaths (FSID). (Details are in the appendix on p. 340.)

A dummy (also known as a pacifier or comforter): This is controversial. Some experts warn against dummies, others say they are an acceptable way to calm a baby. Either way, it's recommended that you don't introduce one for around four weeks if you're breastfeeding, to give the feeding regime a good chance to become established. (For more information about dummies, see pp. 28 and 268.)

Baby toiletries: They may smell lovely, but these really aren't necessary for small babies, and certainly aren't to be recommended for those with dry, sore or very sensitive skin. Plain warm water is all you need, along with two small, soft sponges – one for each of your baby's 'ends'. You may want to have some olive oil or aqueous cream on standby for use on cradle cap and/or dry skin.

A cot mobile or activity centre: These provoke different views. Some babies can soothe themselves by 'fixating' on visual cues, so a well-placed mobile, hung from the ceiling slightly to the side of her cot and/or changing area, may be calming for her. The flipside is that they can prove a distraction when you want her to go to sleep.

Toys: Your baby will no doubt get some of these as gifts, so you may not want to buy any yourselves. In any case, she doesn't need anything more than conversation and cuddles with you to keep her entertained in the early weeks and months.

A baby gym: These are a great way to keep your baby safely entertained after the age of about six weeks, when you need to put her down for a few minutes and get on with something else. Some more sensitive babies may find them a bit overwhelming to begin with.

Breast pump: If you hope to breastfeed for a while, you may want to have one of these at the ready in case you want or need to give her a bottle but don't want her to miss out on the benefits of breast milk. However, they're expensive: it's worth bearing in mind that some mums find hand expressing even more effective; and that electric breast pumps are available for hire. For more on expressing, see p. 67.

A bouncy chair: One of these is useful for keeping your baby safe and reasonably upright for short periods of time, so she can get a good view of what's going on around her, which she can't while lying on the floor. Bouncy chairs are easily moved around, so you can take her into different rooms with you. Some play music or vibrate, which adds to the fun. Be warned, though – if she comes to like the vibrate setting, you may find she'll require it every time, which could be a problem if you run out of batteries or you're not at home and don't have the chair handy. It's also vital for safety reasons that you keep chairs on the floor and don't put them on a high surface, because they may fall off.

A book like this one: Every new parent needs a reliable source of reference, after all!

Buy, Borrow or Bypass?

A quick poll of Netmums to see which baby buys (other than the really obvious ones) they thought were essential, and which weren't, revealed the following results.

Must-haves:

- Muslins
- Simple sleepsuits
- Baby sleeping bag
- Sling
- Baby gym or bouncing seat

Don't-bother-withs:

- Nappy bin
- Cot bumper
- Expensive, heavy, complicated travel systems
- Baby toiletries
- Changing unit

A matter of opinion:

- Baby bath
- Changing mat
- Moses basket
- Special towels
- Baby nest (sometimes known as a doughnut, these are inflatable rings that provide a cosy place for babies to sit in safely).

The First Month

Welcome to your first month of motherhood

Congratulations – you're a mum! The long, difficult haul of pregnancy and birth is over and your reward for sticking it out is a wonderful new baby, and the precious gift of motherhood. To say it takes time adapting to such a challenging new role is an understatement. For many new parents, this early period can be as bewildering, scary and exhausting as it is joyous.

The first six to eight weeks of your baby's life is a learning period – you don't have to worry about anything other than getting through it as best you can. Take things super-slow, accept whatever help is offered and concentrate on getting your strength back, and on getting to know your baby. This is, after all, your 'babymoon' . . .

Health, Growth and Development

Baby milestones

In the first few days of her life, your baby will typically:

- Show a 'Moro response' by throwing out her arms and arching her back when startled by a sudden movement or noise.
- Display a 'rooting' reflex, turning towards a touch on the cheek, or the side of the mouth, and suck instinctively when offered a nipple or teat.

- Demonstrate a number of newborn, reflex behaviours – she will take steps if held upright with her feet on a firm surface, bend her legs under her body when placed on her tummy, as if trying to crawl, and grasp hard on something placed close to her palm. She won't be able to do these things after a few days, and will need to re-learn them later on in her development.
- Be sensitive to light and sound, turning towards a major source of light and appearing startled by a sudden loud noise.
- Be able to focus on and see things up to 20–25cm away, showing particular interest in your face, or anything with a sharp outline or a bright, bold colour.
- Move her arms and legs.
- Gaze up at the adult holding her.
- Vocalise her feelings and needs by crying in a number of different ways.
- Have a sense of smell and taste.

Your baby's medical checks

During the first month after birth, you'll have the support of a network of health professionals who are charged with keeping a close eye on all new babies and their parents. For the first ten days after birth (although this may vary, depending on where you live), you and your baby will be under the care of a community midwife and you should receive several visits from her during this period. The precise number depends on your health authority, and your assessed need. You should also be offered a series of checks, tests and treatments for your baby, including:

- Her first full medical once-over, within three days of her birth, carried out by an appropriate healthcare professional. In hospital, before you've been discharged, this is usually a paediatrician or midwife. At home, you'll be visited by a GP. During the head-to-toe examination, your baby will be weighed and her length and head circumference measured, and her overall well-being checked, in particular, her eyes, heart and hips. Boys will have their testes checked.
- A newborn blood spot test (also known as the heel-prick, or Guthrie test), usually carried out at home by your visiting midwife, between five and eight days after the birth. This test, involving a small prick in the heel,

checks for a number of specific inherited conditions that can be successfully treated if diagnosed: phenylketonuria (PKU), which prevents the processing of a substance in food called phenylalanine and, if untreated, could cause a serious mental disability; congenital hypothyroidism (CHT), a lack of the hormone thyroxine, which could lead to serious physical and mental disability; and sickle cell disease (SCD), in which the red blood cells become stuck in the small blood vessels, causing pain, serious infection and even death; cystic fibrosis (CF), which affects the digestive system and lungs, making digestion and breathing difficult and shortening life expectancy; and medium chain acyl-coA dehydrogenase deficiency (MCADD), which causes problems with breaking down fats, leading to serious illness and even death. All these conditions are rare and the vast majority of babies have normal results.

- An automated hearing test, within the first few weeks after birth, while still in hospital, at a clinic, or at home. This is a quick, reliable test of your baby's hearing, and you'll get the results straight away.
- Vitamin K, given either by a single injection or in several doses by mouth. This will be offered to your baby soon after birth, to prevent vitamin K deficiency bleeding (VKDB), which occurs in a very small number of newborn babies. (For more detail on vitamin K and VKDB, see the Health A–Z at the back of the book.)
- In some high risk areas, babies of one month may be offered a BCG injection to protect against tuberculosis, as soon as possible after birth.

Your health visitor

At some point after ten days, your midwife will sign off responsibility and your health visitor will introduce herself. She will make one or more home visits, and provide you with a Personal Child Health Record (often known as the 'red book') in which healthcare professionals, and you, can make a note of all significant health and development information during your child's early years. She will let you know where and when to find your nearest baby clinic – these are run regularly in health centres and GP surgeries and will usually be the place to go for routine tests and immunisations, and for weighing and measuring sessions. They're a good place to meet other parents, although your health visitor may also run a separate postnatal group with the aim of introducing mums to others in the area.

In the past, parents were encouraged to have their babies weighed and measured weekly but it's now considered pointless for this to be done so frequently – it may even cause unnecessary anxiety. So it's recommended that full-term babies are weighed and measured no more than six times in their first year.

When help isn't immediately at hand

If you are in doubt about any aspect of your baby's health (or about your own) and you are unable to see or talk to your midwife, health visitor or GP, you may be able to get the help you need by calling NHS Direct (NHS 24 if you are in Scotland), which offers 24 hour advice. These numbers are listed in the Health A-Z and Useful Addresses appendices at the back of the book – make a note of them and keep it pinned up by the telephone.

It's official: Registering your baby's birth

Don't forget that, by law, you must register your baby's birth within 42 days (or 21 days, if you live in Scotland). You may be able to do this at the hospital before going home, or you may have to visit a register office to do so. There's more information about registering your baby's birth on the website of the General Register Office (see appendix for details).

When you register your baby's birth, you'll be given a birth certificate and a pink registration card, which you'll need to fill in and sign before taking to your doctor's surgery, so that your baby can officially become a patient there. It's a good idea to get this done as soon as possible, just in case your baby needs to see a GP before her first routine check, at around six weeks.

Weird and wonderful: What your newborn baby may look like

Let's face it, newborn babies can be weird-looking little things, but there'll probably be an explanation for any physical oddity you may notice. The main ones are listed below (for more details, see the Health A–Z at the back of the book). If in any doubt about a feature of your baby that seems unusual, you should check with your midwife, health visitor or GP.

Cord stump: The remains of the umbilical cord (the link between the baby and the placenta during pregnancy) will be attached to your baby's tummy for a little while after the birth but shrivels up and drops off within a fortnight or so. In the meantime, it needs to be kept clean and dry, because these stumps are prone to infection. When you wash or bathe it, always be careful to dry the area thoroughly afterwards by gently dabbing it with tissue or a soft, clean towel. Once the stump drops off, it can take another week or so until the area is healed. It's normal for the stump to appear a little weepy during this time, but if you're worried, ask a health professional to check it.

Head: Babies' heads are often a bit misshapen, or 'moulded', at first. They may be slightly pointed, flattened or swollen as a result of birth, particularly if forceps or a ventouse were involved (these can also leave marks, which will fade after a few days), but this will usually be temporary. The bones in a new baby's head are not yet joined together and a careful feel will reveal the fontanelles, two soft spots. The smaller of these closes in about six weeks, the larger in about 18 months.

Eyes: It's common for newborn babies to squint, because they haven't yet learned to control the muscles round the eyes. If the eyes are yellowish, it may indicate jaundice (see Skin, below). Sometimes they may have a crusty discharge, which suggests a mild infection known as sticky eye, which can be treated with frequent bathing of the eye and, if necessary, antibiotic drops. This is not the same as conjunctivitis. (For more details about sticky eye and conjunctivitis, see the Health A–Z at the back of the book.)

Skin: This may well be blotchy, spotty, patchy, dry or uneven in colour. A newborn baby's skin is very sensitive and prone to all sorts of rashes and spots, including milia (milk spots). These tiny white spots, which occur on the nose or cheeks, are harmless and extremely common. It's also common for babies to be slightly jaundiced in the early days because of the immaturity of their livers – this is indicated by a yellowish tinge. In most cases it's harmless, but your midwife will keep a close eye on it. You may also notice traces of vernix (particularly in premature babies), which is the greasy white substance that protects a baby's skin from amniotic fluid in the womb. Don't be tempted to wash it off – any left on the skin after birth will be absorbed naturally, and until then it can help keep the skin moisturised.

Birthmarks: These are also common and they come in many different forms. A red mark may be the result of pressure on the skin during the birth, and this will quickly fade. (For more information about birthmarks, see the Health A–Z at the back of the book.)

Hair: Babies may have plenty of hair or very little at birth. In any case, it's likely to fall out over the coming months, and what grows back may be an entirely different colour or texture. It's not unusual for babies, particularly pre-term babies, to have a fine covering of body hair. This soft fuzz – called lanugo – protected them in the womb, and drops out over time.

Nipples and genitals: These may be swollen due to an overflow of mum's hormones finding its way into the baby. It's just temporary. You may also notice a little blood in a baby girl's nappy, for the same reason. Boys' testicles come down into the scrotum just before birth but, occasionally, one (or, rarely, both) may remain undescended. This is usually temporary, but may sometimes need a small operation to correct later on. Your doctor, midwife or health visitor will be alert to the possibility during routine examinations.

What the netmums say

What newborns look like

I remember when she was born and turning to my husband to say, 'Oh my God, she's got bow legs!' and immediately thinking that she would need surgery. I didn't realise this was entirely normal. She was hairy, too, and had big red blotches on her eyes from the birth and a cone-shaped head and swollen nipples.
Alex from Kings Langley, mum to Niamh, seven months

He didn't look anything like I had imagined he would. He was solid and round, and purple with bruises.
Jen from Chorleywood, mum to Jack, four and Theo, one

Feeding

Breast, the best

You'll most likely have made a decision on how you hope to feed your baby before she was born. The majority of new mums breastfeed initially, and there's no doubt that it offers the best possible start for a baby – in fact, the advice of the Department of Health, based on a comprehensive review of scientific information carried out by the World Health Organisation, is that exclusive breastfeeding is the best way to feed your baby in the first six months of her life.

Almost all women have the physiological wherewithal to make a success of breastfeeding – although a minority may not be able to breastfeed for specific medical reasons – and those who encounter difficulties have a very good chance of getting through them if they persevere, and with the right help. At the outset, breastfeeding can be really hard work, it's true. Your nipples can get extremely sore until they toughen up and while you work out how to get the positioning right, and, in the early weeks, the sheer amount of time that babies want to suckle can be draining. On top of that are the emotional factors – the worry that she's getting enough milk, and the guilt if you don't think she is. Feeding your baby in the best way you can is the top priority for any new mum, so if for one reason or another you're struggling to do so, it can lead to misery.

Once you're over the early hurdles, though, breastfeeding invariably becomes easier, and even, for many mums, a great pleasure. You should be given all the advice and support you need to get started by your midwife or health visitor – if not, there are a number of organisations you can turn to for help (they're listed in the Useful Addresses appendix at the back of the book). You'll also need moral support and plenty of practical help from your partner, and from other close relatives and friends. In particular, you'll need someone who's prepared to take over the bulk of household chores, and bring you sustenance while you're pinned to the sofa for long stretches of time in the early days. So make sure everyone around knows about your decision to breastfeed, and that you've got their backing.

The benefits of breastfeeding

- Breast milk is 100 per cent natural and contains all the nutrients your baby needs. It provides the perfect food and drink for her. It's also free!

- It's easily absorbed and digested so she is less likely to have colic or constipation.

- It's rich in antibodies, which help to protect against infection – research shows that breastfed babies are less likely to develop gastrointestinal and respiratory illnesses, and ear infections.

- It may help to delay the onset of certain allergic conditions, such as eczema.

- Some research suggests that breastfeeding may lower the risk of cot death.

- Mums who breastfeed reduce their chances of developing breast cancer and some ovarian cancers, and osteoporosis (weakening of the bones).

- Breastfeeding helps the uterus contract back to normal in the days after birth, and helps you lose your baby weight because it uses up calories.

- It's ultra-convenient. The milk is on tap, and there's no bottle-washing, sterilising and preparation to worry about, or equipment to lug around when you're out and about. You don't need to venture into a cold kitchen for night feeds, either.

- You get lots of cuddly, skin-to-skin contact with your baby while feeding her.

- Once established and comfortable, breastfeeding gives you the perfect excuse for sitting down and relaxing with your baby for long stretches of time. (And you should make the most of this time with your first – you may not be able to give subsequent babies the luxury of devoting so much time to them when you have older children to tend to!)

Get ready

Be prepared for breastfeeding in good time for the birth by reading up on it, and make sure you have what you'll need in advance – several well-fitting nursing bras, a good supply of breast pads and plenty of loose, comfortable tops that either lift up easily or open at the front. Don't forget to have a good stock of bibs to hand, or better still, a multipack of muslins.

Give them the 'gold top'

For the first few days after birth, the breasts provide a special sort of milk called colostrum. This rich, creamy, yellowish substance is thick with antibodies and nutrients that help provide resistance to infection, so is particularly beneficial.

On the third or fourth day after birth, a new mum's breasts fill up with regular breast milk – be prepared. It can come as rather a surprise to wake up with very tender boobs that feel close to bursting, and most women find there's a certain amount of leakage to cope with, especially at first. You may need a sense of humour and a good supply of breast pads for a while. It can be an extremely uncomfortable period. Make sure you have a bra that's well-fitting and supportive and try a cold or hot pack, available from chemists, to relieve pain. Putting Savoy cabbage leaves in your bra is an old-fashioned remedy that can actually help, although there's no medical evidence to explain why.

Are you sitting comfortably?

Before you begin breastfeeding, make sure you're comfortable and relaxed – not easy at first, admittedly, but you'll get there. You may prefer to hold your baby across your lap – if so, pillows to support your back and arm, and a footstool or pillow to raise your lap and elevate the baby so she's level with your breasts can be a great help. You can buy a special, boomerang-shaped breastfeeding pillow, but the ordinary sort piled up will do fine. Some mums find the rugby ball position works well – holding the baby under your arm with her legs tucked round your body. Others like to breastfeed lying down, especially those with very large breasts, or if they are very sore after birth, particularly after a Caesarean, which can make breastfeeding challenging at first.

Getting the 'latch-on' right

Finding the right positioning and getting your baby to latch on properly is key to getting her to feed well, and avoiding the agony of cracked and sore nipples. It may not come naturally at first – for either baby or mum – but can be mastered with practice and perseverance. Much like having new shoes, you need to accept that your nipples may hurt while they are being 'worn in'. However, extremely sore, cracked or bleeding nipples almost certainly mean you've yet to get the positioning right.

Start with the baby's nose opposite the nipple and allow her head to tilt back. Move her mouth gently across the nipple until she opens it wide – this is known as the rooting reflex. Bring your baby towards the breast quickly, making sure her whole body is closely tucked in, in a straight line, facing yours. Aim the nipple towards the roof of her mouth and allow her to get a big mouthful of breast – you may need to support your boob underneath with your hand to guide it in. She's latched on correctly if her chin is resting firmly against the breast and her lower lip is rolled outwards. You'll know when the milk is on its way because you'll feel a tingling release as it gathers behind the nipple and areola (the dark skin around the nipple), and you'll know when she's feeding because she'll be taking big, rhythmic gulps. You may also notice that her ears are wiggling slightly!

If she isn't latched on properly and she obviously doesn't have enough nipple in her mouth, start again – don't tug the nipple out as if it was a cork from a bottle, though, or it will hurt like hell. Break the suction cleanly by inserting a finger into the corner of her mouth.

A two-course meal

Let your baby feed for as long as she wants. Milk comes out of the breast in two stages – first the thirst-quenching foremilk, and secondly the fat-rich hindmilk. So always let her empty the first breast you offer before moving her on to the second. You can tell when a breast is empty simply by the look and feel of it, or by squeezing it slightly to see what's left. She may not empty the second breast as well, so be sure to offer that one first at the next feed. Some mums find it helpful to put a safety pin into the bra strap on the side they need to start with, to help them remember.

Supply and demand

These days, it's recommended that babies are allowed to 'demand feed', which means offering them the breast whenever, and for however long, they want. It's the best system for feeding because breast milk is made on a supply and demand basis, so the more you feed her, the more milk you'll make, which is why, if you stop for any length of time, it can be hard to start again.

Don't be surprised, in the early days, by just how demanding your baby may be. A lot of new mums are rather overwhelmed by how often they find themselves whipping their boobs out and how long they must sit there feeding. Sometimes your baby may not even be that hungry, just hankering for the comfort of a suck. This is just a temporary phase – after six to eight weeks she will generally settle into a more widely spaced and regular feeding pattern, as she becomes adept at suckling and so can take what she needs in a shorter time, and as her stomach capacity grows.

Feeding yourself

You don't need to eat especially well to ensure your production of milk, but it's advisable to eat a balanced diet. Try to eat at regular intervals throughout the day. It's recommended that breastfeeding mums consume 400 or so calories a day more than they would normally, and the Food Standards Agency (FSA) now recommends that all women take 10mg a day of a vitamin D supplement while breastfeeding.

You'll need, and will probably want, to drink lots of fluid, preferably water, since breastfeeding can be dehydrating. But it's wise to keep an eye on your intake of caffeine and alcohol, because small quantities of these things can filter through to the milk and may affect your baby. That doesn't mean you need to be a saint – a glass or two of wine a couple of times a week, or three or four small cups of coffee each day, are fine, particularly if they're going to relax you and help to motivate you to keep on breastfeeding. Just try to leave a few hours between consuming them and feeding your baby.

A history of allergies

Current government advice is that women with a history of peanut allergy, or of an allergic condition, such as eczema or asthma, in the immediate family, should aim to avoid eating peanuts and peanut products while breastfeeding (and during pregnancy) because it increases the likelihood of a peanut allergy developing in the child. However, recent publications from allergy groups and the American Academy of Paediatrics have highlighted that there's very little evidence to support this, and in fact, there is some evidence to suggest early exposure may be beneficial. Research is ongoing and so, currently, it's not clear whether or not it's important for high-risk mums to avoid peanuts while breastfeeding.

One thing doctors do agree on is that breastfeeding seems to help protect against asthma, eczema and allergies, and so exclusive breastfeeding for the first six months is *particularly* advisable if there is a family history of these problems. If breastfeeding is not possible, you may be able to give your baby the same hydrolysed formula milk that is given to babies with an allergy to cow's milk (see Problems with formula feeding, p. 27), so it's worth discussing it with your GP.

Foods that may be a problem

Some babies seem to be affected by the food their mums eat while breastfeeding. Likely culprits include spicy dishes, vegetables such as cabbage, broccoli, onions and sprouts, and acidic citrus fruits or juice – if your baby is excessively windy, uncomfortable or colicky, the condition may be eased by a little attention to your diet.

Rarely, a baby may have an allergic reaction to something her mum has eaten, resulting in symptoms such as a rash or diarrhoea. Common allergens include cow's milk protein, wheat, eggs, nuts and soy. You'll need to take advice from your GP if you suspect your baby is affected in this way.

Burping the baby

After a feed you can help to bring up any excess air your baby may have swallowed, which could otherwise cause her discomfort, by burping her. Place her over your shoulder, face down on your lap or in a well-supported sitting position, and gently pat or rub her back. You may or may not get an audible reward for your efforts!

Give up smoking, if you can

It's not a good idea to smoke if you're breastfeeding, because traces of chemicals, including nicotine, can pass through to your baby – and heavy smoking is believed to affect milk production. However, you shouldn't be put off breastfeeding just because you're a smoker. It still represents a healthier way to feed your baby.

Smoking in the house is a bad idea generally with a new baby around, because it increases the risk of cot death and makes her more prone to colic and illness, and to serious breathing problems. If you're a smoker and you weren't able to give up during pregnancy, perhaps you could now? At the very least, be sure to smoke outside the house, away from your baby.

Is she getting enough milk?

Many mums worry that their baby isn't getting enough breast milk, because they can't see what's going in. If a child is feeding regularly and producing plenty of wet nappies, she will be doing OK and, if not, you should seek the advice of your health visitor or GP. But don't be tempted to stop trying – health professionals will rarely advise a mum to ditch breastfeeding in favour of formula, although if there's a genuine problem they might recommend it as a supplement.

In the longer term, you'll be able to see if your baby is thriving by her progress on height and weight charts. Bear in mind that all babies, however they are fed, are expected to lose between 5 and 10 per cent of their birth weight over the course of the first week or so, before gradually gaining weight after that. Be guided and advised by the health professionals who are looking out for you. However, a mum's own intuition is the best gauge of her baby's health and progress, and you will need to have faith in your own feelings.

What to do when it's not working

If you encounter problems with breastfeeding, try not to panic. Keep on trying as best as you can and get advice as soon as possible from your midwife, health visitor, or from a local breastfeeding counsellor, or by calling a breastfeeding helpline (see the Useful Addresses appendix, p. 334).

Breastfeeding twins

As long as you feed on demand, your breasts can produce enough sustenance for more than one hungry mouth, so it's quite possible to breastfeed twins successfully (and even triplets, or more, if you're committed enough). You may have to feed your babies separately until the routine is well established, but once that's achieved, you can latch on two at a time – a V-shaped breastfeeding cushion is particularly useful for this. (Details of some useful organisations and information sources for multiple births may be found in the appendices at the back of the book.)

Common breastfeeding problems

Blocked duct: This occurs when milk builds up, causing a hard, painful lump in the breast. A good feed can help relieve it, or you can try massaging the lump. If left, blocked ducts can lead to mastitis (see below), so are best tackled.

Engorgement: The breasts become painfully full of milk, usually because of a delay in emptying them. The best way to resolve the problem is to feed your baby, but if they're too full for her to get a hold of, you may need to massage your boobs and express a little milk to relieve the fullness first. Like a blocked duct, engorgement can lead to mastitis.

Mastitis: This is a painful inflammation of the breast, which may be infectious if caused by bacteria entering the breast tissue through a crack in the skin; if caused by a build up of milk (known as milk stasis), it's not infectious. You may notice that a patch of the breast is red, hot, sore or swollen, or you may have flu-like symptoms. Taking paracetamol may ease the symptoms and won't harm your baby. You should also drink plenty of water and try to get whatever rest you can. Cases of infectious mastitis (the sort caused by bacteria) require antibiotics. It's perfectly safe – in fact, it's advisable – to carry on breastfeeding during a bout of mastitis. Feed from the affected breast first, so it's completely drained, or express any milk left in it at the end of a feed. You can help prevent mastitis by feeding your baby whenever she wants, so the breast is being regularly emptied, and by making sure your positioning is right to avoid cracked nipples.

Sore or cracked nipples: If you get these, you need help from a health professional or breastfeeding counsellor to check that you're correctly positioned and that the baby's latching on properly. Inevitably, once nipples become sore, it's painful to keep on feeding. So get all the help you can in adjusting your position – and meanwhile, you could try holding your baby differently, in the rugby ball style, perhaps, or lying down, or however you haven't been doing it up until then. Expressing may be the only way to keep the milk coming if your nipples are really sore.

A traditional remedy for sore nipples is to wipe a little breast milk on them after each feed, and this is no old wives' tale. Breast milk contains healing antibodies. You can also buy soothing creams, but use one of these only when you're sure you're going to get a break from feeding for a while, so it has time to soak in. Nipple shields may help, but they make it harder for the baby to suck – and there's also the worry that your baby will come to prefer the shield's teat to the real deal. Keep your nipples clean and dry, allow them fresh air whenever possible, and keep breast pads changed regularly. Very sore nipples may occasionally be a sign of thrush. (See the Health A–Z at the back of the book.)

What the netmums say

Breastfeeding

One thing I did in the very early days was to keep a breastfeeding journal. I'd note down the time, how long she fed for and on what side. It really helped me keep on top of the feeds and helped make sure I fed her enough and evenly on both sides. The funniest thing for me was leaky boobs. Who knew a woman could produce that much milk?
Sophie from Glasgow, mum to Ava Charlotte, one

I was determined to breastfeed. However, I found it incredibly difficult and painful, and then developed mastitis in both sides. At that point I decided to give both me and my son a break and move to formula. The failure to breastfeed properly was

devastating and I felt tremendous guilt for a long time (still do, if I'm honest).
Sharon from Rotherham, mum to Edward, two

I was determined to breastfeed, and had I not been so stubborn about it I might have given up many a time. How much has she had? Is she still hungry? Is she getting enough hindmilk? Is she latching on properly? These were the thoughts that occupied me constantly. I could cope with the pain, which only lasted a couple of weeks and was greatly helped by the cabbage leaves I kept in the fridge, but it was whether she was feeding enough that bothered me. If I'd taken a step back I would have realised that week after week she was putting on weight and thriving, so my breast milk must have been giving her enough!
Alex from Kings Langley, mum to Niamh, seven months

Don't give up on breastfeeding is my advice. I was told by a midwife to give her formula 24 hours after she was born but after some minor setbacks she breastfed wonderfully well. There are so many positives to breastfeeding. I cannot say anything bad about it.
Danni from Higham Ferrars, mum to Olivia, seven months

I don't think midwives are entirely honest in telling you just how frequently a newborn baby will feed! I felt like all I did all day was feed him, change his nappy, and feed again.
Debra from Rotherham, mum to Finn, four, and Louis, two

I wanted to breastfeed her, but had heard such horror stories that I planned to have on-going targets. The thought of doing it for six months was just too scary, so I said to myself that I would see how it went. Amazingly, nearly five months on, I'm still feeding her myself. I'm hugely fortunate that I haven't experienced any pain or discomfort and I always felt as though I had just the right amount of milk, or at least if I felt I was short one day, I seemed to get more the next day and it seemed to satisfy her. At the beginning, though, I honestly thought my nipples were the wrong shape as it took her

ages to get latched on, up to half an hour sometimes. My husband was great and did everything else (well, not quite, but nearly!) in the first two weeks so that I could just concentrate on the feeding. And the thing about breastfeeding is when it's going well, you feel so proud that they have doubled their birth weight because of you and you alone. But when it's going badly, it's so lonely, as you're the only one who can do it, no matter how tired you are!
Louise from Sidcup, mum to Emma, five months

Choosing not to breastfeed

A minority of mums choose not to breastfeed at all (or may be unable to do so for a specific reason) and statistics show that of those mums who start, a high proportion give up well before the six months that's recommended by the Department of Health.

Although bottlefeeding with infant formula milk is not as beneficial as breastfeeding, it's a very good alternative as long as scrupulous attention is paid to hygiene and the making-up instructions. If you decide it's the right option for you, don't waste a moment feeling guilty about it.

The benefits of bottlefeeding

- It's not difficult to master and there's no pain involved.
- It's not such a tie – other willing adults can do it, and enjoy the closeness of feeding, taking the pressure off mum.
- You know exactly how much milk she's getting.
- Formula milk is more filling than breast milk, and feeds tend to be quicker. Once she's finished, she's finished, whereas breastfed babies often like to linger a while. So there'll be longer spaces between feeds.
- She will probably wake less frequently at night and, a couple of months down the line, is more likely to sleep through the night.
- You don't have to keep tabs on what you eat or drink.
- You never have to bare your boobs in public.
- It will be easier to go back to work if and when you want to.

What you'll need to bottlefeed

The essentials are a constant supply of infant formula milk, at least six bottles with teats and lids, and the appropriate equipment for cleaning and sterilising them.

Sterilising bottles and teats properly is absolutely vital during the first year, when a baby's immune system is still weak, to keep bacteria at bay and prevent her from becoming ill. You can use a steam steriliser (some of these are designed to work in the microwave), or a container of cold water with a sterilising solution. Although official advice is not to rely on a dishwasher to sterilise bottles, many health visitors and doctors feel it's fine to do so once your baby is six months old, as long as you always use a very hot cycle (80°C). If you're ever stuck without the means to sterilise feeding equipment, you can do so effectively by simply boiling what you need in a pan of water for ten minutes.

If you choose a steam steriliser, check you have the right sized bottles to fit the one you choose, and take care when lifting the lid to avoid being scalded. Before sterilising them, you need to clean bottles and teats very thoroughly with hot soapy water and a bottlebrush, making sure all traces of formula are gone, since even small marks can harbour bacteria. The surface on which you make up formula feeds must be spotlessly clean, and you should wash your hands thoroughly beforehand.

Making up formula feeds

Follow the instructions on the formula tin scrupulously when making up feeds. Current advice from the Department of Health is to make up a bottle every time you need it, rather than storing it in the fridge for any length of time, using freshly boiled water of at least 70°C (in other words, not left to cool for longer than half an hour). If she's hungry and you need to cool it down in a hurry, hold it under a cold tap for a few minutes, then test on your wrist before offering it. You can buy cartons of ready-made formula these days, which are extremely convenient, especially for travelling, but rather pricey. Babies are usually happy to drink these as it comes, straight out of the carton. (Although some may object, at first, to the fact that it tastes different from the tinned stuff.)

How much?

Just as with breastfeeding, you should offer your baby a formula feed as and when she appears to want it at first. She may take small amounts, up to around 90ml (3fl oz), at this stage, and needs vary from baby to baby. Working out how much and when to increase what you give her will usually be a case of trial and error – aim to always have a little left in the bottle, so you know for sure she's had her fill. It will be obvious she's getting hungrier and you need to offer more when she begins to drain her bottles.

Once a bottle of formula is finished with, always throw away any remaining milk immediately. Milk left lying around will quickly begin to develop bacteria.

It's now recommended that formula-fed babies are given supplements of vitamins A, C and D when they are over six months old and drinking less than 500ml (17½fl oz) of formula per day. In some areas, where vitamin D deficiency is common, supplements are recommended from birth or one month.

Problems with formula feeding

Constipation is sometimes a problem with formula-fed babies (for more, see Nappy talk, p. 34). For this reason, it's vital to use the right quantity of powder, and to be wary of 'hungry baby' versions of formula, which are not suitable for newborns.

Rarely, a baby may be allergic to, or have an intolerance of, the cow's milk proteins in formula milk. If this happens, your GP may prescribe a special hydrolysed formula milk – this is made from cow's milk products, but is specially treated so that the proteins are broken down, removing the allergen factor. Never be tempted to diagnose an allergy or intolerance yourself, or to give your baby an alternative, such as goat's, sheep or soya milk, because these may also cause an allergy and, in any case, are nutritionally substandard (as is rice milk). Always seek advice from your doctor if you suspect your baby has a problem of this kind. (For more information about food allergies and intolerances, see p. 166.)

Never prop your baby's bottle against something and leave her to feed herself. She could easily end up choking. Later in her first year, when her fine motor skills are developed enough for her to hold her own bottle, and she's got enough strength to hold herself upright, she may be happy to feed herself – but even then, you should always stick around.

Help from the government

If you qualify for certain benefits, you may be able to get free formula milk and vitamin supplements under the government's Healthy Start scheme. Ask your health visitor for more information, or look online at www.healthystart.nhs.uk.

Don't forget that all parents are entitled to child benefit, regardless of their income. If you have a hospital birth and receive a Bounty pack, you will find an application form inside it. Otherwise, you can apply online at the HM Revenue & Customs site: www.hmrc.gov.uk/childbenefit/claiming

Bringing it up again

Babies fed on any sort of milk may bring up a surprising amount after a feed. This is known as possetting and is perfectly normal. You can help avoid it by keeping your baby still and upright for a while after a feed. If the amount she brings up is excessive, if she is doing it very frequently, or if the vomit is projectile (very forceful), you should ask your health visitor or doctor for advice. Two specific medical conditions can cause excessive vomiting during or after feeding – gastro-oesophageal reflux and pyloric stenosis (see the Health A–Z at the back of the book, p. 299).

Mixed feeding

Many mums successfully combine breast and bottle feeding, but if you want to do both you should put off introducing a bottle for the first month, to give breastfeeding a good chance to get established and to avoid your baby becoming confused between nipple and teat. (For more on mixed feeding, see p. 66.)

The great dummy debate (part one)

Strong opinions rage on either side of the dummy debate. Lots of mums find a dummy a useful aid for soothing and settling their babies in the early weeks and months. However, there are some potential disadvantages to weigh up before giving your baby one of these comforters. (For more information, see p. 268.)

Suck it and see: The facts about dummy use

- Experts advise against giving a dummy for at least the first four weeks or until breastfeeding is well established, in case it interferes with your baby's ability to suck, or her preference for the breast. (After this period, many breastfed babies will reject a dummy in any case.) There's also the risk that a dummy may be offered when it's a breastfeed that's needed – you need to be certain your baby is not genuinely hungry before giving her a dummy to suck on instead.

- If you do give your baby a dummy, choose an orthodontic variety with a flat, rather than rounded, teat to minimise any potential effects on her teeth. (For more on dummies and teeth, see p. 115.)

- Dummies can easily pick up bacteria, which can be passed through the mouth, causing an increased risk of ear and stomach infections, so be sure to sterilise daily in a steam or microwave steriliser or by putting through a hot dishwash cycle or soaking in sterilising solution. Throw away dummies if the teat shows any sign of damage, and never suck a dummy yourself in order to clean it – our mouths are full of bacteria!

- Never dip a dummy in anything sweet because this will give your baby a taste for sugar and, once she has teeth, could cause decay.

- Try from the start to give your baby a dummy only when she really needs it, for soothing or sleeping, so that it never becomes a too-frequent habit. Don't put a dummy in her mouth if she doesn't particularly seem to want it.

- Recent research suggests that, although it is not clear why, consistently giving your baby a dummy at night, for the first six months, may help to reduce the risk of cot death where there are other risk factors present. (For more on safe sleeping, see p. 31.) However, a baby who relies on a dummy to get to sleep may wake up and cry until you put it back in her mouth for her!

- Speech therapists recommend that dummies are dispensed with by the time a baby is a year old. (For more about this, see p. 268.)
- One thing to be said for never giving your baby a dummy in the first place is that you will never have to go through the process of taking it away!
- Try not to have any rigid preconceptions about dummies being either good or bad – they work for some people and, used responsibly, cause no harm.

Sleeping

Sleeping like a baby?

New babies' sleep patterns vary enormously, but on average they will spend 16 to 18 hours out of 24 asleep during their first month. One thing is certain – you are highly unlikely to get an uninterrupted night's sleep in the early weeks and, in most cases, for quite a long time after that! It's just one aspect of parenthood you have to come to terms with.

Very young babies wake up at night because they're hungry – they have tiny tummies and need regular top-ups. A breastfed baby may wake four or five times a night in need of a feed at this stage (a bottlefed baby probably less so), and she will stop crying only if you give it to her. The upside is that she will sleep a lot during the day, in theory allowing you to catch up on a bit of the rest you've missed the night before.

Early days (and nights)

In the first month, there probably won't be any semblance of a routine to your baby's sleep and there's little point in rigorously trying to introduce one. Newborns don't understand the difference between day and night and, besides, most parents like to keep them permanently close by, which is why a portable Moses basket or carrycot is useful. So go with the flow – let her nap whenever and for however long she wants to, and simply accept it when she is awake. You may find your baby is more content and comfortable being swaddled – wrapped firmly in a blanket, to emulate the snug environment of the womb. However, it's recommended that to avoid overheating, you always leave a baby's arms out in the open when you swaddle her.

Even at this early stage, it's worth getting her used to the idea of being put down for sleep while still awake. That's because later on, when you're aiming to get her sleeping through the night, you'll need her to be able to drop off independently. It's never too early to start practising this! Babies have six states of alertness – deeply asleep, light sleep, drowsy, quiet alert, busy alert and crying. As you get to know your baby, you'll be able to recognise when she is getting drowsy. She'll be yawning and stretching, and her eyes will be gradually taking longer to open and shut. This is the best time to put her down for a sleep.

It's also a good idea to get her used to sleeping against a certain amount of background noise, so don't tiptoe round her when she's asleep, or talk in whispers – it's just not realistic to aim for total quiet every time she naps.

Safest in her own bed

It's important to encourage your baby to sleep in her own cot, crib or basket right from the start, so she learns it's a happy and comfortable place to be. Lovely as it is to have her curled up against you when she's little, it's a precedent you might want to think twice about setting – it's also very risky to fall asleep yourself while holding her on a sofa or chair. Another thing you can do now is to teach her that night-times are for sleeping, and not for partying – keep night feeds brief and to the point (if possible!), your voice low and the lights dim.

Some people choose to have their baby in bed with them because they feel it's convenient and pleasurable. Many more find their babies end up in with them anyway, because it's the easy option when you're tired. It can certainly make night feeds easier if you're breastfeeding. But most health professionals, as well as experts from the Foundation for the Study of Infant Deaths (FSID), believe it's safer for a baby to sleep in her own cot, because bedsharing is linked to a greater risk of cot death.

Goodnight, sweetheart: All you need to know about safe sleeping

Since a major awareness campaign was launched in 1991, the number of cot deaths in the UK has fallen by 75 per cent, but 300 babies a year still die suddenly and unexpectedly in their sleep, for no obvious reason.

According to the Foundation for the Study of Infant Deaths, there are a number of things you can do to reduce the risk:

- Always place your baby on her back when you put her to sleep. Following this golden rule means that babies need plenty of opportunities to spend time in other positions while awake, to avoid a misshapen head. (For more about this condition, positional plagiocephaly, see the Health A–Z at the back of the book.) If she chooses to turn over on to her tummy once old enough to do so, the advice is not to worry about flipping her back again – by the time most babies are capable of rolling, they are likely to be past the main risk age for cot death.
- Put her with her feet at the foot of the cot, and with her covers firmly tucked in, to prevent her from wriggling down under the covers.
- Never give your baby a pillow during her first year.
- Don't let her get too hot. Babies' rooms should be 16–20°C, which isn't especially warm. In most weathers, you won't need to keep the heating on overnight and you should never put her close to a radiator or other source of heat. Always keep her head uncovered when she is asleep. Check body heat by touching her to see that she is not too hot, or sweaty – if necessary, remove a layer of bedclothing. Use lightweight layers of blankets, not a duvet or quilt. Baby sleeping bags are a safe option, as long as they are the right size for her age, lightweight and hoodless.
- Make sure your baby's mattress is kept clean and dry. It's best to buy one new when you're preparing for a new baby – evidence shows babies may be at risk from bacteria that can proliferate in an old mattress.
- Don't smoke anywhere near your baby, or allow anyone else to do so.
- Never fall asleep with your baby on a sofa or armchair.
- Put your baby down to sleep, at night and for naps, in her own crib or cot.

- Keep her crib or cot in your room for the first six months.
- Don't bedshare with your baby. If you do, however, be sure to pay careful attention to the safety guidelines outlined on p. 100.
- Breastfeed your baby – research shows that breastfed babies are less likely to succumb to cot death.
- Seek immediate advice if your baby seems unwell.

General care

Handle with care

Picking up, holding, carrying and dressing a baby all sound simple enough tasks, but unless you've done it before, it's by no means obvious how you go about any of them – and since newborn babies seem so small and fragile, it's nerve-racking trying to get it right.

Babies like to be held firmly and securely, so it's important that you feel confident – besides, it's the only way you're ever going to get a really good cuddle with her. As with so many other aspects of babycare, practice makes perfect.

Lifting and holding

When lifting and holding your baby aim to keep your movements slow and gentle, and be sure to keep her head and neck supported, as she's not strong enough to do this for herself in the first month or so. You can hold a new baby in the traditional way, with her whole body resting on an arm, or you can let her lie against your chest with her head nestling into your neck, supporting her bottom or back with your other hand. In time, as her neck muscles strengthen, she'll enjoy looking over your shoulder while in this position.

Putting your baby's clothes on (and taking them off)

Babies often dislike being dressed and undressed, so it's important to be able to do it quickly and gently – and why simple sleepsuits are the best choice of clothing when they're tiny. Make sure she's as warm as possible while she's being dressed and undressed. Put her on a warm surface and cover her naked bits with a towel or muslin. Most babies dislike having things pulled over their heads because it covers up their eyes, noses and mouths, so aim to do this with speed – scoop your thumbs into the neck of the garment and stretch it before pulling on or off. With sleeves, be sure to pull the garment rather than her arms in order to get her into it. As for poppers – you'll get there with practice!

Nappy talk

Poo-filled nappies are one of the less pleasant aspects of babycare. Think of them as reassurance – if she's producing regular poos (or stools, to give them their correct medical name), and the colour and consistency come within the normal range, it's a good sign that feeding's going OK.

During her first few days, your baby's poo will consist of meconium, a dark, sticky substance that builds up in her intestines in the womb. It looks disgusting and can be hard to clean off, but it means her bowels are working correctly. It soon changes, becoming yellow or greenish, rather runny, and with breastfed babies often has a seedy texture – it's firmer and less brightly coloured in bottlefed babies. Poo tends to be less smelly, and less frequent, in breastfed babies, too. Don't be surprised or concerned by very runny or 'explosive' poos – these are normal. Once your baby is eating solid food you'll notice her poos become more regular and much less messy (though, unfortunately, even smellier).

Keeping regular

How often babies poo varies. Breastfed babies may go several times a day or they may go for several days without one – this is nothing to be concerned about. They are very unlikely to suffer from constipation. Bottlefed babies are more prone to constipation and really need to go at least once a day to avoid a build-up. They can be given a little cool, boiled water to drink to soften their stools, if necessary.

Wet and dirty nappies are an important sign that your baby's feeding well, so keep an eye on them – as a general rule, she should be producing between five and eight wet and/or dirty nappies in 24 hours. It can be hard to gauge when a disposable nappy is wet since they're so absorbent, but they'll feel heavier. Any fewer than this and you should mention it to your health visitor or GP. Consult them, too, if you are concerned that your baby may be constipated, have diarrhoea, or her stools do not look normal.

Time for a change

Change your baby as soon as possible after she's produced a poo or a wee, to help avoid nappy rash. A good tip is to make sure you have everything you need close by before you start, including mat, wipes, clean nappy and change of clothes if necessary. Be sure to clean the whole area thoroughly, front and back, using plain, warm water and cotton wool, or wipes. These are undoubtedly convenient, but rather cold. Some contain ingredients that may exacerbate nappy rash, so choose the alcohol- and fragrance-free varieties. Always wipe girls from front to back to avoid the spread of germs, and gently clean around the penis and balls when changing boys – but avoid pulling back the foreskin. Pat dry afterwards with tissue or a soft towel. A smear of barrier cream, such as Vaseline, can help to prevent nappy rash but shouldn't be necessary if you've cleaned and dried properly. (For more information on nappy rash, see p. 93.)

Finally, don't forget to wash your hands before and after every nappy change.

Reusable versus disposable nappies

Reusable nappies are:

- Generally reckoned to be better for the environment – even if you consider the energy and detergents required to wash and dry them.
- Cheaper in the long run – it's estimated they could save around £500 over the course of several years' nappy use.
- Well designed these days, so they are easily put on, stay in place and don't leak.
- Natural – they don't contain chemicals, as disposables do.

Disposable nappies are:

- Much more convenient – especially when out and about.
- Readily available in all supermarkets and chemists.
- Highly absorbent, so can take lots of wee before causing discomfort.
- More affordable, in that the cost is spread.

What the netmums say

Nappies

I'd been so saturated with information about pregnancy and then when they put Sam in my arms I thought, 'Damn, nobody has told me anything about the baby.' I didn't have a clue. Luckily, the midwives were really good and showed me how to change a nappy, dress, feed and bathe him. However, we did have problems. When he was a few days old, I noticed that every nappy I put on him leaked. I was changing his clothes about eight times a day and was totally baffled. Eventually I realised this was because I was fastening his nappies with his willy pointing up!
Elaine from Lincoln, mum to Samuel, four months

We wanted to use real nappies but I totally regretted going down that route with a demanding baby. I could never put him down and washing nappies was an added stress. It got easier as he grew older but I wished I hadn't bothered using them in the first couple of weeks, and just enjoyed my new baby.
Claire from Letchworth, mum to Oliver, four and Daisy, two

Topping and tailing

Although it's OK to put babies in a bath right from the start, even if they've still got their umbilical stump, many dislike being submerged at first. Most come round to the idea of a bath eventually, but you may find it easier just to avoid it for a while and simply 'top and tail' her once a day. To do this, undress her in a warm room, wrap her in a towel and put her securely on a changing mat or hold her on your lap. Gently wipe her face with dampened cotton wool or a soft sponge, and – in the early weeks, at least – use cooled boiled water to clean her eyes. Wipe from inside to outside to avoid infection, using a new piece of cotton wool each time. Clean gently around the ears with cotton wool or a sponge, but not inside them – and never be tempted to push a cotton-wool bud into the ear canal. There's no need, anyway, since the insides of babies' ears are self-cleaning. The same goes for noses. Give her neck and hands a wipe, keeping her as warm as possible with the towel in the meantime. Don't forget to pay attention to the folds of skin under her chin and her armpits, because dribbled milk can gather here, go nasty (and smelly) and cause soreness.

Bathing your baby

After a few weeks you'll probably feel more confident about bathing her – and although most babies are wary of the bath at first, many come to adore a splash around in some warm water. She doesn't need a bath every day, but it can become a useful part of a bedtime routine, so if she's willing, make it a regular thing.

Begin by half-filling the bath with warm water – put the cold in first, then add hot, so that it's never scalding, just in case you drop her. Test the temperature before you put her in. Undress her and wrap her in a towel, then wash her face as if you were topping and tailing her. If you want to wash her hair (and it's not particularly necessary at this stage), do so while she's still wrapped up in a towel by holding her over the bath and pouring a little water carefully over her head. Then unwrap her and lower her in, carefully supporting her head and shoulders with one arm, and keeping the other free to wash, rinse, tickle and splash her. Keep the towel handy so that when you lift her out, she's not dangling in cold air for any longer than necessary, and pat her completely dry, especially in all the creases. Finish off with a nice clean nappy and a fresh vest and sleepsuit – then cuddle her to make the most of that lovely, clean-baby smell. It won't last long! (For more about bathing your baby, see p. 179.)

Leisure and learning

Out and about

The outside world can sometimes seem a scary place when you've just given birth, but there's no reason not to take your new baby out as soon as you feel up to it. Wrap her up warm if it's remotely chilly, strap her safely into her pram or sling, and show her what fresh air feels like.

Talk to your baby!

Communicating with your baby is as vital as feeding, clothing and cuddling her – it's the best way to stimulate her, teach her all-important speech and language skills, and encourage brain development, a process that kicks off from day one. It's never too early to start playing and talking. Even the youngest babies are social creatures who enjoy interacting with the loving adults around them.

From birth, babies can focus on items that are close enough to their faces, so your baby can see you perfectly when she is lying in your arms, and she will happily take in the sights and sounds you present to her. Babies can hear, too, and she will probably recognise and be reassured by your voice immediately (she'll have heard it enough while in the womb). So chat away to her as much as possible, especially when you're doing things together, such as feeding, getting dressed or nappy changing – it doesn't really matter what you're saying, as long as you're saying something. Most babies prefer a higher pitch, so keep raising yours slightly when talking to her. Babies also love to hear adults sing to them. Don't worry if you can't hold a tune. She'll enjoy hearing your voice, however out of key you may be!

The best time to get your newborn baby's attention is when she's alert and content – there's no point in trying if she's sleepy, or if she has something else on their mind, such as food. If you get up close and gently talk to her during this time, she'll usually respond by making little noises or pulling different facial expressions. Try copying her actions and noises – this is known as baby mirroring and is a great way to get to know your baby and help her to learn about communication.

Toy story

Although your baby won't get much use from toys at this early stage, she may be interested in looking at something in a bright primary colour or bold black and white pattern, carefully fixed or held within her vision. If you have a mobile, hang it so it's close enough for her to see clearly, and slightly to the side rather than directly above her, as newborns tend to focus on what's to their left or right rather than directly ahead.

All About You

Your body after birth

Although experiences vary greatly, giving birth takes a major physical toll on the vast majority of women and, during the first month, your other focus will be on getting your own strength back. Your midwife will make a number of visits (and should also be available over the telephone) to help with this process, and to keep an eye on any possible complications. In the immediate weeks after birth, your body will probably be feeling the consequences of the event in many different parts.

Five rounds with Ricky Hatton: What having a baby may do to your body

Lochia, or postnatal bleeding: A discharge of leftover blood, mucus and tissue from the uterus (womb), this is like a heavy period. It will continue for up to ten days, after which the flow should lessen, although it may carry on for several weeks more. It usually starts off bright red, and will often have clots in it, changing to pink or brown and then a yellowish white. You'll need some heavy-duty maternity pads, which are longer and softer than ordinary pads. Tampons aren't recommended because of the risk of infection.

Afterpains: Similar to labour or bad period pains, these are caused by contractions of the uterus as it shrinks back to normal size after the birth. They're often particularly noticeable while breastfeeding – and if you breastfeed, it can help to speed up the process – but should occur for up to seven days only. If necessary, you can take a painkiller, such as codeine or paracetamol, but double check with your midwife first.

Soreness, scars and stitches: Some level of pain and discomfort down below is inevitable after a vaginal birth, and after a Caesarean section if you experience normal labour beforehand. The perineum (the stretch between the vagina and the anus) will commonly be bruised and sore – even if it didn't tear during the birth, it's still had a battering – so sitting down can hurt for a while. To avoid infection, keep it clean and change your maternity pad regularly, being sure to wash your hands before and afterwards. It may hurt to wee for a while, too – try waiting until you're just getting out of the bath, or pouring a jug of warm water over your bits when you're on the loo. Pain and discomfort is likely to be even worse if you had stitches after the birth because of a tear or an episiotomy, which can take up to four weeks to heal. You may find some relief from a warm bath or shower, a chilled gel-filled pad, a local anaesthetic spray or cream, an over-the-counter painkiller, such as ibuprofen, or a homeopathic remedy, such as arnica (check with your midwife before taking anything). Lie down as much as possible and use a soft pillow to sit on. You may want to look into hiring an inflatable 'valley cushion' from the NCT (see Useful Addresses at the back of the book). If you've had a very serious tear, you may be referred to an obstetric physiotherapist for extra help. Stitches will usually dissolve within a fortnight. If you've had a Caesarean section, recovery times vary. The pain tends to be acute for a few days but then subsides. You may be immobile for a while – it is major surgery, after all. You'll need painkillers to get you through the first week or so, and loads of practical help when you get back home, especially if you're breastfeeding and struggling even to pick up your baby.

Painful boobs: Your breasts can expand to what feels like bursting point if you delay a breastfeed when it's due. Nipples may be extremely sore until an effective latch-on is established. If you've decided not to breastfeed, there will be an uncomfortable or painful period while the milk dries up naturally over the course of a day or two. Painkillers and a supportive bra can help.

Aches, pains and exhaustion: After giving birth, it's not unusual to feel as though you've emerged from a big fight. General pains and aches in the pelvis, chest, tailbone, back and legs are all normal.

Saggy tums and stretched skin: Immediately after birth you'll lose up to a stone in weight, and inevitably you'll have a very saggy stomach as a result. Postnatal stretch marks, which can appear on the tummy, breast and thighs, affect some women, but not others (the cause is thought to be a simple matter of genetics). They fade over time and become silvery but will never disappear completely, so if you have them, you'll just have to embrace them as a proud mark of motherhood. Meanwhile, a good moisturiser will ease any itchiness.

Poo, wind and piles: Bowels can be sluggish after a delivery, and this physiological problem can be worsened by psychological ones. You may feel as though your stitches are going to burst open when you try to open your bowels (they won't!) and it may help to hold a pad or wad of tissue in position to protect them. If you're badly constipated, your doctor or midwife may advise you to take a stool softener such as lactulose solution – this is available over the counter, but check with your doctor or midwife first. Eating a balanced diet that includes plenty of fruit and veg, and drinking lots of liquid, will help keep your movements soft and less likely to cause a problem. Excessive wind is common, because the muscles and nerves around the bowels can be stretched and even damaged by childbirth. Occasionally, postpartum faecal incontinence (leaking poo) may occur for the same reason. Haemorrhoids (piles) are varicose veins just inside the anus and are extremely common after birth, caused by the pressure of pushing during delivery. Over-the-counter or prescription creams and plenty of fibre and fluids can help.

Sweating and weeing: You may notice you're doing a lot more of both these things, as the body releases all the extra fluid that's stored up during pregnancy. The good news about this is that if you suffered from puffy ankles, face and hands in the build-up to the birth, they will soon begin to go down. It's essential that you have a wee within eight hours of birth to avoid urinary tract infection, which is why your midwife will always check to make sure you've emptied your bladder.

Weakened pelvic floors and leaky bladders (stress or urinary incontinence): Loss of muscle tone in the perineal area can affect the bladder and cause leakage – doing your pelvic floor exercises will help if this is a problem (see the box on p. 43 for more information). They also improve the flow of blood to the vaginal area, which speeds up the healing process.

Sheer exhaustion: You've given birth, you're emotionally overwhelmed, and you're caring for a new human being 24/7. You're going to be very, very tired for a while!

When complications become serious

Post-pregnancy complications may occasionally lead to a serious medical condition. Your midwife will be alert to possible symptoms, but you should seek immediate treatment if you develop any of the following:

- Sudden or extremely heavy and bright red blood loss or very large blood clots, particularly if accompanied by racing heartbeat, faintness or dizziness; feverishness or shivering, or bleeding that smells unpleasant.
- Swelling, tenderness or pain in the legs.
- Sharp chest pain or shortness of breath.
- Severe or persistent headache, dizziness, vomiting or blurred vision.
- Swelling, redness or oozing at the site of a Caesarean incision.
- Difficulty or pain in urinating.
- Persistent pain in the abdomen or perineal area.

What the netmums say

Pain after birth

I remember vividly the physical pain after having my first daughter. I had a lot of stitches and I couldn't sit, walk, lie down. I wanted to sit and cuddle her all day, but it hurt too much.
Andrea from Derby, mum to Emily-Rose, ten, Lucy-Mae, nine, Korben, eight and Tyeran, five

The main physical pain I had, which no one warned me about, was going for a wee. Getting acidic urine on raw skin was traumatic and painful, and lasted for around two weeks after the birth. It took a little while for my womb to settle down, too. It felt like a huge torn muscle.
Erin from Leeds, mum to Connor, ten months

After-birth exercises

Pelvic floor exercises, sometimes called Kegel exercises after the physician who pioneered them, are vital to help you regain strength in your pelvic floor, the layer of muscles that support the bladder, uterus and bowel, which can become stretched and weakened by pregnancy and birth. Even if you haven't done the exercises during pregnancy, you can still start now! They can help reduce or prevent leakage or incontinence, speed up healing down below, and enhance your sex life (once it's up and running again).

First you need to establish exactly where your pelvic floor muscles are and this can be tricky. Since they commonly feel rather numb in the immediate weeks after birth, it won't always be obvious. However, once you've got over that hurdle, the exercises are not difficult to master and you can be do them more or less any time, anywhere – even when you're busy with something else, such as feeding your baby, washing up or watching television.

A bit of a squeeze: How to do pelvic floor exercises

- Tighten the muscles around your back passage and draw them up, as if trying to stop yourself from passing wind. At the same time, tighten the muscles around the front passage and draw them up as if trying to stop passing water. Don't practise this while actually weeing, though, because it could put you at risk of urinary tract infections. Alternatively, you could try putting a clean finger in your vagina – you'll feel the squeeze.

- It's really important to breathe normally and avoid squeezing the muscles in your legs or bum, or pulling in your stomach – these aren't the muscle groups you're working on!

- Once you've worked out what you're doing, aim to hold the squeeze for a few seconds, then relax for a few seconds. Gradually increase these times until you can hold the squeeze for up to ten seconds, and repeat ten times. Then try another variation by tightening the pelvic floor muscles quickly and strongly, then relaxing quickly, up to five times.

- Practise both at least three or four times a day – and aim to do a set a day for the rest of your life, to keep your pelvic floor strong and better able to cope with any future pregnancies, and to guard against any problems developing in the future.

Regaining some strength in your stomach

Although the first few months is definitely not the time to attempt any sort of strenuous workout, there's no reason why you can't very gently begin to regain some strength in your abdominal muscles, if you feel up to it, by softly pulling in your tummy and holding it for a few seconds, whenever you get a moment. Try to do this regularly during ordinary activities, such as walking, and particularly when feeding, changing or lifting your baby, because it will help to prevent backache or strain, a common after-effect of pregnancy and birth.

(For more about exercise and bodies after birth, see the sections on the second and ninth months.)

Ups and downs

It's not just the way you feel on the outside that can take a battering after birth – your state of mind will also need some TLC. While you may well feel intermittently high, there may also be times when you feel very low. These postnatal mood swings – probably caused by a combination of hormonal changes, anxiety and exhaustion – are experienced, to some extent or another, by just about all new mums. They can be heightened if you've been through a particularly difficult delivery, if you're finding breastfeeding hard going, if you're really struggling with one or more of the physical consequences of birth, if you're isolated from friends and family, or if your partner is not around much, perhaps because he's had to return to a demanding job.

Often called the baby blues, this period of changeable emotions won't last long and is best tackled by getting as much rest, sympathy and practical help as you possibly can. The development of full-on postnatal depression (PND), on the other hand, is something to watch for because you may need some professional help to get through it. (For more information about this condition, see p. 81.)

You will probably feel a strong rush of love for your baby very soon after birth – but you may not. For some mums (and dads), the bonding process can take a while and those deep feelings of love may take several weeks or more to kick in.

What the netmums say

Baby blues and bonding

I'd been constantly told that as soon as I saw my baby I would feel an overwhelming sense of love, so I felt awful when this didn't happen. I didn't feel that bond – I just felt numb. It wasn't until about week four that all of a sudden I just couldn't bear to be apart from him. Now I'm absolutely loving it, although I still feel like I've got a constant hangover from the lack of sleep! But none of that matters when he looks at me and smiles.
Carly from Norwich, mum to Finley, seven months

Bless her, I did not enjoy my baby for the first month, and it took me a while to bond. I felt terribly guilty, and used to pretend that I loved her. I was all blown up with water retention, leaky breasts and painful episiotomy scars. And I didn't think I was ever going to get a good night's sleep again. But now, she is the light in my life. With my next baby I'm going to relax, and enjoy the first few weeks if I can.
Sally from Matfen, mum to Lily, one

The first few weeks for me were so amazing. I hadn't bonded with my bump at all and didn't really feel like I was going to have a baby, so when my son was born and put on my chest I felt such a rush of love for him (and amazement that I had a baby). I know it will be a feeling that I will never forget – or ever be able to describe. The first few days I just watched him sleep but felt a bit afraid of holding him in case I dropped him, then three days later I couldn't stop crying as every horrible thing that might happen to my baby went through my mind. By the time he was two weeks old I'd got over that and felt like a pro. I was so confident that I was the best mum for my baby and I felt on top of the world.
Jenna from Wolverhampton, mum to Jude, one

I couldn't bond with my first daughter, initially. I loved being pregnant and feeling the baby move inside me but when she was born I felt

completely empty. I expected to be like they are on the telly, all crying and smiling, but there was nothing, just a total void. I just went through the motions, not really sure what I was doing, making the right 'happy' faces at staff and visitors alike. We spent five days in hospital because she was small for her dates. She couldn't breastfeed and I felt rejected. I tormented myself terribly, believing I must be a bad mother because I couldn't breastfeed my own flesh and blood. Anyway, about three weeks later something changed in an instant. My daughter was asleep in the middle of our bed and I called my husband upstairs. I couldn't take my eyes off her. Suddenly she was so innocent and vunerable and beautiful . . . and she was mine. My heart felt so full of love for her that I thought it would burst right out of my chest. Through tear-stained eyes I said to my husband, 'We made that,' and smiled. That was the turning point for me.
Kellie from Norwich, mum to Aimee, six and Alfie, four

A helping hand

If there's one piece of advice you should follow in the first month, it's to take it easy. Do the bare minimum of housework – aim to keep food preparation areas and toilets reasonably clean and the floor clear enough that you don't trip over things. Live on ready meals and speedy snacks (but not out-and-out junk food), and delegate anything that doesn't involve looking after yourself or your baby to someone else, if possible. Most new parents will have at least a couple of good friends or relatives who are willing to help in some way – exploit them, and let them know how much you appreciate the chance to do so. And don't forget to ask for help – people may not realise you're in need, or they may not want to offend you by offering.

At the same time, you may need some peace and privacy during this period, so if your mother-in-law's bustling is causing you stress, or the constant flow of visitors is getting you down, you'll just have to say so – and put a politely phrased 'please do not disturb' note on the front door, to discourage impromptu visits that you're just not up to. But whatever you do, don't try to go it alone in this month – if you're a single parent or if your partner has a demanding job and isn't able to take time off, take help wherever you can find it.

What the netmums say

Mums and mums-in-law

I have a mother-in-law from hell who came round every day for the first week for three hours at a go and just stared, and that got uncomfortable when I had to feed him. She even just sat there in the room while the midwife visited. I don't think you can explain how difficult all the visits are that first week. Does she not remember what it's like to have a newborn baby?
Carly from Norwich, mum to Finley, seven months

I am lucky my mum was great, she confined me to bed, made all my meals and did my housework for me for a week. She said she was doing things the old-fashioned way and that in her day, mums didn't do anything other than feed and change their baby for the first two weeks. I wasn't going to complain. I spent some great time with my baby and we really had a chance to get to grips with breastfeeding. Mum has got some funny ideas about things and some of her advice is way out there, but when it mattered, she really helped out.
Karen from Morden, mum to George, two months

Grab a kip, when you can

Sleep deprivation is unavoidable, but any amount of rest and relaxation that you can come by is worthwhile – if your baby is asleep, ignore the fact that there's ironing to do (who needs neat-looking clothing, anyway?) and grab a power nap while you can. Eating well is also important now – home cooking might be a tall order, but simple nutritious snacks such as wholemeal sandwiches, jacket potatoes, beans or egg on toast, cartons of fresh soup, oatcakes and cheese, yoghurts, salad and fruit should see you through.

Don't forget to tuck your baby into her pram and get out in the fresh air with her as soon as you feel up to it. Going out can be a real tonic for your physical and mental health – being stuck permanently inside can send anyone a little stir crazy. Just don't try to go far, or do too much.

What the netmums say

Sleep deprivation

I do remember the sleep deprivation making me feel a bit mad and down. I don't think I had baby blues, it was just tiredness making mountains out of molehills. I never felt anything but overwhelming love for the baby but my husband got the rough end of my tongue several times in those first weeks. I remember finding it hard to achieve anything other than feeding and sleeping and even going to the loo or having a shower was hard to fit in.
Amanda from Otley, mum to Dylan, six, Fraser, four and Bethan, two

I was pleasantly surprised how much my newborn slept in the day. When people spoke about being sleep deprived, I assumed they meant they were up all the time, day and night. I found that napping in the day when my son slept meant I didn't feel so out of it.
Jenna from Wolverhampton, mum to Jude, one

The Netmums ten-point plan of recommendations for new mums

At Netmums, we know only too well that life as a new mum can be hard going. That's why we came up with the following ten-point plan, based on what we know to be the common experiences and needs during the first year of motherhood. If you can find the time during your first month, do read it through – then come back to it from time to time as you pick your way through the rest of the year. This advice is also available online, at www.netmums.com

1. First steps

After your baby is born, your health visitor will usually run a baby clinic and/or a postnatal group where you can go for advice, to get your baby weighed and meet other mums with new babies. These mums will be going through the same experiences as you, and good friends can be made here. Your children will take their first steps at about the same time, learn to speak at the same time and perhaps start pre-school and even school together.

2. Toddle in

Check out the Netmums listings of local parent and toddler groups and activities in your area. Be brave and be prepared to talk to other mums there. Don't give up . . . like starting a new school or new job, it can take some time to stop feeling like the new girl and to start feeling that you fit in, and are part of the group. As you get to know other mums a bit, invite one or two you feel you have something in common with to your house with their kids for a coffee and a play; or invite them for tea – always a trying time of day. Based on our survey results, six out of ten mums would like to make new friends – so statistically, that mum you start a conversation with will be just as pleased to talk to you . . . maybe she is shyer than you are!

3. Toddle out

Get out of the house. Anything is better than sitting at home with a baby all day every day watching daytime TV. There's plenty going on for parents and kids every day in your local area: toddler groups, toddler swimming classes, indoor play centres, parks, farms. It's hard work trying to entertain a baby at home alone. Get your old clothes on, and get stuck in!

4. Meet a Mum

Netmums run a Meet a Mum board in every area of the country. It's an online local board where mums post a little note about themselves and other mums reply and then they arrange to meet. Thousands of successful friendships have been made through these boards and we have recently launched our very own Netmums Meet Ups.

5. The Netmums Coffee House

If you're not quite ready for the Meet a Mum board, visit the Netmums Coffee House to chat to other Netmums around the country. You can ask advice, offer advice, have a laugh and make friends – all without getting dressed. Many a Netmum has become efficient at one-handed typing with a baby on the other arm.

6. Back to school

You need driving lessons before you can drive a car, a licence to own a dog – but why are we expected just to 'know' what to do with a sleepless baby, a terrible toddler or an anxious child? Well, we don't. There are classes in parenting in most areas, which include simple but amazingly effective techniques to help you deal calmly and sensibly with your child. Highly recommended by Netmums!

7. Find time for yourself . . .

A Netmums survey revealed that 75 per cent of mums find that lack of 'me time' is one of the major stress factors in their lives. A bit of mutual support can give you the little bit of breathing space that makes all the difference. As you get to know local mums and their children, offer to babysit while they go to the hairdresser's or dentist, or even for just a couple of hours child-free shopping. They may then offer to reciprocate and it could become a regular thing. Babysitting circles are one way to fill the gap left by absent grandparents.

8. . . . and your partner!

Four out of ten mums find their relationship with their partner stressful, but seven out of ten of us turn to them when we are feeling down. So find time for each other – that babysitting circle could be just the thing.

9. Get help

If you are struggling, *find some help*. There are support groups for almost everything, probably in your area. It is not a weakness to ask for help. You can't expect to be a good mum unless you are well supported yourself. That's what these groups are there for. Start with www.netmums.com, which has listings for many sources of help.

10. Everybody needs good neighbours

If you are lucky enough to be one of those mums with loads of friends, think about the instruction you would give your own children: if someone looks lonely or left out, be the one to talk to them and include them in the group. These days, we all live in boxes and rarely talk to anyone we don't know. Let's talk to each other . . . look out for each other . . . be good neighbours.

Memories are made of this

You won't have much in the way of spare time this month, it's true, but do try to find a few moments to record all the important details of your baby's birth, such as the time, and how much she weighed. These may seem like unforgettable nuggets of fact right now, but there'll come a time one day when you just don't remember – and you might wish you'd made a note of it!

You may have received a baby record book as a gift – although they can be fairly exhausting to keep up because they demand a great deal of information – but if not, you could simply fill the pages of a pretty album with photographs and a few written details. Some pages are included at the back of this book for you to jot down any special thoughts, memories or milestones. Alternatively, you could start a memory box, into which you could put all sorts of keepsakes, such as your baby's hospital identity bracelet, her very first pair of bootees, and all the congratulation cards you received. Some other ideas for items or facts that you might want to preserve or record appear throughout the book. One day, when your baby is a bit older, she'll adore sifting through these priceless memories, and so will you.

What the netmums say

Keepsakes and memories

I can't bear to throw away or pass on some of my girls' baby clothes as they have too many memories and too much sentimental value. So I've cut squares of the material out of sleepsuits, dresses, tops,

etc, and stitched them together to create a patchwork effect. I keep it in my bedroom as a hanging and it's absolutely lovely!
Katharine from Alfreton, mum to Madeleine, five and Harriet, two

With James, I kept a few of his very tiny baby clothes, as they still bring back difficult but nice memories of when he first got out of his incubator and into a cot and could finally wear some clothes! I have a wee hat (which looks like it would fit a doll), a sleepsuit and a wee outfit and cardigan. I kept quite a few of Kayla's wee cute outfits, too.
Catherine from Singapore, mum to James, four and Kayla, one

I kept so much! I kept her baby book on the table all year and stuck her hospital band in, a lock of hair, her first sock, footprints, handprints. There are photos galore, a family tree, birthday, christening and Christmas cards, her newborn hearing test report. When she was born and at her christening, I got close friends and family to write her a message, so they're all in there. Now that she's nearly three, and the book is almost finished, I've started a scrapbook for her instead. I love to look at it with her, and remember all those great days. And if you do a tiny bit every time, it's really no trouble at all. I've done the same for my son, too. We also have thousands of digital photos saved (and backed up!), and a camcorder to catch each new thing.
Helen from St Asaph, mum to Ceridwen, two and Ceirion, nine months

We had his fingerprint set into solid silver, which I wear on a bangle and have never taken off – every time I look at it, I think of him at earlier stages of his little life.
Rachel from Wallingford, mum to Max, four

I started off with such good intentions and consequently have a baby record book, which was kept immaculately until three months, when it tails off to nothingness. Still it's more than my parents left me. Both died and I'm an only child; consequently, I only have a handful of photos of me as a little girl. So I'm determined to do better for my son. I've kept his birth announcement from the *Times*; birth congrats cards and letters; his first babygro; the little woolly hat he had when newborn (knitted by old ladies for the maternity unit); his hospital tag; a lock of his hair; and his first shoes. I've also taken hundreds of photos and every three months I compile one of those lovely 'photo books' that you can order online. It's funny how this job always ends up being Mummy's job, isn't it? My husband doesn't have a clue what I keep!

Sarah from Poole, mum to Arthur, one

My parents wrote about us every month as little ones and now I am doing the same for Isabella and will do for my next one. My siblings and I love, even now, to look back on what we did, and it's interesting to compare my little one with me as a baby. Also it made me feel really precious to my parents, that they were interested in every detail of us. I want my kids to feel the same. It's also interesting to see how the traits we had as toddlers are the same we have as adults!

Jo from Crawley, mum to Isabella, two

I had my son's DNA profile made into a piece of artwork and displayed in a frame, and took black and white pictures of his tiny feet and his hands gripping both mine and my husband's fingers. These are now all together in a triple frame. I also decided to have his feet cast and framed.

Rachel from Braintree, mum to Ben, seven months

I kept Josie's umbilical cord when it fell off! It's in a plastic bag in my jewellery box. Hers was a homebirth and she didn't have an identity bracelet, which I had for Sam, so I wanted something!

Emma from north London, mum to Sam, four and Josie, 11 months

The Second Month

Welcome to your second month of motherhood

With the first month of motherhood under your belt things may be settling down a little – some mums find that six weeks is a bit of a turning point, and life gets somewhat easier. You may even have some semblance of routine in place. You'll probably be in better shape, too. After six weeks, you should be over the worst of the physical consequences of birth. However, don't expect too much. It's still very early days and for many new mums, life remains in disarray at this point!

You should soon be starting to get something back for your troubles, though, as your baby will be responding happily to the sight and sound of you – and by the end of this second month, will probably have shown you how much she appreciates you with her very first smile!

Health, Growth and Development
Baby milestones
Now that she is one month old, your baby will typically:

- Be able to lift her head briefly when placed on her stomach.
- Stare at and focus on your face.
- Notice a sudden or prolonged noise, such as a vacuum cleaner, and pause to listen.

- Be stretching out her limbs and fingers, uncurling her body from the foetal position she's kept in the early weeks.

And she might also:

- Be able to 'track' with her eyes a moving object held about 20cm from her face.
- Hold her head steady for a few seconds when you support her in an upright position.
- Make 'happy' noises, such as cooing and gurgling.
- Give you her first proper smile!

Milestone focus: Smiling

On average, babies produce their first meaningful smile once their facial muscles are strong enough, some time between four and eight weeks – any earlier than that and, truth be told, it's probably just a reflex action, usually occurring when she's asleep, or wind-stricken. As well as being a heart-melting, emotional moment for any proud parent, her first smile is developmentally significant because it shows she's using her brain to process images – those of you smiling – and responding in the appropriate way.

Babies learn to smile by copying people who smile at them, so the single most important thing you can do to help her reach this milestone is to beam at her whenever you get the chance. If you're not feeling like smiling much during this period because you're suffering from postnatal depression, try to arrange for another adult to spend time with your baby and give her lots of loving smiles in your absence. And please do seek help, because no one can trigger a joyful response in your little one quite as well as you can. (There's more on PND on p. 81.)

Your baby's very early smiles may be given in response to any friendly face that enters her horizon, but rest assured that in a few months she will definitely be saving her broadest smiles for you – the people she knows, and is beginning to love, best of all.

An important note about baby milestones

All babies develop differently. Some take longer than average to reach the various milestones, others are well ahead. Of course, all parents are keen to see their baby passing each stage – it's a sign that all is well – but a baby's first year isn't a race. How soon she reaches certain points is no indication of how clever or able she is, and no reflection on how much she'll achieve later in life. She'll get there eventually.

Lists of the developmental norms you could expect of your baby, month by month, are included in this book just because baby milestones are so important to parents. These offer very general guidelines based on averages, so please don't be concerned if your baby doesn't conform to them strictly. However, if you're worried that a major developmental milestone is significantly delayed, it's a good idea to chat to your health visitor or GP about it. Just occasionally, it can signal a problem that needs addressing.

Mums of pre-term ('premmie') babies should always bear in mind that their babies will usually take longer than full-termers to reach the various milestones. A premmie's achievements should be measured against her adjusted age – in other words, from the time when she *should* have been born, not when she actually was born. (Bliss is the main UK charity devoted to supporting parents of premature babies, and contact details are included in the back of the book.)

Big and small

A baby's growth will normally be quite rapid in the early months. However, growth patterns vary hugely from child to child and are dependent on many factors other than how they are feeding, including their general health, birth weight, gender, racial background and genetic make-up.

There are no hard and fast rules – some babies may gain as much as half a kilogram (roughly 1lb) per week, others may put on 100 grams (a few ounces) – but how much they gain (or don't gain) in any one week is not really important. A gradual rise over the course of several weeks, or even months, which should produce a rough but steady curve on the weight centile chart in their Child Health Record, is what counts.

Breastfeeding mums must bear in mind that their babies tend to grow at a different rate from formula-fed ones, gaining weight more quickly in the early weeks, but then becoming lighter on average, and growing at a slower pace. This difference in growth rate is *not* a sign that your breastfed baby isn't thriving.

Weighing it up
Try not to fret about how much your baby is growing, and never be tempted to compare your baby's progress with others. Unless your baby was premature (in which case she will be weighed more regularly) or your health visitor has specific concerns about her progress, there's no need to rush to the clinic every week to get her weighed – an average of six weighing sessions in her first year is now reckoned to be plenty. However, any dramatic drop, or rise, on her centile chart is something you should discuss with your health visitor or GP.

Meanwhile, you should be reassured that your baby is feeding well and thriving if she is producing lots of wet and dirty nappies, by the gradual 'rounding out' of her face and body, and the fact that, as the weeks and months pass, she is regularly outgrowing her sleepsuits.

The six- to eight-week check
Your baby will be offered a medical check or general review when she is six to eight weeks old. This is usually carried out by your GP, either during your own routine check-up (see p. 78) or on a separate occasion. The review involves a brief physical examination – she will usually be weighed and have her length and head circumference measured, and checks made on her heart, hips and eyes. Boys also have their testes checked. This appointment is a good opportunity for you to ask your doctor any questions you may have about your baby's health.

Her first jabs
At or around the point she turns two months old, your baby will offered the first of a series of immunisations, carried out by a practice nurse or GP, probably at a special immunisation clinic. These include one injection of a

five-in-one vaccine – you'll see it described in literature as the DTaP/IPV/Hib vaccine – that gives protection against some serious diseases. These are diphtheria, tetanus, pertussis (whooping cough), polio and Haemophilus influenzae type b (Hib) – an infection that can lead to a number of major illnesses including septicaemia (blood poisoning), pneumonia and one particular form of meningitis. On the same occasion, she will receive a second shot, which protects against pneumococcal infection, one of the commonest causes of bacterial meningitis as well as ear infections and pneumonia. This a relatively new vaccine, which you'll see described in literature as Pneumococcal conjugate vaccine, or PCV.

Your baby will be due for further jabs at three and four months. Depending on the policy in your area, you won't necessarily get a reminder about these, so you may have to make a careful note in your diary to book subsequent appointments – or perhaps book them at the first session.

Will it hurt?

Although distressing for your baby, the discomfort of an injection lasts for just a few moments. About one in ten babies experiences some mild side effects, including high temperature, irritability or swelling and redness around the site of the injection. In the case of a high temperature, you can bring it down with an appropriate dose of infant paracetamol (suitable from two months old) or ibuprofen (suitable from three months, and only if your baby weighs more than 5kg [11lb]).

Rarely, a child may suffer an allergic reaction in the form of a rash or itching after immunisation. Even less likely (thought to be about one in a million), a baby may show signs of an extreme allergic reaction to a vaccination, causing serious breathing difficulties and collapse. If any severe reaction occurs, you should seek immediate treatment, at your local A&E if necessary.

While a small number of people have concerns about immunisations, virtually all health professionals believe them to be safe and there's no concrete evidence to suggest otherwise. Having your child immunised means you are protecting her from the risk of a number of extremely serious but preventable diseases. You're also playing your part in protecting the whole community, as well as babies and children who cannot be immunised because they are too young, or for medical reasons, because widespread immunisation keeps these diseases at bay.

Colic and crying

It's normal for babies to cry a lot – it's how they communicate their needs and feelings to their carers, and the average baby will cry for between one and three hours a day. But a significant number of babies, thought to be somewhere between five and 20 per cent, will cry excessively and without any particularly apparent reason, even after you've checked for and attended to all the obvious possibilities for their distress, including hunger, tiredness, a wet or dirty nappy, boredom and discomfort. These bouts of unexplained crying are usually called infant colic. It's not a specific medical condition, but simply the term that's used for the relentless crying of a baby who appears to be in pain and is impossible to comfort.

What is colic?

No one's entirely sure what causes colic. Typically, it starts when a baby is a few weeks old, and will almost always stop at around three months or soon after. It can happen at any time of day but often begins in the early evening and may go on for several hours, and is characterised by loud, relentless screams or cries. A baby with colic may go red in the face, and pull her legs up, as if in pain.

Some experts say colic is a reaction to pain, caused either by wind or the digestive deficiencies of an immature gut. It may be that once a baby starts crying, she gets into a vicious circle, because she is taking in gulps of air, which just cause further discomfort. More specifically, there's a theory that colic in breastfed babies occurs when they aren't allowed to drain one breast completely before swapping to the next. As a result, the baby takes too much of the lower-fat foremilk and not enough of the more filling hindmilk, demands more frequent feeds and thus consumes a larger volume of milk than her tummy can cope with.

Others suggest that excessive crying may affect babies who have structural stresses and strains in their heads and bodies, caused during birth, and report that cranial osteopathic treatment (an alternative therapy which involves gentle pressure being applied to the baby's head and body) can alleviate it.

Another, completely different, school of thought is that colicky crying is not a response to pain at all, but rather, a mini breakdown in babies who are simply unable to cope with life outside the womb, or, more specifically, with a sensory overload at the end of the day.

What can you do?

Whatever the cause (and there's not much in the way of evidence to prove any of these theories), one thing is certain – a baby with colic can cause distress and confusion for a parent. Unfortunately, there's no 'cure', and nothing you can do to prevent it. However, there are lots of things that may help. You could try:

- Giving her a commercial preparation, such as Infacol, Colief or gripe water, all available from chemists. There's no scientific evidence that any of these work, but some parents report an improvement after their use.
- If breastfeeding, always ensuring she empties the first breast completely before you offer the other side, so she is getting all the hindmilk available.
- Keeping an eye on what you eat to see if your consumption of caffeine, alcohol, strong vegetables, such as cabbage or broccoli, or citrus fruits seem to be linked to the crying. Don't make any dramatic changes to your diet without consulting a doctor, though.
- If bottle feeding, keeping the bottle upright so there is always milk covering the neck of the bottle to reduce the amount of wind she swallows. Also, making sure that you are not overfeeding her.
- Experimenting with anti-colic teats or bottles, which aim to reduce the amount of air going in.

Soothing a colicky baby

There are a number of things you can do that may, or may not, soothe a baby in the midst of a bout of colic – a process of trial and error is the only way to put them to the test. Don't forget to check for the obvious things first, and be certain she is not ill (see 'When it's an emergency', p. 92). Then, you could try:

- Taking her for a walk in the pram or keeping her close to you in a sling.
- Putting her in the car seat and taking her for a drive.
- Holding, cuddling, jigging or rocking her rhythmically in your arms.
- Singing to her or playing her music.
- Letting her listen to the 'white noise' of a washing machine or vacuum cleaner.

- Giving her a warm bath.
- Allowing her to suck on your boob or a dummy – but avoid a dummy for at least the first four weeks, or until breastfeeding is well established.
- A spot of baby massage – lie her on her tummy and gently rub her back, or lie her on her back and gently rub her tummy. (For more on baby massage, see p. 75).
- Putting her in a vibrating or rocking chair/crib.

Coping with colic

It can be unbearably hard to cope with colic, because you feel so out of control – nothing you do for your baby seems to console her and it's easy to assume it's your fault. But colic is only ever a phase, and one that will come to an end within a couple of months.

Enlist as much help as you can when trying to cope with the crying. If you find yourself at breaking point, make sure your baby is in a safe place and leave the room for a while. (For more ideas about how to keep cool when you're under stress, see p. 275.)

Other explanations

In a very small number of cases, babies with colicky symptoms may be having a bad reaction to lactose, the sugar found in milk (including breast milk). Lactose-intolerant babies will usually have other symptoms, though, such as diarrhoea. If you suspect this is the problem, you should seek advice from your GP.

Another potential medical explanation for excessive crying is gastro-oesophageal reflux, the regurgitation of acid from the stomach into the gullet, which can cause vomiting, coughing and pain during or after a feed. (For more information about this condition and its treatment, see the Health A–Z appendix, p. 312.)

Colicky crying on its own need not be a cause for worry, but if the crying is accompanied by any other problems, such as vomiting, diarrhoea, failure to gain weight, fever, constipation or dry nappies, seek medical advice.

Be sure to tell someone about it, too, if the crying is causing you such grief that you are worried you may harm your baby, or if it is causing or worsening any depression you may be feeling.

What the netmums say

Colic and crying

My son cried and cried and cried. He just seemed so hungry all the time. I stopped breastfeeding at ten days, because I was starting to feel sick when he woke for a feed and was terrified I would hate him, and then felt awful for stopping. I couldn't look at the cards or presents we'd been given, as I felt I didn't deserve them. Then, at about two weeks, the colic started, and he screamed from 4p.m. until 10p.m. every single exhausting day until he was about three and a half months old, when it suddenly stopped. It was as though the skies had cleared and it all suddenly made sense. The funny thing is, throughout it all, I still felt the most overpowering love for him.
Jen from Chorleywood, mum to Jack, four and Theo, one

I wish someone had prepared me for the colic! We spent night upon night walking her round and round and round. My dog thought it was brilliant – I don't think he has been walked so much in his life! In the end, we found that sitting her upright and bouncing her helped to ease it.
Sarah from Southend, mum to Madison, two

We struggled after our son was born. He screamed and screamed. You know how the point of antenatal classes is to meet people to make you feel better when you all realise you're going through the same thing? Well, we were the people who made everyone else feel better. Every time we spoke to someone else with a baby we were left wondering what on earth we were doing so wrong. We were told that Kieran had colic, and this was the source of our woe. We tried everything: Infacol, Colief, Dentinox, baby massage. Nothing worked and we were so tired. We felt we couldn't complain, because we knew we were blessed to have this baby. But why was it so hard? Everyone was full of advice. One doctor sent us straight to the children's ward at hospital when he heard how intense the crying was. But the consultant's diagnosis was extreme colic. The remedy? Nothing. Just keep surviving. Exhausted and broken, we decided to take him to a cranial osteopathy session – afterwards, he began to improve immediately. Turned out that his head had been totally mashed from his traumatic delivery. After about three or four sessions, he started sleeping through. Light at the end of the tunnel! If you're finding life with a newborn tough, then you're not alone, don't beat yourself up about it, it's not your fault. When they grow up a bit, they're fantastic. We absolutely adore our son and would never be without him. So much so, that I am a totally gutsy mother now!

Kate from Macclesfield, mum to Kieran, one

My daughter screamed from the first night she was born and a good 80 per cent of the time after that until she was four months old, except for when she was feeding or sleeping (on me). The doctor put in her notes that she was irritable and difficult to examine, and she had a LOUD cry, which made me really paranoid about annoying our neighbours. She was a big baby and after being two weeks overdue I was induced, so my theory is that she was happy where she was and not mentally prepared for the outside world – along with the fact that our stress made her feel worse. She was a good feeder, never sick and extremely alert, but just couldn't switch off when she got tired. She still has trouble sleeping now – but I wouldn't change her for the world.

Karyn from Brighton, mum to Abigail, one

It's very challenging to keep your temper in check with a very small baby who won't stop crying. You're sleep deprived and absolutely shattered, and there's no way of knowing what's wrong and how to stop their piercing cry, which after all is specifically designed to make a mother react. I remember my partner asking: 'What's wrong with him? He won't stop crying.' He was fed and burped, changed, the right temperature. It wasn't until a bit later that we realised babies just want a grizzle sometimes, and that crying is their only way of communicating. If I felt as though I was going to lose my temper,

I put him in a safe place like his cot and left the room for a couple of minutes to calm down. Then I could go back with a cool head and react rationally.

Carly from Norwich, mum to Finley, seven months

Feeding

Breast . . . still the best

If you're breastfeeding, you should have got the hang of it and passed any initial difficulties by the second month. You should begin to notice that your milk supply is more in tune with your baby's demands, and that feeds are taking up a bit less of your time.

Some mums make it through the first, painful stage only to stop at this point because they're fed up with the commitment. If your enthusiasm's waning, it might help to remind yourself of all the benefits of breastfeeding (see p. 16), which carry on well beyond the first month.

Milk machine

Babies very commonly have a growth spurt at around six to eight weeks, and may seem hungrier than ever for a couple of days. This can cause some breastfeeding mums to worry that they're not providing enough milk for their babies, and may prompt them to offer a formula top-up. However, if you continue to feed her whenever she seems to want it, she'll almost certainly be getting enough. You may have to accept that for a few days at least, you're no more than a human milk machine – if you can keep up with her demand over these few days, your breasts *will* rise to the challenge.

Bottlefed babies may also seem noticeably hungrier, evidenced by the way they drain their bottles. You could try giving her a little extra, experimenting if necessary until you've worked out how much she needs to satisfy her. Never try to give her more than she seems to want, though, and never be tempted to use more powder in feeds than the instructions say.

What the netmums say

Growth spurts

I breastfed on demand and spent the first few weeks in my pyjamas as it seemed easier. There was one day when we'd asked some friends around for a barbecue and I was looking forward to feeling a bit more human, but on this day, Clara decided to have a growth spurt! I spent most of the day either laying in bed with her attached to my boob, or on the settee watching everyone enjoying themselves out of the living-room window. I must admit, tears did roll down my cheeks due to the frustration. But it only lasted three days and she was back to normal.

Sharmaigne from Peterborough, mum to Clara, one

Mixed feeding

If you're breastfeeding and want to try your baby with a bottle – perhaps because you'd like to give some expressed breast milk feeds, or because you would like to introduce formula, or mixed feeding – the ideal time to start is when she's six to eight weeks old. Leave it any longer and you may find she's so accustomed to the breast she won't be very open-minded about other possibilities. Any earlier, though, and it might interfere with her ability to drink from the breast, or even lead her to reject it altogether.

It's perfectly possible to make a success of mixed breast and formula feeding, and many mums find this is a good compromise if they want to carry on giving their own milk but need to plan for a return to work, or simply want a break from the commitment of breastfeeding. A word of warning, though – once you stop exclusively breastfeeding, your supply of milk will decrease to match the reduced demand, and once your baby is happily taking the bottle, the temptation to give up on breastfeeding altogether may grow strong. You need to be fairly certain it's the route you want to go down.

What the netmums say

Expressing milk

I fully intended at least to partially breastfeed my child until she was one (and possibly beyond) but for economic reasons had to return to work when she was four months old. I tried expressing but after shutting myself in a room at work only for the cleaner to walk in, I gave it up as a bad job. (I have to say, expressing made me feel like a cow and I did not like it, although I was prepared to do it for the sake of my child.) I still continued to breastfeed in the evenings and at night, but when my daughter was nine months old I had to admit that I had dried up.

Andrea from High Wycombe, mum to Angharad, three

My sister helped me to get my daughter on a bottle of expressed milk before six weeks, which is apparently the point by which it's best to try, by phoning me at five weeks, six days and telling me to do it *immediately*! It worked, and the transition from breast to bottle was totally painless. It was really nice for my husband to feed her so early, so everyone was a winner. To make the bottle feeding easier, I collected milk in shells [soft shell-shaped containers worn inside the bra to collect excess breast milk] when I leaked, or expressed from one breast while feeding from the other, and I always had seven or eight feeds in the freezer.

Adilla from Bideford, mum to Alice, three

Milking it: How to express with success

Expressing your own milk for bottle feeds can be a great solution for mums who want to give their baby all the benefits of breast milk but are having physical difficulties with breastfeeding, or need someone else to do the feeding sometimes. However, it does require some commitment and determination, because it's slightly undignified and time-consuming.

It's possible to express reasonably efficiently by hand – in fact, for some women hand expressing will yield more milk than a device because this method aids the release of the hormone oxytocin, which stimulates the flow of milk. Gently massage your breast towards the nipples to stimulate the let-down reflex. Milk will begin to gather behind the areola. Gently squeeze the breast between the first finger and thumb, and keep pressing and releasing. Be sure to squeeze the breast and not the nipple, which would be painful and ineffective.

For speedier or more regular expressing, you may be better off with a manual or electric breast pump. The electric versions are particularly effective and, although expensive, may prove a good investment if you intend to use one a lot. Otherwise, you can hire one through the National Childbirth Trust (see Useful Addresses at the back of the book).

Always express into a sterilised container (you can buy pre-sterilised bags or bottle liners for the purpose). Expressed milk can be stored in a bag or bottle with a secured top in the back of the fridge at between 2°C and 4°C for three to five days – don't forget to label each container so you know when it went in. Breast milk tends to separate when stored, with the cream rising to the top, so you'll need to give it a shake. It can be successfully frozen, although it will lose some of its antibodies in the process. Allow frozen breast milk to thaw overnight in the fridge, or by running the container under warm water – don't be tempted to put it in a microwave because, as well as the risk of hot spots that might burn your baby's mouth, you may lose yet more of its beneficial properties. Use within 24 hours and, once out of the fridge, always use a breast-milk feed within five hours. Don't attempt to re-freeze breast milk that's already been frozen and thawed in case bacteria have developed in the meantime, and because re-freezing it will destroy valuable nutrients.

Boob to bottle tips

Some babies who are accustomed to being breastfed are happy to accept a bottle and teat immediately. Others need some convincing – particularly if you're also introducing formula for the first time, which tastes very different from breast milk. You may need to keep persevering until she gets used to it. When making the move from breast to bottle, there are several things to bear in mind:

- Babies often reject a bottle or formula feed when mum offers it, perhaps not surprisingly – if she can feel and smell your breast in the vicinity, she might wonder why you're trying to fob her off with a fake! It may help if you get her dad, or any other adult she's comfortable with, to offer the bottle first.
- There's a huge variety of types and shapes of teats available, so if your baby rejects the first one you try, give another one a go (but don't go mad trying out every single one on the market, because there are loads). Teats are usually made from either silicone or latex. Babies used to a real nipple may prefer the latex sort because they're softer.
- Check you've got the expressed or formula milk at the right temperature – your baby will probably prefer it slightly warm. It's now advised that you make up forumula feeds with cooled, boiled water as you need them, rather than making them and storing in the fridge beforehand, so you will have to cool feeds down, rather than warm them up. However, if you do need to warm a bottle of milk, use a bottle warmer or a cup of hot water rather than a microwave, which can cause hot spots that could burn her mouth. If you *do* use a microwave, bear in mind that different models vary in wattage levels – and that it's vital to shake the bottle very thoroughly before offering it.
- Get the timing right. Offer the bottle when she's hungry, but not so ravenous that she'll be feeling sensitive.
- Try feeding in a different place from usual, or try giving the bottle in the dark.
- If she's having none of it, wait a day or two before trying again. Give yourself plenty of time to make the introduction – if you know you're going to be returning to work at a certain time, make sure you offer a bottle well in advance.
- Try not to become anxious or unhappy if she doesn't take to the bottle as quickly as you'd like. Unless you are in a real hurry (perhaps because you need to return to work), or are genuinely concerned that she's not getting enough from the breast, it shouldn't be a cause for worry.

- Drop breastfeeds gradually, to avoid painful engorgement and a dramatic drop in supply. Start by offering a bottle just once a day at first.
- Some babies never take to the bottle – especially if you're late in trying. You may have to bypass bottles altogether and introduce a cup when appropriate. (See p. 174.)

What the netmums say

Mixed feeding

I had some trouble breastfeeding because I never felt like she was getting enough – even though she would feed for forty-five minutes every two hours sometimes, she would still cry in between. So at eight weeks I introduced a bottle and she immediately became a much calmer baby. Also, because I knew she was getting her 'fill' from the formula, it gave me the confidence to keep breastfeeding her at least twice a day to ensure she was getting the goodness of breast milk as well. The best of both worlds, as far as I was concerned.
Michelle from Brighton, mum to Freya, one

I really wanted to breastfeed but I've found it so challenging. I was prepared for some pain but continuously feeding her every couple of hours on demand caused very sore nipples – even with the help of midwives, my health visitor and a breastfeeding counsellor. I've done a lot of soul searching and now breastfeed three times a day, the rest of the time she has formula. Although this wasn't my plan, I realise that a happy mum equals a happy baby. I was beginning to dread feeding times and it wasn't a healthy atmosphere for either of us.
Rachel from Preston, mum to Lila, aged six weeks

Sleep

A bedtime routine

A few lucky mums find that their babies begin to sleep through the night early on, but for the majority, one or more night wakings will still be a feature in the second month, and well beyond. One thing you can do, though, to pave the way to a solid night's sleep in the future is to begin a bedtime routine for your baby.

Having a habitual process that takes place at the same time each and every evening before she's laid down in her cot will get your baby used to the idea that sleep is invariably what comes next! Before long, she'll get to a point where she has no idea there's any other option, an advantage that will help you towards peaceful evenings – and, eventually, nights – and stand you in good stead for many years ahead.

Bath, story, bed

For many babies a bedtime routine starts with some combination of a bath, a feed, a story (it's never too early – for more on reading to your baby, see p. 104) or song, and a cuddle. Do it all with the lights dimmed and in a low voice, and make sure her room is dark when you leave her so she knows that it's night-time and, therefore, time for sleep.

Some parents think that a completely darkened room, which can be achieved with special black-out blinds, helps their baby to get to sleep quickly and can even ensure a lie-in the next morning. However, if you go down this route, you may find she won't settle in a room that's not completely dark, which could be a problem if you're staying away from home. A much cheaper, and portable, alternative to blinds is a piece of black-out fabric, available by the metre at all good haberdashers, which can be unrolled and attached temporarily to any window with the aid of a bit of masking tape.

Remember that it's far better to put your baby in her cot awake, if you can, so that she can learn how to settle herself to sleep – something you'll want her to do later when you're aiming to get her to sleep the whole night through, without waking you!

What the netmums say

Bedtime routines

Each baby is different, but personally I like having a routine, and it made sense for me to get my daughter into a pattern as soon as was practical. We established bath, bottle, bed at 6.30p.m. from

when she was five weeks old (with a late-night bottle at about 10p.m.) and from eight weeks old she's gone through the night consistently. Now, at two, she still goes to bed no later than 6.30p.m. and sleeps for 12 hours. She has always had a nap during the day, but I would not let her sleep beyond 4p.m. I found this invaluable.
Amanda from Milton Keynes, mum to Sienna, two

At around six weeks I found she did start settling for as much as eight hours a night. I've stuck to a routine of bathing her just before her bedtime, and now as soon as she is bathed I know I can put her to bed awake and she settles because she knows it's the end of her day.
Nina from Nuneaton, mum to Sabrina, five months

I'm a bit of a routine freak, to be honest, and got him into a routine as soon as possible. By the time he was 16 weeks he was sleeping from 7p.m. to 7a.m., with one nap during the day. He's three now, and still sleeps almost 12 hours a night. We had, and still have, a structured bedtime. When he was small, he would get a nice bath, bottle, story and bed. He's slept brilliantly ever since. Now he knows when it's time for bed and he goes without any fuss, happy to put on his pjs for a story, drink, pee, then bed!
Nicola from Aberdeen, mum to Blaine, three

Daytime naps

Your baby will still be napping frequently and for long stretches in her second month, but you may notice a pattern emerging, which will help you to plan your day a little more easily. You can encourage her towards a good daytime routine, too, by putting her down to sleep at the same time each day, whenever possible.

The Foundation for the Study of Infant Deaths advises that the same safety advice applies to nap time as well as night time – so for the first six months, it's best to remain nearby when your baby is sleeping.

Leisure and Learning

Out and about

By now a regular walk with the pram or sling, or a drive in the car, may be a favourite part of the day – it will almost certainly be a good way of getting her to nap if she needs to, provided she's had a feed beforehand. You may also be more confident about taking your baby on necessary trips, such as to the shops or visiting – although, for some mums, getting out and about with very young babies can cause a good deal of anxiety. As your baby gets older, less demanding and more predictable, it does become easier.

One of the challenges of getting out and about with your baby is remembering to take everything you might need. A good tip is to fix a checklist to the front door or fridge – or better still, keep a bag packed and ready, with all the necessities, by the door.

Packed and ready: What you might want to take when you go out with your baby

- Several nappies, changing mat and wipes (also useful for mopping up spills). Nappy sacks are useful for disposing of smelly nappies and mucky wipes, and muslins are indispensable.
- At least one (easy) change of clothing in case of accidents.
- If you're bottlefeeding, whatever she'll need for a feed, even if she's not likely to be due one while you're out – in case you get stuck somewhere. Current advice is to make up feeds when you need them, so take a pre-sterilised bottle and teat, sealed by the lid, and either a carton of ready-made formula or a flask of hot water and a small container of powdered formula.
- If you're breastfeeding, a change of breast pads – and a muslin, if you are modest about baring your boobs in public.
- An extra layer of clothing for your baby, and/or a blanket in case the weather gets colder. A sunhat, sunshade and sunscreen if it's sunny, or in case it becomes sunny.
- A distraction of some kind, such as a small rattle or fabric book (but a set of car keys can work as an alternative!).

Driving lessons: What you need to know about car-seat safety

If you're travelling in the car, be certain you've made all the safety checks you need to. Make sure your baby's car seat is fitted correctly. Never put a rear-facing infant car seat in the front with an airbag – in fact, the best place to put a baby seat, generally, is in the back. You can buy a little mirror to fix on to your front windscreen, which allows you to check behind you without turning round.

Don't put heavy objects in the car where they might move in transit and hit the baby, and when getting your baby in and out of the car, do so on the kerbside. Never leave your baby alone in the car, and take care in the heat because parts of a car seat's strap can get very hot.

Bear in mind that babies shouldn't sit in car seats for more than a couple of hours at a time, because it may place a strain on their spine. There's also some evidence that babies left sleeping unsupervised in car seats for long periods – especially if born prematurely – may be at risk of a restricted airflow (possibly because their heads can flop forward, although it's not known for certain why). So, although it may be tempting to leave your sleeping baby in the car seat once you're back home, it's advised that you always transfer her to a cot as soon as you can.

For more information on car seats and travelling safely with your baby, take a look at the website of the Child Accident Prevention Trust (CAPT), or the Royal Society for the Prevention of Accidents (RoSPA). (See Useful Addresses at the back of the book.)

Fun and games

Soon, your baby should be able to 'swat' at things dangled close enough for her to reach comfortably. This is a good way for her to develop her hand-eye coordination as well as being good fun. You can encourage the game by carefully holding or fixing a piece of string with a safe, suitable target, such as a plastic rattle or small soft toy, attached to it above her.

Baby massage

You might want to enrol in a baby massage class now, or try some simple massage techniques at home. Baby massage is a wonderful way to bond with your little one, and to relieve your own stress and tension – in fact, research has shown it can even help to alleviate postnatal depression. It also offers a host of recognised physical benefits – it's said to ease colic, improve the digestive system and even aid sleep. It's becoming increasingly popular, so you shouldn't be too far away from a course or class, if you want to try it under the guidance of a qualified instructor. The International Association of Infant Massage has an online register of these (see the Useful Addresses appendix, p. 333), or you could ask your health visitor if she knows of a local class. Otherwise, you can teach yourself some simple baby massage techniques – some are outlined below – and do them regularly at home. Some massage techniques shouldn't be used until after your baby has had her eight-week check because they involve moving the hips around, but a simple stroking massage is safe.

Before you start, choose a time of day when you're both fairly relaxed, and your baby isn't too tired. Don't try it too soon after feeding – let her have half an hour or so to let her milk go down. Make sure the room is warm. You could also perhaps dim the lights and put on some soothing music. Use an oil to help, but pick the right one – something natural and unscented, such as olive or rapeseed oil, is a good choice. Avoid a nut-based oil, such as almond oil, because of the risk of allergic reaction. Make sure you put a towel and changing mat under your baby, in case she decides to wee or poo mid-massage. Undress her and lay her gently in front of you on her back. Then get into a comfortable position, remove rings or bracelets, and give your hands a rub with the oil to warm them up. Then you're ready to go!

Touchy, feely: A short, simple baby massage session to try at home

These techniques can also be found on the Netmums website, www.netmums.com

- Start by placing your relaxed hands on your baby's shoulders and gently stroke down from her shoulders, across her chest and tummy, to the feet. Pressure should be light, but not so light that it tickles. Make sure that the whole of your hand and fingers comes into contact with her body. Do this stroke six times.

- Now place your hands flat at the top of her chest and stroke upwards and outwards going over the collarbone, shoulders and then down the arms. Repeat this six times.
- Stroke down your baby's body again from shoulders to feet, six times.
- Very lightly circle your fingertips over her tummy in a clockwise direction. Then massage the sides of the belly by stroking hand over hand first from one side to the belly button and then from the other side to the belly button.
- Stroke down your baby's body again from shoulders to feet, six times.
- Add some more oil to your hands if you need to, then hold one of your baby's legs at the top of the thigh and move your hand slowly down to the foot. Just as you're about to let go, place the other hand at the top of the same thigh and start to move down the leg. This is a nice rhythmic technique but remember to keep it slow, smooth and gentle. Repeat several times and then move on to the other leg.
- Stroke down your baby's body again from shoulders to feet, six times.
- If she will tolerate it, turn her over on to her tummy and stroke down her back and the backs of her legs with alternate horizontal hands.
- Finish the massage, either on the front or back, by placing your hands warmly on either the base of the back or the shoulders for a few seconds and then remove gently.
- Wrap your baby in the towel to absorb any excess oil before dressing her.
- This session should take about ten minutes, but if your baby starts to cry at any point, stop and try again another day.

What the netmums say

Baby massage

I took my daughter to baby massage from about six weeks until she was about ten months. She loved it, and I really feel it helped us bond more and have some time that was just ours. I showed my other half how to do it too and we used to give her a massage after her bath, before bed. It helped her to sleep better, and also helped her colic. Now she's four, and she still loves getting her back rubbed.
Sharon from Alexandria, mum to Jessica, aged four

When I had my first son I went to baby massage classes when he was about three months old. We both loved it, and I felt we had such a strong bond during the massage. We continued the practice at home, it was our one-to-one time together and a truly wonderful experience. He still loves being massaged, at three. When my second son arrived last year, I again went to classes with him, and all those precious feelings returned. Both my babies were very relaxed and so far we've not had any sleep problems. Because of my interest in baby massage, I've trained in it and am now qualified to teach. I'm delighted to be able to pass on the art of massage. Touch is a wonderful gift to be able to give to your child!
Roisin from Belfast, mum to Zack, three and Corey, one

Talk to your baby some more!

By now your baby should be showing lots in the way of responses to your face and voice, so keep giving her loads of opportunities to do so by talking to her, singing and making eye contact. Try imitating her when she makes a noise or pulls a face – it should become a popular game and will help her to understand that imitation is one of the best ways of learning. (For more on the importance of talking to your baby and ways to do it, see p. 271 in The Eleventh Month.)

All About You

Your postnatal check

Some women will find they are physically back to normal after six weeks, but for others it will take longer – particularly if you had a difficult birth. Your midwife and/or health visitor will remind you to go for your all-important six-week postnatal check, which is usually carried out by your GP, a practice nurse or sometimes, if you had a complicated delivery, a hospital doctor.

What happens at the test will vary from doctor to doctor. You may well have an examination to make sure your uterus has fully contracted back to its pre-pregnancy state and that there is no sign of infection around your scars, as well as routine blood pressure, urine, weight and blood checks. Your doctor may ask you how feeding is going, whether your lochia (the postnatal blood flow) has stopped or slowed, and whether your bowels and bladder are functioning normally. You may also be offered a smear test. It's a good chance to chat to your GP about any physical or emotional concerns, so it's important that you speak up if you feel you're suffering in any way.

Assuming you're fit and well, you'll get the go-ahead to have sex if you want to and haven't already. A small number of women find their libidos are still intact and their bodies sufficiently recovered to resume lovemaking within a few weeks of the birth, although most prefer to wait for the six-week go-ahead, particularly if they had stitches or a Caesarean section. Even if you had a straightforward delivery without stitches, your vagina may still be bruised, strained or sore, and plenty of couples wait for much longer than six weeks. If you're not in the mood, still suffering physically, or just too tired to have sex, don't worry. You're not alone. Many women still don't feel that way inclined at this point.

You'll also be asked about what sort of contraception you plan to use, and since few women are keen to become pregnant again too soon after giving birth, this is a question you'd be wise to address. (For more information about sex and contraception, see p. 125.)

Losing your baby weight

Once you get the nod from your doctor at your six-week check, you can make a gentle start on getting back into shape if you want – and if you've got the time! For most mums, though, this will come pretty low down their list of priorities. And it's very important to bear in mind that baby weight rarely drops off quickly – it takes nine months to gain, and for most women, it will take at least that long to shed.

If you do want to take an active approach to regaining your old body, it's vital to do so gently. Avoid dieting, especially if you're still breastfeeding, which, incidentally, will help you lose weight more quickly than if you are not. Stick to a healthy balance of different foods, eating lots of fresh fruit, salad and veg, and cutting down on fatty, sugary snacks. And if you want to begin a proper exercise regime, do so with caution. Your body will still be vulnerable to the lingering affects of relaxin, the hormone that's released during pregnancy to loosen the joints and ligaments, increasing the risk of strain and injury. So high-impact sports, such as aerobics or running, are best avoided for six to nine months after the birth in favour of low-impact activities, such as swimming or power walking – in fact, just getting out and about with the pram or sling and covering a fair bit of distance at a quick pace, regularly, is a great way to raise your heartbeat and shed the pounds. It's not just about physical benefits, though – keeping active, especially outside in the fresh air, is good for your state of mind, too. Your baby is pretty much guaranteed to sleep on the move, so a nice, long walk provides the opportunity for some much-needed peace and reflection.

Diastasis recti
In the majority of women, a condition called diastasis recti occurs naturally during pregnancy. It happens when the pressure of the growing baby stretches the connective tissues between the two bands of the main tummy muscle – the rectus abdominus – causing them to separate from one another. It's a temporary condition that almost always begins to right itself immediately after delivery, although it takes the muscle four to six weeks to realign and several months to strengthen to its original state.

All new mums suffer from stretched and weakened abdominal muscles to some extent, though, and these muscles need time to recover after delivery. So it's best to avoid intense exercises, such as sit-ups, curl-ups or crunches, for four to six months after the birth. In the meantime, you can work on getting your tummy muscles back in shape by regularly pulling them in and holding for a few seconds before releasing and repeating. Pelvic tilts are also effective: stand with your back to a wall, slide a hand into the gap between your lower back and the wall and use your abdominal muscles to tilt your pelvis backwards. You'll know you're doing it right if you can feel your lower back pushing against your hand. Both these simple exercises can be done any time, any place, anywhere.

Pilates is also an effective and safe form of postnatal exercise – but only under the guidance of a professional instructor, to whom you should point out that you have recently had a baby. Some elements of this sort of workout may not be suitable right now.

Weight loss, celeb-style

Don't get sucked in by the strange modern assumption, fuelled by a media obsession with 'yummy-mummies', that it's somehow possible to squeeze back into your old dress size within a few short weeks of having a baby, just in time for that all-important film première or lucrative magazine photoshoot. For most of us, it isn't. These people have plastic surgeons, personal trainers, chefs and maternity nurses – and, if all else fails, photographic airbrushing – at their disposal. In other words, they don't live in the real world! (For more information on bodies after giving birth, including some other ideas for getting back into shape, see p. 239.)

What the netmums say

Bodies after birth

It was the shape of my body that got to me and made me tearful. I breastfed, and loved it, but hated the size of my boobs, and the rest of me. I did lose all the weight very quickly, so looking back I was silly to worry. But I think with your first baby, it can be quite shocking to lie in the bath and stare down at what has happened to your body. You don't think it will ever be back to normal.
Chantelle from Christchurch, mum to Daisy, five, Ruby, four and Dylan, one

I spend everyday out and about walking with my little boy and I did expect to get back into shape a little quicker, but I'm so preoccupied enjoying my little man I don't have much time to dwell on it. My philosophy is it took me nine months to put all the

weight on, I'm giving myself nine months to take it off! I feel proud of my post-birth body. I feel womanly and I wear my stretch marks with pride!
Carly from Norwich, mum to Finley, seven months

The return of your periods

If you're not breastfeeding, you may find your periods start again between four to six weeks after the birth. If you're exclusively breastfeeding, you may not have a period for as long as you keep the feeding up – it's nature's way of offering some contraceptive protection during this period (but see p. 126 for more information before relying on this method).

Postnatal depression

While the mild and commonly experienced baby blues will be over now, a significant number of mums suffer more serious emotional difficulties. Postnatal depression (sometimes known as postnatal illness, or postpartum depression) often sets in during the second month after giving birth, although it may kick in some time within the first month, or some months afterwards, and typically lasts for several months. It is thought to affect up to 20 per cent of mums and can be experienced at different levels, from mild to severe.

Other than having a baby, there are no particular trigger factors for postnatal depression; it affects women of all circumstances from all walks of life, although some women may be more vulnerable to developing it – those with a previous history of depression, for example, or who have depression in the family. Women who have no support from family and friends, or who have a difficult relationship with their own mum, or with their partner, may be more prone to developing PND, as may those who have been through a traumatic period before or after the birth. A problem with the baby, or a particularly difficult birth may be other factors.

The good news is that something can be done to help women suffering from PND. The bad news is that a great many women suffer in silence.

How PND can make you feel

- Low, tearful, unhappy, irritable
- Anxious or even panic-stricken
- Stressed
- Struggling to cope
- Lethargic
- Unable to relax, laugh or show interest or excitement in anything
- Guilty
- Exhausted (but not necessarily able to sleep)
- No appetite
- Unable to concentrate or make simple decisions
- Indifferent towards your baby or partner
- Convinced something bad is going to happen to your baby
- Completely uninterested in sex or intimacy

Why me?

The causes of PND are unclear. Hormones may be involved, but as the usual changes to hormone levels tend to happen immediately after the birth (and are probably largely responsible for the mild, short-lived and extremely common baby blues) they can't be entirely blamed for full-blown postnatal depression. Usually the sheer difficulty and exhaustion involved in having a baby will be a factor, and if one or more stresses and strains is at play, then that can trigger depression.

What's vital is recognising that you have PND, and acknowledging it. Until that happens, you won't be able to get the help you need to get better. Not everyone realises they've got PND, while many others may suspect it but be unable to confront it. Health professionals these days are very clued up to the possibility, which is why you'll be asked how you feel a great deal in the weeks after the birth. New mums are usually asked to complete some kind of Maternal Mood Assessment questionnaire, such as the Edinburgh Postnatal Depression Scale. Do be honest when you fill one of these in, however bad you're feeling. No one will judge you – and you can't get help unless you let someone know you need it.

If you are suffering, the best thing to do is to tell someone about it, ideally a health professional, but your partner or a close friend or relative would be a good start. PND sufferers invariably need support from one or more health professionals, but equally from a patient partner, who can offer both practical and emotional support, and/or other close family members and friends.

How is it treated?

Postnatal depression will get better eventually. However, it can cause a good deal of grief and may affect your relationship with your baby, so it's much better to seek help sooner rather than later.

Treatment may come in the form of counselling or a more specific psychological treatment, such as Cognitive Behavioural Therapy (CBT), which aims to help you change the ways you think and behave. Medication in the form of anti-depressants, which affect the activity of chemicals in the brain, may be prescribed if the depression is severe or has gone on for a long time – they usually take a couple of weeks to kick in and you may have to take them for around six months. Some may have side effects, such as nausea or sleepiness. Generally, you will be advised to stop breastfeeding if taking anti-depressants. In many cases, though, the most useful treatment is the sort that can't be prescribed – adequate support and rest.

(For contact details for a number of helpful organisations, see the Useful Addresses appendix at the back of the book, p. 339)

Beat the blues: How to help yourself win the battle against PND

- Talk about how you feel, whether to someone in your family or a health professional, such as a GP or your health visitor.
- Find someone who's going through it too, so you can help to support one another. (If you can't find anyone, go online and find someone to talk to through Netmums.)

- Get as much rest and sleep as you possibly can, cat-napping if need be. Let other less important tasks, such as housework, go by the wayside.
- Try to get some gentle exercise, which can help you sleep better and helps trigger endorphins, the body's natural painkillers.
- Eat well – healthy but easily prepared food that doesn't need much cooking.
- Find some time to spend with your partner.
- Spend a little time with yourself, letting someone else take care of the baby for a while.
- Don't take on any other major stresses, such as a house move.
- Don't blame yourself, or your partner, for the way you feel. Remind yourself that it's an illness, and no one's fault.
- Don't be frightened by the diagnosis. It's a common condition, countless women have been through it and you will get better in time.

When PND is dangerous

Rarely, a new mum may suffer from puerperal psychosis, which is the most severe form of PND and affects one or two in every thousand women. It generally occurs suddenly and fairly soon after the birth. It's thought that the sudden hormonal drop in the days after birth is what triggers it, although it is most likely to affect someone with a personal or family history of mental illness.

A mum with this condition may become manic – going through phases of being extremely excited, elated, invulnerable and overactive, followed by a plunge into feelings of depression, anxiety, panic, guilt and inadequacy. She may even have delusions. At worst, she may become suicidal or consider harming her baby, so it's essential that anyone suffering from it has immediate help.

What the netmums say

Postnatal depression

I was probably fairly depressed for around six weeks. In fact, it took 'til she was eighteen months for me fully to discover the new version of me. I don't think I'm unusual though: I reckon nearly all the mums I know experienced some kind of depression in the first year. I believe PND should be considered a spectrum that covers just about all new mums, rather than something awful that happens to a few of us.
Clare from Sheffield, mum to Hannah, three and Sophia, one

I was in a fog for the first year, if I'm honest. But the worst thing I did was to pretend everything was fine. I told the health visitors what they wanted to hear, and put on a great act. My husband was great and if it wasn't for him, I don't know what would have happened. I have two regrets about the first few weeks of my daughter's life. The first one is that I was in complete denial about having postnatal depression, because I now realise that was what was wrong with me. And the second one is that when I look at photos of my daughter aged just a few weeks old, I don't remember a thing about it. But it hasn't put me off. We're trying for number two, and if we're lucky enough to have another, this time I'll know I'm not Superwoman, and the hoovering can wait.
Mags from Bellshill, mum to Eve, two

When Connor was six weeks old, I started getting very angry. Anger was the start of it. I would throw things, yell and scream, and break down crying. I isolated myself from everyone. I still really enjoyed time with Connor, but everything else was going downhill. Soon after, I was diagnosed with severe postnatal depression and have been on anti-depressants and having weekly counselling sessions ever since. I feel because of the depression that I've missed out on really seeing Connor grow through his first ten months of life. It feels like it's gone in the blink of an eye, and I don't remember much of it. I want my little baby back, but I want to be well enough to enjoy it and do it properly.
Erin from Leeds, mum to Connor, ten months

The Third Month

Welcome to your third month of motherhood

Most new mums have got a bit more into the swing of things by now. Feeds and naps should be more regular, allowing you to plan your day, and your baby will be spending more time awake during the day, allowing you to enjoy her company.

Assuming all's well, she'll be steadily growing. Perhaps she'll be busting out of her early outfits, or needing to move from her Moses basket to a proper cot. As her development progresses, she may be demonstrating new and exciting skills – holding her head up for short periods, reaching out, grabbing, laughing and chattering away to you in the form of gurgles and coos. These are the beginnings of conversation – who knew a tiny baby could be so talkative?

One of the best things you can do for yourself now, if you haven't already, is to get out and about in the community with your baby. Whether you live in a city or a village, there's sure to be at least one other mum in your position living somewhere near you. All you have to do is get out there and meet her!

Health, Growth and Development

Baby milestones
Now that she is two months old, your baby will typically:

- Be able to lift her head for a little while, when lying on her stomach.
- Wave her arms and kick her legs.
- Listen with interest to your voice.
- Be able to 'track' with her eyes a colourful object moved about 20cm from her face.
- Make 'happy' noises, such as cooing and gurgling.

And she might also:

- Lift up her head and upper chest for a little while, when lying on her tummy.
- Smile back when you smile at her.
- Laugh or squeal with pleasure.
- Grasp a finger placed against her palm.
- Copy you, if you put your face close to hers and stick your tongue out at her!

Milestone focus: Cooing and babbling

Early as it may seem, your baby's talking skills are in development even now. In her first few months, her 'chat' takes the form of adorable coos and gurgles, using vowel sounds like 'aah' and 'ooh', but she's not just doing it to melt your heart – she's practising the movements of lips, palate and tongue that are required to form proper speech, and she's learning that her sounds make things happen around her.

From three or four months, she'll begin to make consonant sounds such as 'b' and 'd', and somewhere between four and seven months she's likely to start joining vowels and consonants together repetitively. This important stage in her language development is known as babbling – and although you may delightedly think she's already learned your names when she says 'ma-ma' and 'da-da', the truth is, it's just a coincidence. She makes these sounds early on because they're among the commonest she hears, and also the easiest for her to say – although, if you respond to them, they will become the words you're looking for before too long.

Gradually this babble begins to sound almost like actual conversation, as she adds intonation to her strings of chattering sounds. And usually she'll love nothing more than experimenting with the sound of her own voice – so you can fully expect her to exercise it loudly and frequently!

You can encourage and boost her babbling skills by joining in – listen to the noises she's making and, when she's reached the end of her 'sentence', copy her. This is a good way to demonstrate to her how conversation works, taking turns to have your say. And don't forget to keep on talking, singing and reading with her, too.

Second round of injections

At the end of this month, your baby will be due for her second routine five-in-one injection for diphtheria, tetanus, pertussis, polio and Hib. At this point, she will also have a separate meningitis C jab, which offers protection against one type of meningitis. It doesn't offer protection against all forms of meningitis infection, so you still need to be aware of this disease's symptoms (see the Health A–Z appendix at the back of the book, p. 318).

When your baby is ill

Small babies may be frequently poorly. They have underdeveloped immune systems, which makes them vulnerable to minor illnesses, such as colds, coughs, and tummy bugs. It can be stressful and frightening when your baby is ill, and often very hard to decide on the best course of action – wait to see if she gets better on her own, check with your health visitor, contact a doctor, or rush her to an A&E unit. Your instincts will guide you, but it's always best to err on the side of caution. Keep a close eye on her if you suspect she's poorly – being so small, she can get worse quickly. Excessive vomiting or diarrhoea, for example, can soon lead to dehydration, and if left untreated, this can cause serious problems. Babies also have small lungs and airways, so simple viral infections can cause significant breathing problems.

Who can help?
Your health visitor will be able to give you advice on minor health problems, and you will usually be able to make contact with her on the telephone the same day. If it's something she thinks should be looked at, she'll suggest you call your doctor's surgery. There may also be an NHS walk-in centre or other drop-in clinic in your area – check with your surgery, ask your health visitor or call NHS Direct to find out more about these. You can also consult a pharmacist about many minor ailments.

It's a good idea to find out how your GP's out-of-hours arrangements work, as these things vary. Usually, if you call your local surgery at weekends or overnight, you'll be redirected to a dedicated out-of-hours centre.

Sometimes you may feel that you don't want to trouble your GP with what may be a perfectly ordinary childhood ailment. However, most family doctors are sympathetic to parents with a sick baby or child, and will often agree to see you without an appointment, or at the beginning or end of surgery hours. There may be a nurse practitioner at your surgery, who'll have experience of many child-health issues and may be available to see you if a doctor isn't. Another alternative is to consult your doctor on the telephone. Be sure to let the receptionist know your child's age and what the problem seems to be when you call the surgery.

The next best thing
For immediate medical advice, you can call NHS Direct, 24 hours a day, 365 days a year (in Scotland, the equivalent service is NHS 24. As yet, Northern Ireland does not have one). Keep the number stuck to the fridge or somewhere else prominent, because at times when you cannot get an appointment with your doctor, a chat to one of its nurse advisers may be the next best thing. (The numbers are listed at the top of the Health A–Z and also in the Useful Addresses appendices at the back of the book, p. 299 and pp. 336–7.)

Knowing she is ill

A detailed list of common childhood illnesses and other medical issues, including their symptoms and what you should do about them, may be found in the appendix at the back of this book.

However, some general indications that a child is poorly are worth knowing about. Be sure to make a careful mental or written note of exactly what the symptoms are before consulting a doctor or NHS Direct nurse adviser, to help him or her make an accurate assessment.

General symptoms

You should make an immediate appointment with your doctor, or call NHS Direct for further advice, if your baby:

- Has bruised or discoloured skin.
- Seems listless or unusually drowsy.
- Is crying persistently or differently from normal – especially if moaning, whimpering or screaming in a high pitch – and usual methods of soothing aren't helping.
- Is not interested in feeding.
- Appears to have severe leg pain or tenderness.
- Has a rash, particularly if it's accompanied by a fever. You can check for meningococcal septicaemia by using the glass test (for details, see the Health A–Z appendix at the back of the book, p. 318).
- Seems irritable and does not like being touched.
- Has a fever (a high temperature over 38°C or 100.4°F) or is flushed, hot and sweaty.
- Is not wetting or soiling her nappies as normal.
- Has had diarrhoea for more than 12 hours, or has blood-streaked poo in her nappies.
- Is vomiting excessively, as opposed to possetting (bringing up normal amounts of milk after a feed), particularly if the vomit is green (which indicates bile), bloody or projectile (very forceful).
- Has a discharge of any sort from ears, eyes, navel, penis or vagina.

When it's an emergency

If you are very concerned because your baby is displaying one or more of the symptoms below, take her to the nearest accident and emergency unit, or dial 999 and ask for an ambulance.

- She is not breathing, is breathing much faster than usual, or is having difficulty breathing and is grunting or wheezing.
- She is not conscious or is semi-conscious.
- She looks very pale, or her skin is blue, or she is dusky around the lips.
- She has a convulsion (fit) and has not had one before. (For more on this, see the entry for Febrile Convulsions, in the Health A–Z appendix, p. 311).
- She has cold hands or feet but also has a fever (a temperature over 38°C or 100.4°F).
- She feels floppy or limp, and is unresponsive.
- She will not be woken, or appears not to recognise you.
- She has a purple rash anywhere on her body that does not fade or lose colour when you press a glass against it.
- She has a raised, tense or bulging soft spot (fontanelle) on her head. This may be a sign of raised pressure on the brain, seen in meningitis or after a head injury. However, it can also occur in perfectly healthy children, for example after a spell of crying or after immunisation. It's worth getting your baby checked but if she is otherwise well, she's likely to be OK.
- She has had an accident involving a burn, deep cut, significant fall or bump to the head, or has swallowed something that could be harmful. (For more on how to deal with accidents and emergencies, see First Aid, p. 329.)

A sore subject: All you need to know about nappy rash

Nappy rash is a very common irritation of the skin on a baby's bottom and/or genital area. It's usually caused by prolonged contact with urine and/or poo, which can turn to ammonia, resulting in soreness and an outbreak of pink or red spots or blotches. It can also be caused by a fungal infection, such as thrush, which can develop in warm, damp conditions.

Most nappy rashes are mild and will clear up with the aid of an over-the-counter healing cream, such as Sudocrem. You should also change your baby's nappy more frequently than usual, and take extra care in keeping the area clean and dry. Accepted advice is to stick to cotton wool and water and to avoid using soap – however, you may find that a change of cream, cleansing method, wipes or even brand of nappy may help. It will also help to leave the nappy off altogether for short periods to allow the air to get to her skin. More severe or persistent nappy-rash symptoms can sometimes develop and your doctor may be able to prescribe a stronger cream for these. A nappy rash that refuses to clear up may possibly be the result of fungal infection and your GP may prescribe an anti-fungal cream that should soon resolve the problem.

Occasionally, a bacterial infection develops in the nappy region, often when ordinary nappy rash is left unchecked. This can become inflamed and very sore and may also cause a fever. You'll need to see your doctor, because it will probably need treatment with antibiotics.

Rarely, nappy rash may be caused or exacerbated by an underlying skin condition, such as eczema or contact dermatitis. (For more information on all these conditions, see the Health A–Z appendix, p. 299.) If your baby is diagnosed with one of these, you may be referred to a dermatologist (a skin condition specialist).

As well as frequently changing your baby's nappy and taking extra care in cleaning and drying the area during changes, you can help to avoid nappy rash by making sure nappies and clothing are not too tight, so there's room for air to circulate, and letting her go nappyless for short periods, whenever practical. Applying a barrier cream, such as zinc or petroleum jelly, will help to protect her skin from contact with her own waste.

What the netmums say

Nappy rash

When Jamie's nappy rash was bad, I swore by Metanium [a brand of nappy-rash ointment, available over the counter]. It's simply magic stuff – oh, and plenty of nappy-off time too!
Ruth from Lancaster, mum to Jamie, two

My first child had very bad nappy rash for the first ten weeks of his life, and it was so uncomfortable, he cried all the time. We went to the doctor's with him repeatedly and were given various creams – some seemed to do the trick, others made it worse. In the end, I just changed the brand of nappies we were using and within four days the rash had gone.
Rachel from Lincoln, mum to Sean, five and Naomi, two

I found that when I stopped using water and cotton balls to clean my son, he got nappy rash. It took ages to clear up and I tried every cream going – Bepanthen [another brand of nappy-rash cream] is fantastic. I now use fragrance-free baby wipes but then wipe over the cleaned area with a little water before blotting dry with kitchen paper and applying the cream.
Sam from Bristol, mum to Oliver, one

This is an issue in our house. My daughter had constant nappy rash for her first ten weeks, often ending up with thrush. I'd read somewhere that if they're particularly sensitive, they should be washed only with cotton wool and water, so that's what I did. But one day we were out and I didn't have any and tried some sensitive wipes – and the rash really diminished. I thought it was just a coincidence but when I went back to the cotton wool it flared up again. I wish I'd thought to experiment a little rather than just assuming the accepted wisdom must be right. It's worth trying to do things slightly differently if your baby is suffering. You never know what might work.
Sara, from Stafford, mum to Noor, three and Jasmine, 11 months

My little one has suffered with nappy rash twice only, but each time it was very nasty – blisters and raw skin. The first time, she had pooed in her sleep and by the time she woke up in the morning, the damage had been done. The second time, I haven't a clue as to the cause. I find Sudocrem to be ideal for her bum, or I let her spend time nappyless as much as I can, with towels everywhere. I always avoid wipes with alcohol as they're drying and can sting (try them on yourselves – you may be surprised!) so I use a variety with aloe vera.
Kath from Cardiff, mum to Mali, one

Feeding

A more regular intake

Now that you're in the third month, you should be over the period of seemingly endless feeding. Even if you're breastfeeding – which generally takes longer than bottlefeeding to settle into a reasonably spaced pattern, because breast milk is not so filling – a more regular schedule for feeds will probably have emerged by now and most babies will be taking approximately six feeds in any 24 hour period, approximately four hours apart. However, all babies are different and if yours is still requiring a couple more breastfeeds than that a day, it's nothing to worry about – although it's worth checking that your baby is definitely hungry when she cries, rather than feeling bored, or looking for a comfort suck. You may be able to help eke out time between feeds a bit by distracting her with play, or a trip out.

Watch out for genuine hunger caused by possible growth spurts, though, as these can occur at any point during the first couple of months. If she seems ravenous for a few days, you'll just have to bow to her demands until things have settled back into a more widely spaced pattern of feeds again.

How much formula?

Formula-fed babies will take different quantities of milk according to birth weight and growth, but as with breastfeeding, you still need to be guided by her at this stage. Between 113g (4oz) and 170g (6oz) per feed is a good general guideline around now. Aim to have a little milk left at the end of the feed, so that you know she is full – if she's draining 142g (5oz), for instance, try giving her 170g (6oz) next time. Never force her to finish a bottle – she knows best how much she needs.

Sleep

All the way through the night?

Sleeping through is generally defined, when babies are this young, as a solid six-hour stretch overnight – if you're really lucky, you may have a baby who sleeps for even longer, but on the other hand, she may not! Babies vary wildly in their sleeping habits and this particular turning point seems to be just the luck of the draw. At this stage, there's not much you can do to influence it, although sticking with a regular bedtime routine is still a good bet, and keeping night feeds swift and calm will help to reinforce the idea that it's time for sleeping, and not being awake.

Keeping wakings to a minimum

Many two-month-old babies still need at least one feed (or even two) to get them through – if she wakes in the night, it will probably be from genuine hunger, so you'll simply have to give her the benefit of the doubt and feed her. She's still too little for any major sleep-training techniques. (For information about these, see p. 200.)

She should, however, be able to sleep for more than just an hour or two – if she's still waking up very frequently, you may be able to help her settle for longer periods. Don't jump up immediately when she whimpers or cries, or rush to give her a feed. Wait a few moments to see if she settles back to sleep on her own, or try soothing her a little by stroking her.

By now, you can probably get away without changing her nappy at night (check after you've fed her that she hasn't pooed or made it so soggy it's uncomfortable), which means you can get her back into her cot even quicker.

Will a bottle help?

Some breastfeeding mums find that introducing a bottle of formula for the last feed helps them get a bit more sleep at night. That's because the addition of thickeners and a different balance of milk proteins in formula means it stays in the baby's digestive system for longer, so she doesn't get hungry so quickly. And as it can be given by your partner, it also means a break from the commitment for you.

However, don't let the lure of a night's sleep tempt you into putting baby rice or any other sort of thickener in her bottle. Her digestive system is a long way off being ready for solids at this point, and in any case, putting anything other than milk in her bottle could put her at risk of choking or dehydration, and, done regularly, could even increase her chances of being obese later on.

If you do decide to go with the formula last thing at night, bear in mind that once you've introduced that first bottle, your breasts will respond accordingly and will soon cease to produce milk for that feedtime, so you won't easily be able to change back again.

What the netmums say

Sleeping through

Perhaps I was one of the luckier ones as my son slept through from the age of 13 weeks. I'll never forget the first night he did it. I woke in the early hours, realising he hadn't woken, went in his room to check on him and he was fine. I went back to bed and the next thing I knew it was 6.45a.m.! I thought at first it may have been a fluke but ever since that night, he's slept right though. It was almost like flicking a switch.
Ruth from Lancaster, mum to Jamie, two

My daughter slept through the night from nine weeks and my second daughter was seven weeks. I put it down to them both being very contented babies, and we also had a great bedtime routine. I can remember both times when they first slept through the night. My husband and I woke with a panic when his alarm for work went off and we leapt from bed to check on them only to find them still sleeping soundly.
Gail from Glasgow, mum to Brodie, six and Zoe, four

My son has only been sleeping through since he was 14 months old. We had a routine and followed advice of varying kinds but nothing worked – although we did eventually crack it four months ago. My daughter is nine weeks and we did exactly the same with her: bath, story, bed. She sleeps from 7.30p.m. until 2a.m., when she has a feed, then sleeps until 7a.m. again. It's convinced me that it's down to the baby, not you!

Sheridan from Melbourn, mum to Seth, one and Stella, five months

We were lucky with our eldest son – he was sleeping 12 hours a night from seven weeks. He always slept a lot and we didn't have to encourage good sleeping patterns. I used to wonder why all the other mums were complaining they were tired! Our younger son is completely different, though, and at 14 months, he's only recently stopped waking in the night. He would scream for up to four hours, no matter what we did, even if we held him and rocked him. Even now we have to sit in the room with him until he drops off. For more than a year, we were exhausted. I don't know how we coped really – we were like zombies some days. But you just have to get on with it.

Emma from Radstock, mum to Jayden, two and Finley, one

My daughter has always been a great sleeper. She did wake up to feed every three hours at the start, but always went straight back to sleep after her bottle. She has slept through the night from six weeks, from 7p.m. to 8a.m. She has slept in a baby hammock [a type of baby bed that is suspended from a frame, designed to provide gentle motion, and to keep the baby lying on her back] since birth and still does. She's always had the same routine: bath, a nice quiet bottle in her room, then bed. I'm sure the baby hammock has helped as she rocks herself and it looks so comfy. I'm dreading when she gets too big and has to go into a cot.

Julie from Ffynnongroyw, mum to Elsie, eight months

From cradle to cot

You may find your baby is simply too big to fit in a Moses basket comfortably by now, in which case it's time to move her to a proper size cot. You can ease her into the change of surroundings by putting her Moses basket in the cot for a few nights, or putting her in there for daytime naps, if you don't already.

If your baby has ordinary bedding, don't forget to put her in the 'feet-to-foot' position, making up her sheets and blankets at the bottom of the cot, tucked in tightly so she can't wriggle down under the covers and risk overheating. Baby sleeping bags are a popular alternative, and as they ensure the baby can't wriggle out and then get cold, are generally considered to aid sleep. Make sure it's lightweight and hoodless, and bear in mind that you shouldn't put any heavy extra bedding, such as a duvet, over it, although something lightweight, such as a cellular blanket, is fine if it's cold. Safety experts have advised against cot bumpers in the past, but the latest research suggests they are not dangerous, at least until your baby is old enough to use one to help her climb out of the cot. However, you should never let a baby under the age of one have a pillow, or overload the cot with soft toys, to avoid the risk of suffocation.

Nursery or bedroom?

Where to put your baby to sleep is a subject that provokes some very different views. Some parents are keen to move their baby's cot out of their bedroom as soon as possible (usually because babies can be rather noisy at night, as they tend to fidget and 'snuffle' so much). However, research has shown that – although it's not clear why – babies who sleep in the same room as their parents are less at risk of SIDS (Sudden Infant Death Syndrome, or cot death), so current advice is to keep your baby in with you for the first six months, after which the risk of cot death drops dramatically and it's fine to move her into her own room.

Some parents choose to have their baby in bed with them. However, there are risks attached to this and the government, safety campaigners and most health professionals emphasise that the safest place for babies to sleep is in their own cot, in a room with you.

Is bedsharing really that bad?

Parents have some very divided views on bedsharing with their babies – and the fact that official advice is strongly slanted *against* bedsharing doesn't really reflect the reality, which is that around half of all mums in the UK have had their baby in bed with them at some time.

Campaigners stress that, while there's nothing wrong with bringing your baby into bed for a feed and a cuddle, research has found a proven association between SIDS and sleeping together with your baby in the same bed.

Whether or not specific factors, such as suffocation, crushing or overheating, are to blame is unclear, because it's usually impossible to pinpoint the actual cause of such deaths.

Crucially, it seems it's not just bedsharing but bedsharing combined with one or more other factors that seems to increase the risks of a baby dying while sleeping in an adult bed, and so health professionals emphasise that it should be avoided if:

- One or both of you smoke (regardless of *where* you smoke).
- One or both of you has consumed alcohol.
- One or both of you has taken any kind of drug or strong medication that may alter your mind or make you drowsy.
- One or both of you has an illness that could affect your state of consciousness, such as diabetes or epilepsy.
- One of both of you is very obese.
- One or both of you is excessively tired.
- One or both of you – or the baby – has a fever or any sign of illness.
- Your baby is under three months old.
- Your baby was born before 37 weeks, or weighed less than 2.5kg (5½lb) at birth.

If you *do* choose to share a bed with your baby, there are a number of precautions that you can take to reduce the risk of accident and overheating.

- Make sure your mattress is firm and flat.
- Make sure your baby can't fall out of bed or get stuck between the mattress and the wall or bedhead, or any other gaps.
- Check the room is not too hot (16–20°C is about right).
- Check your baby is not overdressed – she shouldn't be wearing any more in the way of nightclothes than you are.
- Don't allow your covers to come over her head.
- Make sure that when she's not feeding, she is lying on her back.
- Don't leave her alone in or on the bed, even if she's too young to roll over.
- Make sure your partner knows your baby is in bed with you.
- Don't let an older child sleep next to the baby – it should always be you or your partner.

- Get a king-size bed, if you don't have one already.
- Never allow pets in your bed.
- Check your sleeping position. It's vital your baby doesn't slip under the covers or go into the pillow. Forming a c-shape with your body, so that it is curved around your baby, facing her, and with an arm in between her head and the pillow, will help to prevent her from moving up or down the bed. Most breastfeeding mums instinctively take this position, anyway.
- Consider investing in a bedside cot, which is designed to fit snugly against your bed.

Other reasons not to sleep with your baby

Safety apart, many parents find they get more sleep without a snuffling, fidgeting baby in between them – and that it's easier to be intimate with one another without a third party present.

The other factor to consider if you share a bed with your baby is that it can become a habit that's difficult to break – in fact, many older babies and children who refuse to settle in their own room or bed do so because they spent a long time bedsharing with parents. Unless it's something you're happy to keep up long-term – or you're prepared for the possibility of a struggle in turfing her out later – you'll be far better off introducing her to her own cot as early as possible.

What the netmums say

Sharing a bed with baby

My little one slept in bed with us from the age of four months after she had an apnoea attack [a momentary period where breathing stops] which made me frightened to leave her alone at night. But it's caused problems – she's now two and although she has her own bed we still find her in our bed every morning, and it's become very tiring as we cannot sleep properly.

Kim from Cornwall, mum to Eliza-Jean, two

I'm a single mum who works full-time and I have no family to support me. The last thing I wanted to do was to have to get up if she was having a bad night and then have to go to do a full day's work the next day. It meant I didn't have to get up to feed her and if she was ill she was next to me and she had the comfort of me being right next to her. I have a king-size bed and Lily refers to the left-hand side as 'Lily's side'! When she was small I put a bed guard up on that side so there was no danger of her falling out of bed. She's started to sleep in her own cotbed occasionally now – her own choice – and is soon to get her own 'big girl's bed'. I think it's down to personal preference, and those of us who bedshare shouldn't have to feel guilty about it.

Caroline from Manchester, mum to Lily, four

To be honest, I never even thought about having Amelia in bed with me. I don't think I would have slept a wink from fear of squashing her. I breastfed her and night feeds were never a problem – her crib was always right next to my side of the bed, though, so I didn't even need to get out of bed to put her back.

Lisa from Oxford, mum to Amelia, two

With both of mine, I've had the cot next to the bed – my son until he was seven months, and my daughter is still there now. If my daughter wakes for a feed, I feed her lying down, and if I drift off, I drift off. I always make sure she's safe and sleep curled round her on my side. Mostly she gets put back in her cot until after early morning feeds, when she is less settled, then she naps next to me. My son was the same. He went into his own room once the night feeds became less frequent after seven months, and once I'm down to one feed a night with my daughter, she'll do the same.

Sheridan from Melbourn, mum to Seth, one and Stella, five months

I tried to keep my daughter out of my bed as much as possible. Having her in with us was scary – I didn't want her on the outside of the bed but I thought that putting her in the middle was too dangerous. We kept her in her Moses basket next to the bed and when I was breastfeeding I would take her into bed with me but put her back when she was finished. It also helped that my partner would sit awake with us when I was feeding, so I couldn't have fallen asleep with her in my arms. Sometimes after a bad night, though, (there weren't many) I'd take her in with me during the day for a nap, but as I've always found it difficult to sleep during the day, I didn't think the risk of me hurting her was anywhere near as bad. Although I would like to say that I'd never taken her into bed with me at all, we're not all perfect and some days you just have to do what you can.

Leigh from Glasgow, mum to Eve, one

Despite official advice, I have always shared the bed with my son. He screamed the house down for days (and nights) on end in his crib, and despite our recent attempts to get him to sleep in a cot he is having none of it! As soon as he was in bed with me he would go off to sleep with a lovely smile on his face. I find bedsharing is easier for breastfeeding, too, but you have to be careful. I think there can only be one adult in the bed, and it should be pushed up against a wall so they cannot roll out when they get mobile. Other parents and health professionals have tutted when they have found out I bedshare but I think if you are sensible, then the risks are low.

Leona from Wallingford, mum to Ewan, eight months

I went to sleep on a camp bed in the nursery for the first six weeks. That way I was close for feeding, but we didn't have any awkward transition when we wanted her in her own room. It worked really well, and we never had any problems.

Heather from Leeds, mum to Willow, nine months

Leisure and Learning

More fun required!

Your baby isn't a newborn any more. She'll be spending longer periods awake and will need more of your attention as a result. However, she can be left safely for short periods in her bouncy chair or under a baby gym, which will give you valuable moments to get things done, and as she may be starting to swipe at and grab for things, she should be getting some use out of the attached colourful toys. Don't leave her for long or go far away, and never put her on a bed or other high surface without very careful supervision – you never know when she'll make her first successful attempt to roll over.

This is a good time, too, to start putting her on her front to play. Get down on the floor with her so you can supervise and help to make it more interesting. As well as being a nice change of scenery and position for her, it will help to strengthen her upper body and neck muscles in preparation for sitting later on.

Babies of this age often like to look in a mirror – you may have an activity centre or other toy that has one, or you could try holding her up carefully in front of your mirror, so she can see herself in it. She won't understand who the baby looking at her is, but she'll enjoy smiling back at the friendly face in the glass.

Young readers

It's never too early to begin reading to your baby. Reading to her regularly is a fantastic way to help her develop her language and understanding skills, and can even help her eye muscles to strengthen as she focuses on the words and pictures. It's also the perfect activity for that wind-down slot just before bedtime and a lovely chance to bond – even if she hasn't a clue what the story's about, she'll love hearing the soothing sound of your voice. She may also like to chew the book, so don't be surprised if her early literary collection ends up rather dog-eared.

Start off with books that have large, simple pictures and bold colours. The sort with one word a page, simple rhymes or repetitive phrases and interactive options, such as flaps or textures, are good. Use a slow, lively voice and take your time, stopping as you go to point out pictures and say clearly what they show. Don't ever force it – you may not be able to hold her interest for long, but even very short bursts of reading can be beneficial and enjoyable.

Ten books your baby will love

- *The Hungry Caterpillar* by Eric Carle
- *Peepo!* by Janet and Allan Ahlberg
- *Dear Zoo* by Rod Campbell

- *Everyone Hide From Wibbly Pig* by Mick Inkpen
- *Guess How Much I Love You* by Sam McBratney
- *One Fish, Two Fish, Red Fish, Blue Fish* by Dr Seuss
- *We're Going On a Bear Hunt* by Michael Rosen and Helen Oxenbury
- *That's Not My Puppy* by Fiona Watt and Rachel Wells
- *Clap Hands* by Helen Oxenbury
- *Where is Maisy?* by Lucy Cousins

Memory box

If your baby has a favourite book, give it a prominent place on her bookshelves – chances are, she'll enjoy returning to it for many months, and even some years down the line, she'll be fascinated to see what entranced her as a baby. Once she's definitely passed it over, you can tuck it away in your own memory box. Perhaps one day your baby's baby will enjoy it, too.

What the netmums say

Reading to your baby

I started 'reading' with my son when he was around three months old. I used to lie on the floor or in my bed with him and hold up books with really bright and colourful pictures. Some days he really looked at them, other days he wasn't that interested. He particularly loved a soft plastic Miffy Rabbit book, which he enjoyed chewing on. I found he started to take more interest in books from six or seven months. I now read to him every day. He absolutely loves books now, and he often comes to me with a book in his hand wanting me to read it to him. *Irma from Oldham, mum to Damir, one*

You can never start to read too early or make it too much fun in my opinion! I started reading to Noor at 11 days and my second,

Jasmine, was read to for the first time at just three days old! I'm an avid reader myself and I wanted to instil that love of books and learning in my own children. I make a point of doing special voices for each character, using hand gestures, and making it really exciting and fun. Noor asks for books all the time and even reads to herself and her toys in bed, while Jasmine lights up every time I get a book out.

Sara from Stafford, mum to Noor, three and Jasmine, 11 months

I started reading to Ewan as a newborn, telling him about whatever I was reading! I think the Bookstart scheme [which aims to provide every baby in the UK with a free bag of books, usually delivered through your health visitor or local library when your baby is seven to nine months old] is great but they should offer books even earlier, to encourage mums to read to their children. I started reading soft play books when he was three months old as he could grab the pages and take part, but we graduated to hardback nursery rhyme books by four months, when he could turn the pages and touch the pictures.

Leona from Wallingford, mum to Ewan, eight months

As a soother I read to my son from day one, from whatever I was reading. As soon as we started a bedtime routine at about three months I read from his own books. By six months he was having four books a night, pointing to them in order of preference. My daughter has had to listen to all Seth's stories since she was born and she's now come to expect this as 'quiet time'. It calms her before her last feed.

Sheridan, from Melbourn, mum to Seth, one and Stella, five months

I read to my bump! And once Harrison arrived, I continued to read to him almost every night. He loves books (eating them, as well as reading!). At bedtime we sit in the chair next to his cot and have a story, then another and another and another. He screams if I try to put him down before we've worked our way through the whole box.

Kelly from Birmingham, mum to Harrison, one

The earlier the better! I started all mine on books from around three months and, as I'm also a registered childminder, I now read to all my 'mindees' and I enjoy it as much as I ever did. You may think they don't understand, but months down the line they're suddenly pointing, touching and saying things, so it's all going in! My three kids are now all avid readers, so I must be doing something right.
Kay from London, mum to Jamie, 15, Sarah, 12, and Sophie, nine

All About You

Making friends

If you haven't already done so, now's a good time to start attending a postnatal group or find some other way of meeting fellow mums and their babies. Spending time with other new parents can be a great way to make the step back into real life, counter loneliness (it may even help prevent or ease postnatal depression) and gain some valuable peer advice.

Don't assume that having children in common will guarantee a firm friendship, though – it doesn't always. And never be tempted to compare your life or your baby with other mums'. You may meet women who appear to be coping far better than you are. If they are – and do remember that appearances can be deceptive – don't let it bother you.

Be careful, too, not to take any one mum's babycare advice as gospel – she may be right, she may not. Ask other mums, read up on the subject and – if necessary – check with a professional before taking any individual's word for it.

Meet-a-mum: How to meet other new mums and their babies

- Ask your health visitor – she'll usually know about (and may have set up) a postnatal support group of mums with similar age babies in your area.
- Check if any other parent and child groups are run in your area by charities, churches and other organisations. Look at the local boards on Netmums, keep an eye on noticeboards or try your

library. There may even be a specially produced booklet or magazine available, listing all such groups in your area.

- Consider joining your local branch of the National Childbirth Trust (NCT), and go along to one of their local coffee mornings.
- Join a privately run class suitable for newborns, such as swimming or baby yoga. You'll find details of many of these on the community boards at Netmums.com, or you could look online, in the local paper or in the Yellow Pages. (For more information about mum and baby activities, see p. 120.)
- Visit a Sure Start Children's Centre, if you have one near you. These government-run initiatives offer a wide range of services for new parents, including social clubs. (Details for Sure Start are given at the back of this book.)
- Ring up anyone you know who gave birth at a similar time and invite them over for coffee.
- Go to the local park. Chances are, you'll soon get chatting!
- Log on to Netmums and make some friends online – or think about going along to one of the meet-ups. There's more detail on the website: www.netmums.com

What the netmums say

Friendship

The one thing that kept me going during the emotional and exhausting first few weeks was our social life. The day my partner went back to work when our son Riley was 15 days old, we got up and walked into town for an NCT coffee morning. There we met other mums and babies and I was able to talk through all my fears and get advice on the many problems – mainly breastfeeding and sleeping – I was having. I now run the local mother and baby group. We arrange walks around the local park, cinema outings with the babies, lunches at baby friendly restaurants, and I have an amazing network of friends, all with babies roughly the same age. We are the ones giving advice and helping the very new mums, yet it's fantastic to know that I can get support from people in the same situation as I am. It's been a lifesaver!

Jayne from Welwyn Garden City, mum to Riley, three months

I was apprehensive about mother and baby classes. I didn't know if I needed any new friends, but I met the nicest people, who've been such a help. It's so reassuring to know your little devil isn't the only one who scratches you when she's feeding, and other mums give you great tips. I'm busier now than I was when I worked full time, going from one group to another or meeting up with friends. I think being able to talk to someone else makes whatever it is you're stressing about so much better.

Louise from Sidcup, mum to Emma, five months

I didn't feel the need to reach out for mummy friends once our baby was born. We saw our further-afield friends often enough and I was too shattered to be overtly social. I did meet someone local who I get on with really well and we go to a playgroup together. But we would have got along, children or not! On the other hand, I have a neighbour with young children who tried her best to make friends when I had our baby but I knew I had absolutely nothing in common with her apart from being a mum. I think if you meet people who have children who you just happen to like a lot, then it is great, but being parents is not the sole basis for an adult friendship.

Leona from Wallingford, mum to Ewan, eight months

I really had no choice but to go out and meet other mums as all my family and old friends were over 100 miles away and the only people I knew were through work. One mum I met by accident at a shopping centre. I asked her if she'd like to meet up the following week and from then on we met every week for a coffee and a walk in the park and it was wonderful to have someone who understood what I was going through. She's still one of my very best friends now. I also met someone through the Netmums 'Meet A Mum' board. She had an older child already so was able to give lots of good advice. She's since gone back into full-time work but we still meet up in the holidays. The thing is, it can be so nerve-racking when you meet up with other mums for the first time, and you do need to be prepared to make the first move and ask them if they want to meet up for a coffee or play date. But the vast majority of mums out there are only too happy to say yes. At first the conversation may be all about babies but you soon find other stuff in common and before you know it, you're on a 'Mums' Night Out' and drunkenly telling them all your secrets!

Debra from Rotherham, mum to Finn, four and Louis, two

To be honest, I found mother and toddler group excruciating at first, but Noor loved it so I forced myself to go every week. I hated the small talk and watched the clock. It was when another scruffy, harassed mum leaned over to me and said, 'God, don't those yummy mummies make you feel sick,' when yet another beautifully turned out mother and baby pair came into the room that I finally found someone I could really talk to. We're now firm friends – and somewhere along the line the offending yummy mummy became one, too! The best thing about mum friends is that when you get past the initial barriers, you soon realise that you're not alone and that everyone finds motherhood challenging to a certain extent. I sometimes wish mums were more honest, though. I spent months thinking that I was a failure because everyone I met gave such a rosy view of motherhood. It took a while to get to the point where new friends let their guard down and gave me the whole story. It's not that I look at motherhood as a struggle, it's just that I had unrealistic expectations of both my baby and myself. Now I can laugh and share the trials, tribulations and sheer joy of parenting with my friends.

Sara from Stafford, mum to Noor, three and Jasmine, 11 months

The Fourth Month

Welcome to your fourth month of motherhood

Once your baby is three months old, you may find you've turned a corner. You'll have adapted to your new life, physically you should feel OK, and feeding and sleeping will usually have slotted into a more regular pattern, which makes life easier all round. Colicky crying tends to stop or ease up now, and your baby will generally be waking fewer times in the night – perhaps even sleeping through (if you're very lucky!).

Your baby is getting more and more adventurous and may be making her first attempts to move around by rolling over, which is an exciting development, and one that has safety implications, so you'll need to be vigilant. Her neck will be growing stronger, which means she can sit on your lap and enjoy a whole new view of the world. And she's becoming ever more aware of you and the important role you play in her life.

Health, Growth and Development
Baby milestones
Now that she is three months old, your baby will typically:

- Smile back when you smile at her.
- Laugh or squeal with pleasure.

- Make 'happy' noises, such as cooing and gurgling.
- Wave her arms and kick her legs.
- Hold her head steady for a few moments when you support her in a sitting position.

And she might also:

- Bat or swipe at objects dangling in front of her, and occasionally hit them.
- Do mini push-ups with her arms when lying on her tummy.
- Have discovered her hands, sucking her fists and observing her own fingers.
- Make her first attempts at rolling over.
- Try to bear weight on her legs when supported.

Milestone focus: Head control

Head control is a vital skill that your baby must master before she can go on to achieve other milestones, such as rolling over, sitting up, crawling and, eventually, walking. At birth, she had little or no control over her head and her neck muscles, which is why it was so important always to support her head while holding her in the first few months. That soon changes, though, and by now she may well be able to support her own head for a few minutes while you're holding her. Her head control will continue to improve, and somewhere between six and nine months it will, typically, be strong enough for her to sit up alone without support.

The most important thing you can do to help your baby develop this ability is to give her lots of 'tummy time' during the day when she's awake, regularly putting her down on the floor on her stomach. You can do this from about one month, when she'll typically be able to lift her head slightly for a few moments, and turn it from side to side. As time goes on, she'll be able to hold it there for longer, and she'll also start to do little 'push-ups' with her arms. Another little 'exercise' that will help is pulling her gently up by her hands from a lying position to a sitting position, then back down again.

Yet more injections

At the end of this month, your baby will be due for her third set of vaccinations – and the last routine injections she'll be having until she reaches her first birthday. This time, she'll be offered three shots: one of the five-in-one diphtheria, tetanus, pertussis, polio and Hib vaccine (DTaP/IPV/Hib), one for meningitis C (MenC) and one for pneumococcal infection (PCV).

Her first tooth

Although teething usually starts at around six months, some babies may begin teething as early as three months, so it's worth keeping an eye out for the signs that her first tooth is on the way from now on. A few children may cut their first teeth even earlier – a tiny handful are even born with teeth – and some won't get their first until they are almost a year old, or even older. The time and rate they come through is determined by genetics.

Commonly, the two bottom front teeth come through first, followed by the top front teeth (central incisors) and then the top and bottom incisors either side. It varies a great deal, but most children cut an average of eight teeth in their first year, with the complete set of 20 in place by the time they are two and a half.

If you're still breastfeeding when the first teeth come through, you may find that your baby tries a few experimental bites of your breast with her new gnashers. You should be able to discourage her by issuing a firm 'no' and stopping the feed. You could also try giving her something else to practise her biting on outside of feed times. Some mums have found relief by wearing a breastfeeding necklace – these are chunky, colourful necklaces designed for mums to wear while feeding, to keep babies distracted so they don't bite, pull hair or generally cause any grief!

Does it hurt?

Different babies respond in different ways in the period just before the tooth pushes through the gum. For some, it appears to be fairly painless and causes few symptoms; for others, it's a highly uncomfortable experience that can affect their mood, sleep and appetite. Symptoms that are linked to teething include:

- Pain
- Fever

- Swollen or bleeding gums
- Red, hot cheeks
- Excessive dribbling
- Sleeplessness at night
- Loss of appetite, or even a refusal to feed
- Increased tendency to chew things
- General irritability
- Diarrhoea or loose bowels, thought to be caused when excessive saliva passes through the tummy, making stools looser than normal. Saliva can also make the stools acidic, and so sometimes causes nappy rash.

Never assume these or any other symptoms are caused by teething, though – especially a raised temperature. They could be the result of something unconnected that needs checking with your GP.

What can I do to help?

If teething seems to be painful, you could try rubbing a little teething gel on the gum with a clean finger. This has a temporary numbing effect that lasts about 20 minutes – check the manufacturer's instructions and make sure you don't exceed the recommended dose. A dose of infant painkiller may help – read the label carefully to check it's appropriate for your baby's age. Homeopathic teething powders, available at most chemists, may also help. Offer her something hard to chew on, such as a teething ring that has been chilled in the fridge (never the freezer – it could cause pain and damage her gums). If she's old enough for solid foods, you can give her a hard biscuit or cold chunk of fruit or vegetable, but be sure to supervise, in case of choking.

You can prevent soreness from all the extra dribble by applying a little Vaseline around her mouth, and a bib is a sensible precaution against permanently soggy clothes.

All smiles: How to look after your baby's teeth

Although this isn't the only set of teeth your child will get (her baby ones start to fall out when she's at primary school, to be replaced with a whole new adult set), these first teeth are very important to your baby. They are vital for efficient chewing and eating, to make space in the mouth for the subsequent set, and for the development of speech and language. So even now, her teeth require looking after.

You can start to clean your baby's teeth as soon as they begin to appear. It's probably easier to use a small piece of clean, soft cloth and a tiny smear of baby toothpaste at first, progressing to a baby-sized toothbrush with very soft bristles as more teeth grow through. Clean twice a day, and in particular, just before she goes to bed, after her milk.

Exposure to sugar can cause tooth decay, so dentists recommend that you don't give your baby anything other than milk or water in a bottle (and stick to plain water in between regular feeds), and that you avoid leaving your baby in her cot at night with a bottle of anything other than water – even milk, which has naturally occurring sugar in it. This is because if she falls asleep with a mouthful of whatever she is drinking, it could sit in her mouth and 'bathe' her teeth for a prolonged period. In fact, dentists tend to discourage bottle use generally, because fluid hangs around in the mouth for longer when sucked through a teat, and recommend introducing a beaker or cup as soon as your baby is old enough. (For more on introducing a cup, see p. 174.)

You don't need to worry, from a dental point of view, if your baby sucks her thumb or a dummy, unless she is doing so for very long periods every day, and even then, her later, permanent teeth won't be affected – by the time these come through, the majority of sucking habits will have been abandoned, or will at least be very infrequent and so unlikely to have an effect. However, you should never dip a dummy in anything containing sugar because of the risk of tooth decay. (For more on the pros and cons of dummy use, see pp. 28 and 268.)

Your baby can have her first dental check-up at any time from six months and it's probably a good idea to get her used to visiting the dentist from an early age so she's not scared later on. You could take her along when you have a routine check-up yourself.

Memory box

Don't forget to make a note in her baby book of when the first tooth appears!

What the netmums say

Teething

What's surprised me most about teething is how different each child's experience is. My first daughter didn't get upset at all; in fact, I only knew her first tooth was on its way when I felt it with my finger! She was seven months and they kept coming thick and fast after that. I'd get an inkling when I felt a bit of roughness on my nipple while breastfeeding for a day or so, then a tooth would appear. My second daughter on the other hand is really grumpy with it and clearly in a lot of pain. Her first came through at seven months too, and she'll chew on anything – even my breast! She also turns into a bit of a drool monster every time, which gives her a rash. A dose of Calpol is the only way to make her comfortable enough to sleep at night.

Sara from Stafford, mum to Noor, three and Jasmine, 11 months

Both of my boys suffered with their teeth. Jack was fine in the day, but he used to be bad in the night. He'd rub his face into his mattress, and scream and scream. The photos we have of him on his first birthday show him with bright red cheeks, and sore patches all over his little face. Theo gets terrible nappies when he's teething. They smell acidic and, when he was very little, they gave him really bad nappy rash that almost bled. When he cut his first couple of teeth, I was changing his nappy every hour.

Jen from Chorleywood, mum to Jack, four and Theo, one

Jayden got his first tooth at seven months. He always got two or three together so he got his bottom front two, and then at 11 months he got three at the top. Finley got his first tooth at

nine months and at 14 months he still only has six! So far, no trouble.
Emma from Radstock, mum to Jayden, two and Finley, one

My son got his first tooth at seven months, and his second a month later. They've come through one after the other since, so he seems to have been constantly teething. He gets a sore face from the extra dribble and whines all the time. He gets very clingy, and sometimes has a sore bum. I just keep thinking, eight down, 12 to go!
Michaela from Chester, mum to William, one

My daughter's first tooth came when she was only three months old. It didn't affect her at all. We didn't even know it was coming through until she started chewing on my finger one day. She didn't get any more after that until she was over nine months old and then she had four come through at once – we knew about it then as she didn't want to leave mine or her Nana's side, and her nappies were really runny for just over a week. Once the teeth had cut through, she was fine.
Lisa from Hereford, mum to Keira, 11 months

Feeding

What next?
You may be preparing for a return to work now, and thinking about who will feed your baby when you're not around, and how. If you're formula feeding, this shouldn't be a problem – although you'll need to make sure whoever is responsible has all the correct supplies and equipment to hand, and is up to scratch on bottle-making matters, feeding times and quantities. If you're breastfeeding, though, and you haven't yet attempted to introduce a bottle of expressed or formula milk, you should try when you have plenty of time available. You may have a task on your hands, because your baby might not be keen to accept one. If so, you might find you're better off bypassing the bottle and introducing a beaker instead. (For advice on ways to do this, see p. 175.)

You may also want to consider what sort of facilities are available at your workplace, if any, for you to express and store breast milk, and to begin building up a store of breast milk in the freezer.

You might be advised by some people you know to start thinking about weaning your baby on to solids now, and it's true that previous generations of mums were doing so as early as three months. But we have more scientific knowledge available to us these days and we know now that this is too soon to give your baby anything other than breast or formula feeds, because her digestive and immune systems have not yet developed enough to cope with solid food. Four months is the earliest you should start , and the Department of Health recommends waiting until closer to six months. There's more on starting solids on pp. 132–6 in The Fifth Month.

Nursing strike: What to do if your baby refuses your breast

Sometimes, even when breastfeeding has been going with a swing for several months, babies can temporarily become reluctant to feed for no obvious reason. This is known as breast refusal, or 'nursing strike', and it can cause a lot of worry and frustration. It may even bring about an earlier-than-planned end to breastfeeding for some mums and babies. In most cases, though, and with a bit of determination and patience, you should be able to overcome breast refusal once you've pinpointed the cause. There are a number of possible explanations:

- Pain in your baby's mouth, caused by teething, a cold sore, or an infection, such as oral thrush. (For more information about this, see the Health A–Z at the back of the book.)
- An over-reaction by Mum to being bitten has alarmed them.
- Your baby has an ear infection that is causing pressure or pain while breastfeeding.
- A cold, or a blocked nose, is making it difficult for your baby to breathe while feeding.
- There's not enough milk in your breast – your supply may have dropped because you've introduced supplementary bottle feeds.

- Your baby is being distracted by noise or other interruptions. This is particularly likely after six months, when she has an increasingly developed interest in the world around her.
- Stress or other major disruption in routine or surroundings, such as a house move or you returning to work.
- You've been separated from your baby for more than a day or two.
- A change in the taste of your breast milk, which may be caused by the return of your periods and therefore changing hormones, something you have eaten, or medication you have taken; or a change in the taste of your skin, if you've applied a new cream, for example.
- Your baby may simply have had enough of breastfeeding and is weaning herself off the breast – this is only really likely after she is nine months old, though.

If your baby is refusing to breastfeed:

- See your doctor first, to rule out any possible medical causes and get any necessary treatment.
- Offer her a bottle of expressed milk if it's the only way you can get her to feed, and don't fret about it – a few bottles won't necessarily stop her from getting back on the breast.
- Keep expressing to avoid painful engorgement, or mastitis, developing.
- Take it easy. Stop if one or both of you is becoming frustrated or stressed out; otherwise, it may be even harder next time.
- Don't wait until your baby is very hungry, or she may be too upset to try.
- Keep distractions to a minimum. Feed her alone, in a quiet room with soft lighting.
- Try feeding her when she's sleepy. She may be too tired to object.
- Move around when you breastfeed, rocking her or walking with her. She may enjoy the motion. You could try experimenting with different feeding positions.

- Make sure you have lots of cuddle time and skin-to-skin contact.
- Keep an eye on her nappies – if she's not wetting around six a day, she may not be getting enough fluid and you should seek advice from your GP.
- Aim to keep her routine as normal as possible.

Leisure and Learning

Activities for the two of you

If you haven't already, you might be thinking about taking up a class, or some other form of activity specially designed for parents and their babies. These can be a fun way to bond with your baby, to encourage her development in a variety of ways, and a good chance for you both to get out of the house and make friends. Don't be tempted to take up too many, though, or you may both end up worn out, and don't take it too seriously. Although these classes are developmentally beneficial in many ways, the main aim is to have fun!

What's available?

There are so many baby-oriented activities on offer these days, with most suitable from around three months. Ask around to see what other parents recommend, look on the noticeboards at your nearest library, sports centre or community halls, or check out the local boards on Netmums, to see what's on offer in your area.

Top of the class: Activity sessions for you and your baby

Music and movement: A vast number of classes offering sessions full of song and dance have sprung up in recent years, which is not surprising since they're highly popular with babies and their parents. One of these classes will boost a whole variety of your baby's developmental skills – social, language and motor – as well as encouraging confidence and creativity.

You can create your own music and movement sessions at

home, with the aid of some toy instruments and fun music. It doesn't have to be kids' stuff – you can get her into whatever you listen to early on!).

Swimming: Most babies love splashing around in the water, maybe because it allows them to move around so effortlessly. It's a good idea to get them used to a swimming pool, so that they're confident and happy when the time comes to learn how to swim. Most larger leisure centres run parent and baby sessions, usually based around fun and building water confidence. Various private companies offer courses, most of which emphasise that babies can be taught to swim from as early as six weeks to three months, although you may want to wait until she's had all her initial immunisation.

Of course, you don't have to go to an organised class to take your baby swimming, although you do need to make sure the pool you take her to is warm – most sports centres have a 'learner' pool that's appropriately heated. You can take her any time from birth, but it might be a good idea to wait a month or two, because swimming pools can be rather daunting places for tiny babies. Keep swim sessions short and sweet – no longer than 30 minutes – so she doesn't get too tired or cold. Kit her out in a swim nappy, take a large, soft towel to wrap her up in afterwards and don't forget a bottle, if you're formula feeding, because she'll probably be ravenous after her session.

Baby gym: Most leisure centres run sessions with fun, safe equipment for your baby to explore, wriggle and roll on, with your help, and private companies run franchises around the country. These sessions are usually very enjoyable, and good for strengthening her muscles, and aiding development of all her gross motor skills.

Baby yoga: A relatively new but increasingly popular activity, baby yoga is based around a series of flowing positions, lifts and stretches. The claims are that it aids bonding, communication, relaxation and general wellbeing in both mum and baby, and also stimulates the nervous and digestive systems, promotes sleep and calm, boosts flexibility, and even settles behaviour in your little one.

What the netmums say

Mum and baby activities

A group of friends and I got together to attend a swimming course when our babies were about five months old – we had four half-hour sessions in a local pool. It was great, as I don't know whether I would have plucked up the confidence to go on my own. Second time round, I just haven't had time to go to anything. Between work, naps and nursery, there just aren't enough hours in the day!
Jen from Chorleywood, mum to Jack, four and Theo, one

I started taking Harrison to baby signing classes when he was just under four months old. [There's more information about baby signing on p. 207.] It was more a way for me to get out and meet new people as I'm painfully shy, but I forced myself to do it. Now Harry's just turned one and seems to enjoy going. He definitely recognises some of the signs and has attempted to do one or two himself, but really it's just a nice morning out with some like-minded mummies for me to chat to, and some other babies for Harrison to play with!
Kelly from Birmingham, mum to Harrison, one

Danny and I go to Baby Rhyme Time at our local library. We learn nursery rhymes and actions, and there are musical instruments to play with. He really seems to enjoy it – there's always plenty of smiles and laughing!
Cathy from Reading, mum to Danny, four months

We go to baby yoga and absolutely love it. It combines small stretches and massage, nursery rhymes and playtime for the little ones. It's great fun and really seems to help her sleep plus we've had no bellyache (touch wood) since we started. A lot of the mums and babies are those I did antenatal yoga with, so it's a chance to continue those friendships.
Danie from Ipswich, mum to Amelie, three months

As well as baby massage, I've also done baby yoga with both my children, which I highly recommend, and story, rhythm and rhyme sessions at our local library. I think the one thing that can be said for any of the baby activities is that it doesn't matter what you do, it's just important to get out of the house, forget the chores and enjoy your babies while you can. I've made some great friends through attending various classes and would be lost without them.
Roisin from Belfast, mum to Zack, three and Corey, one

I had made my mind up when I found out that I was pregnant, that I was going to do everything with my child to give her the best opportunities I could. I joined a singing group call Rhythm Time when my daughter was six weeks, a structured group, which included singing, massage, bubbles, dancing, instruments, and she loves it! We also went to baby signing when she was four months. It was a great class and I learnt a lot, although my daughter never really got the hang of it! I also decided that I didn't want my daughter to be frightened of water and looked at swimming classes but they are so expensive, so my husband and I take her swimming every weekend and we all have a great time splashing around in the pool.
Amanda from Peterborough, mum to Rebekkah, nine months

Me and Josh have been attending baby swimming lessons since he was seven months old. He developed water confidence quite quickly. The benefits also include interaction with other adults and babies, water safety skills, and hand and eye coordination. He now has six certificates and badges to represent the stages he's passed!
Kate from Stoke-on-Trent, mum to Josh, one

We used to go to the library where they did sessions for babies. Someone from the library would read some baby books and sing some songs – a great way to introduce kids (and mums) to the library and to help mums feel confident about reading to their babies.
Nicola from Aberdeen, mum to Blaine, three

All About You

No sex please, we're parents

If you're still not feeling much like making love again several months after having your baby, you're not particularly unusual, and there may be a number of reasons why, both physical and psychological. Maybe you are:

- Still suffering some post-delivery discomfort or pain down below.
- Worried that it's going to hurt or feel different.
- So wrapped up in your new identity as a mummy, you've lost sight of yourself as a sexual being.
- Suffering from postnatal depression, which can often affect your interest in sex.
- Not feeling sexy because of hormonal changes or emotional stress.
- Self-conscious about a still-sagging tummy, stretchmarks or leaky boobs.
- Bothered by the fact that your baby is in the room, or worried you will wake her.
- Scared you might get pregnant again.
- Suffering from a dry vagina, which can occur after birth and while breastfeeding due to hormonal changes.
- Just too exhausted to find the energy!

Gently does it

Sometimes the longer you leave it after giving birth, the less inclined you are to give sex a try. And sometimes, if you do attempt it and it hurts, or you don't enjoy it, that can put you off trying again for a while to come. It's important not to force it, and to take your time.

Meanwhile, you don't have to give up on intimacy altogether – while you're waiting for your libido or energy to return, try making love in other, non-penetrative ways, or just kissing and cuddling.

If it's a simple matter of lack of opportunity, ask someone you trust to look after the baby for a couple of hours, perhaps during the day when you're less tired, and spend the time together. Clear your bedroom of baby clutter, if it helps to reinforce the fact that you're someone's lover, not just someone's mother.

If it hurts

If you have any severe or persistent pain during sex, do talk to your doctor about it because it could indicate an infection or a problem with the way you've been stitched, which may need attention to put right. Dryness can also be an issue after giving birth because of hormonal changes, especially if you are breastfeeding, but a little lubricant will help. It's also a good idea to avoid positions of deep penetration. Sometimes pain or discomfort is exacerbated or even caused by tension. Take your time, use some lubricant, get the mood right with soft lighting and a pretty nightie, or indulge in a glass of wine beforehand – whatever it takes to help you relax.

Talk about it

Do keep talking to your partner about how you feel if you're not that much up for sex. Sometimes it can work the other way round, and a man is put off sex for a while – after all, dads are affected by exhaustion, too, and a man can be affected psychologically by his partner giving birth, particularly after a traumatic delivery, or by changing perceptions of her now that she has such a significantly different role in life.

If emotional problems surrounding sex refuse to go away, you might want to consider telling someone else about it. You could chat to a sympathetic GP or health visitor, or you could contact Relate, the relationships organisation, which charges a fee for counselling sessions. (Contact details for Relate can be found in the Useful Addresses appendix at the back of the book, p. 340.)

Be realistic

It's probably best not to expect too much from sex for a while, even once you have cranked things up again. You're unlikely to be swinging from the chandeliers, if only because you don't want to wake the baby, so give yourselves loads of time to get things back to the way they were – up to a year, or more, would not be especially unusual. Even then, most couples have to accept that, for as long as they've got small children, their sex lives may not be quite the same as they used to be (although they can, and do, come back!).

No plans for another one

Unless you want just a small gap between babies (for more on planning your second child, see p. 260), make sure you've got an effective form of contraception in place before resuming your love life, because it's perfectly possible to conceive from about three weeks after giving birth. If you used a cap or diaphragm, you may need to have a new one fitted, because your vagina could have changed size or shape. If you were on the combined pill or had a contraceptive patch, you'll be advised to use a different type of hormonal contraception while you are breastfeeding, because the oestrogen the pills and patches contain may reduce your milk flow.

Now could be the time to consider changing the method you use – for instance, to an intrauterine implant, such as an IUS or an IUD. These need to be fitted by a doctor or specially trained nurse.

Your chances of getting pregnant before your baby is six months old while you are *exclusively* breastfeeding on demand and your *periods have not returned* are slight. Known as the lactational amenorrhoea method or LAM, this is reckoned by experts to be a *fairly* effective method of contraception – but only if all these factors are in place, and even then, it's not guaranteed. Rely on it with caution.

What the netmums say

Sex lives after birth

It took me ages to pluck up the courage to have sex after having both of my children, and things still aren't right now. First time round, I had a third-degree tear. I was swollen and sore for weeks and it took several months before it felt like it had healed. I couldn't bear to touch myself, even when having a shower, and my husband was scared of seeing it, as he's squeamish (although when he did have a look, he couldn't see a thing!). Also, I was exhausted, not just from lack of sleep, but the whole strain of having a baby, dealing with the house, and then returning to work. I never had a second to myself, so the thought of finding time for sex just seemed crazy. When I did feel more like it, we started trying for our second, which was fine, but after he was born it all started again. This time, it was the breastfeeding – I just couldn't think of myself as being a 'sexual being' at all. It has put a strain on our relationship, although it's better now and we have a good balance.
Lorna from Bingley, mum to Ben, four and Toby, one

I didn't have sex until my little one was four months old, for many reasons! I healed up quite quickly – my labour was very straightforward so that wasn't a problem. I was scared by the thought of penetration, as the last time we'd had sex was months before the birth. Also, our baby was in the same room as us and for me that was really weird. I had the baby blues, too, and felt so unattractive – big wobbly belly, leaky boobs, and since I didn't have any time for myself I felt I looked a state and couldn't believe my husband would ever find me attractive. I will admit the first time we did it I had a couple of glasses of wine to relax, and the baby was in his own room by this point. Our sex life took a long time to recover, and it's still not as active as it could be.

Helen from Liverpool, mum to Joe, three

After my first baby was born, my husband and I didn't have sex for six months afterwards. I had an episiotomy and stitches and I was very sore for a very long time. My husband was a complete angel and understood. We managed other things, but I just couldn't face making love to him in that way. I remember going to the doctor about my stitches and she said just to make sure the first time you do have sex to use lots of KY. We did, and it was fine. I also remember sobbing my heart out after we had managed it, as I was so relieved that my bits were working again and we could enjoy it again. From then on we never looked back.

Theresa from Romsey, mum to Joseph, three and Ryan, one

We first attempted sex about five weeks after my daughter was born. I was a nervous wreck as I'd had a third-degree tear and thought I might split in two! What I hadn't realised was that breastfeeding can leave you a bit dry down there. So we bought a tube of lubricant, and things were much better after that. I was afraid things wouldn't feel the same after a delivery but after a few attempts that were not painful but uncomfortable, things were back to normal.

Mags from Belshill, mum to Eve, two

At the moment I feel as if I don't want to have sex ever again! Although I love my son to bits I certainly don't want to get pregnant again. I had a forceps birth and loads of stitches and I'm really worried it will hurt, and I seem to have lost my sex drive all together. I'm also breastfeeding. One man sucking on my boobs all day is enough!

Karin from Nottingham, mum to Lindsay, two months

The Fifth Month

Welcome to your fifth month of motherhood

Your baby's language skills will be really taking off now – she's probably cooing away and may be babbling, making repetitive consonant sounds, which is her way of talking. She may be becoming fairly mobile, perhaps rolling from side to side or even making her first attempts to flip right over – don't forget to keep a very close eye on her and never leave her alone for a second on a high surface (if you need to leave her for a moment to answer the door or telephone, pop her on the floor before leaving the room – but make sure there are no obvious hazards she could roll towards). She'll be growing ever more attached to you and anyone else who helps to care for her, perhaps showing dismay if you leave the room, or reaching up with her arms and a big, wide smile whenever she wants you to pick her up.

Maybe you're planning a return to work now or in the not-too-distant future. Some mums are keen to get back to old routines, others are enjoying their baby so much they want to look at other options – different hours, a new job, or perhaps a long-term break from work altogether. Take your time weighing things up – it's an important decision.

Health, Growth and Development

Baby milestones

Now that she is four months old, your baby will typically:

- Quieten or smile at the sound of your voice when she can't see you.
- Bat or swipe at objects dangling in front of her, and occasionally hit them.
- Have discovered her hands, sucking her fists and observing her own fingers.
- Listen intently when you speak to her.

And she might also:

- Explore objects by putting them to her mouth (sometimes known as gumming).
- Be rolling over.
- Practise sitting up, by pushing forward in her bouncy chair or on your lap, or pulling herself up on her cot bars.
- Have begun babbling, making consonant sounds such as 'ba-ba, ab-a, da-da, ma-ma'.
- Find her feet fascinating, perhaps putting them to her mouth.

Milestone focus: Sitting up

Acquiring the skill of sitting up is a natural progression for your baby once she's got fairly good head control. You'll know she's on her way when she's able to push up with her arms while lying on her tummy, and when she can hold her head up strongly for a while.

You can give your baby sitting up practice from about four months, in the same way you'd encourage head control skills (see p. 112). You can also let her try it for herself, by sitting her on the floor and surrounding her with a supporting wall of cushions, or propping her up in her baby nest, or doughnut, if you have one. However certain you are that the support is sturdy, though, don't leave her, just in case she wobbles over and falls on to her face.

Once your baby's mastered sitting up, a variety of new

possibilities opens up, such as joining you at the dining table in her highchair, or enjoying the view from a new mode of transport, the back carrier!

As with all other milestones, the timing varies between babies. Some may master a slightly wobbly sitting position from as early as four or five months, others may not do so until nearer their first birthday.

Feeding

A regular routine

Breast or formula feeds should now fit into a regular pattern of four to six times a day. A typical schedule might be a feed on waking, mid-morning, mid-afternoon and early evening, with many babies still requiring a late or night-time feed (or both). They still don't need any other form of drink, although bottlefed babies may need some extra water in hot weather – cooled and boiled – so don't be tempted to introduce anything else, such as juice. (For more information on drinks, see p. 257.)

Don't despair if your baby is still waking in the night for a feed. Before too long you'll be able to help her learn how to get through without one, but not yet – experts recommend that you don't attempt any kind of sleep-training techniques until after she is six months old and weaning is under way, so you can be sure she is definitely not waking due to hunger. (For more about sleep training, see p. 200.) Certainly she won't need more than one night feed at this point, so if she's waking more often than that, don't jump up every time to offer her breast or bottle. As mentioned before, wait a few minutes – she may settle herself back to sleep on her own. If not, you could try offering her water, a comforter or some gentle soothing instead.

If she's begun waking when previously she's slept through, it's not necessarily a sign that she's hungry and ready for solids, as many people believe, but more likely to be due to changing sleep patterns, which occur around now. Don't be tempted to start giving her a night feed, because this will just spark a comfort habit that you'll have to kick later on. Try to get her back to sleep with a cuddle or some other form of comfort instead.

Is now the time to start solids?

You may well notice that your baby seems hungrier around now, perhaps showing dissatisfaction once she's drained the bottle or boob. She may also show a great interest in the food on your plate while sitting on your lap at the table, reaching out to grab and sample grown-up food for herself.

Until about six years ago, mums were advised to start weaning their babies on to solid food from four months. However, it's now recommended by the Department of Health that you wait until your baby is nearer to six months before you start giving her solids (regardless of whether she is breast or bottlefed). This advice is based on recommendations made by the World Health Organisation in 2001, following a review of scientific information on the subject. The WHO's conclusions were based on evidence that the functions of a baby's gut are not yet fully developed in the first six months of life, so early weaning can increase the risk of gastro-intestinal infections.

So what's the truth about weaning?

Many parents still go by the old guidelines and begin weaning after four months – after all, old habits die hard, and many babies do indeed seem pretty hungry by now. In fact, many doctors, dietitians and health visitors are not convinced by the current government advice. They feel that some particularly big and hungry babies may well be in need of solid food *before* they reach six months, and that it will not harm them, as long as you wait until *after* the four month (or 17 week) stage. That view is backed by the British Dietetic Association, which supports the Department of Health recommendations but acknowledges that some parents may wish to wean earlier than six months. Even the Department of Health suggests that its own guidelines are by no means set in stone, when admitting that 'all infants are individuals who require a flexible approach to optimise their nutritional needs,' and that, 'if an infant is showing signs of being ready to start solid foods before six months, for example sitting up, taking an interest in what the rest of the family is eating, picking up and tasting finger foods, then they should be encouraged.' (Department of Health, May 2003: Infant Feeding Recommendation.) There's also some evidence that introducing your baby to fruit and vegetables before they are six months old means they are likely to eat more of them later in childhood.

One thing that does seem quite clear, however, is that four months (17 weeks) is the *absolute earliest* at which you should start the weaning process. And if you do begin before six months, there are certain foods it's advisable to avoid (see the box below). There's more on suitable first foods in the section on the sixth month.

Being alert to allergies

Although doctors are currently unclear about the risks, if any, of weaning before six months where there is a history of allergies or allergic conditions such as eczema, asthma, or hayfever, official advice for high-risk families is that it's prudent to wait until the six-month point, and then to introduce any likely allergens such as milk or milk products, fish, eggs, and wheat one at a time, so you can easily pinpoint the culprit if anything does prove to be a problem. (Your baby's body will also be able to cope better with any adverse reactions if she's a little older.) Where nuts and nut products are concerned, it's currently recommended that babies and children from families with a history of allergies or atopic conditions avoid them for the first three years of life. This guidance is under review, however: do seek advice from your health visitor before weaning your baby if you're concerned about her risk of developing any of these conditions. There's more about allergies on p. 166.

Steer clear: Foods to avoid before six months

Salt: Guidelines from the Food Standards Agency recommend that babies consume less than 1g of salt per day before six months, and a maximum of 1g salt per day after six months, because it's all their kidneys can cope with. (The maximum recommended amount rises to 2g a day for children aged one to three and no more than 3g a day for children aged four to six.) These amounts are to be found in breast or formula milk, so you should never add salt to anything you give your baby at this stage, or give her any commercial product, such as tinned sauces or sausages, which are usually high in salt. Jars and tins of food specifically marketed for babies are not allowed by law to contain salt, so these you don't have to worry about.

Added sugar: Don't add sugar to her food or drinks, or you could encourage a sweet tooth, which could eventually increase her risk of dental decay and obesity. Try to make sure purées are made with ripe, sweet fruits, so they don't taste tart and need sweetening.

Honey: This shouldn't be given at all in the first year – after which the intestines have matured sufficiently to cope – because it can very occasionally contain a type of bacteria that produces toxins in a baby's intestines, which leads to a serious illness known as infant botulism. And honey is also a form of sugar (see above).

Gluten: Current government advice to *all* mums is to delay the introduction of foods such as bread, pasta and breakfast cereals that contain gluten, a protein found in wheat and to a lesser extent, rye, barley, and oats, until six months. That's because of the risk of allergy or intolerance to wheat, and also because sensitivity to gluten can trigger a serious autoimmune condition called coeliac disease. (There's more detail about it in the Health A–Z appendix, p. 304). However, some very recent research from ESPGHAN, the European Society for Paediatric Gastroenterology, Hepatology and Nutrition, suggests there is no benefit to be had from waiting beyond four months to introduce gluten-based products, for families with no history of a problem with wheat – and particularly where a baby is still being breastfed, as this is believed to have a protective effect.

Nuts, nut products and seeds: Research is still ongoing into this complicated subject, but as things currently stand, the government recommends that nuts, nut products and seeds be avoided by all babies before six months, and by children from high risk families with a history of allergy or atopic conditions, for three years. (Whole nuts should be avoided for all children before the age of five, because of the risk of choking.)

Eggs, fish and shellfish: While recent research findings suggest there's no need to avoid these common allergens before six months *unless* there is a history of allergy in the immediate family, undercooked eggs and shellfish may harbour bacteria that can cause food poisoning, so should be avoided before six months for this reason.

Soft or unpasteurised cheeses: These may contain an infection-causing bacteria, so should be avoided before six months.

Let your baby lead you

Perhaps the most important point about weaning is to be guided by your baby. She may be ready for solids, once past four months, if she doesn't seem satisfied by milk feeds alone, is sitting up well with support, seems keen to chew on whatever she can get into her mouth, and is showing a great interest in your food. Rest assured that until that point, breast or formula milk will give her everything she needs. As with just about every other developmental step forward in the first year of your baby's life, getting her on to solids is not a race – even if some other people imply that it is – so don't be tempted to rush into weaning until she's definitely ready. You may have to be firm about ignoring the advice of well-meaning onlookers – in particular, older relatives who brought up babies when views on the subject were very different. And in any case, if you start before she is ready it will be a longer and more difficult process, and you may find you're wasting your time.

Do seek advice from your health visitor if your baby was premature, and don't assume it will mean a later weaning date for them – in matters of weaning, it's the birth age of premmies that's relevant, not the corrected one. (For more details about the process of weaning, see p. 159.)

What the netmums say

When to wean

My sons were both weaned at four months, as that was what the guidelines said then. By the time I had Carys they'd changed, and I waited until she was six months. We then went down the baby-led weaning route [for more on this, see p. 170], which worked really well for us. I found, with Carys, that as I was more experienced, I was less likely to bow to the pressure of the people who said I should have weaned her earlier. I knew my child, and I'd read a lot about the subject. Sometimes with babies it can feel like a race to be the first to hit the milestones – I remember mums with babies three months younger than Carys gloating that their child was already on three meals a day, as though that made them far more advanced than mine! But it's important to have the confidence to do what you feel is right for your child, whether it be your first or your fifth.

Delyth from Aberystwyth, mum to Rhys, five, Siôn, four and Carys, two

The advice for weaning has changed so much over the years. My first was weaned at 12 weeks as was then advised, but it was difficult and he became a messy and fussy eater! Charlie was much the same. When I had Annabel the advice had changed to 16 weeks, which was definitely better. Erica weighed 18lb at five months and although I wanted to wait until six months, I was advised to begin weaning her slowly, and within six to eight weeks she was fully weaned. Now she eats everything that's offered and enjoys finger foods so much more than my earlier children did. I think this is because her hand/eye coordination is more developed and food goes in rather than all over the place! I wish I'd taken things a lot slower with my first two. I also think that all children are individuals and a number of different factors play a part in the decision about when to wean.

Judy from Mountsorrel, mum to Andy, 15, Charlie, 12, Annabel, eight and Erica, eight months

My son started solids at four months because he was showing interest in whatever we were eating and kept trying to put our food in his mouth. I started in moderation and thought he would only have a few spoonfuls at a time but he ended up eating pretty much all of whatever I prepared for him. By six months he was picking up peas and putting them in his mouth and not happy if we gave him mashed or puréed food. He wanted what we were having. I've breastfed exclusively from day one and still give him a couple of feeds throughout the day, but his appetite for food and different types grows all the time. In the end, he was the one who decided he was ready for more than just milk. I was conscious of the six-month guidelines, but they're just that – guidelines. I think that babies naturally seem to know what's best for them.

Ruth from Ealing, mum to Noah, 11 months

Leisure and Learning

Baby walkers and door bouncers

Your baby is probably wriggling or even rolling around now, revelling in her increasing mobility and independence, and on the lookout for new ways to be stimulated and to explore the joys of movement, as well as a change of scenery every now and then. You, meanwhile, still have the washing machine to unload, lunch to prepare and a host of other things that require two hands to get done. And yet you can't really leave her under the baby gym any more in case she rolls off into the sunset, and you may not be very popular if you try to 'imprison' her in a bouncy chair. For many mums, this is where a baby walker or a door bouncer comes in. However, both items come with a number of warnings attached.

The use of baby walkers that have a seat in a square or round frame on wheels, in which the baby sits and uses her feet to scoot herself around the room, is actively discouraged by safety groups such as the Royal Society for the Prevention of Accidents (RoSPA) and the Child Accident Prevention Trust (CAPT). That's because every year, according to the most recent figures available, more than 2,000 babies are taken to hospital after an accident in one, although the European standard has since changed, which means walkers must now conform to safer designs that are much less likely to tip over. Safety campaigners point out that, because babies in walkers can move surprisingly quickly (this is more relevant to the earlier designs) and because walkers raise babies to a height where they can reach for hazardous items, they cause more accidents than any other piece of nursery equipment. The accidents include falls, where baby walkers have tipped over, fallen downstairs or crashed into something, and burns, where babies in walkers have tipped into or against fires, heaters and hot surfaces, or reached out for something hot.

Many health professionals aren't keen on baby walkers, either, not just because of the injuries they may cause, but because if overused, they could delay normal development by restricting a baby's freedom to roll, sit, crawl, play and generally explore her surroundings. Door bouncers are also widely frowned upon, because prolonged use can encourage a baby to walk on tiptoe.

All that said, baby walkers and door bouncers remain popular pieces of equipment with both parents and babies. If you do decide to get one of these, be sure to bear in mind the following advice:

- Make sure you comply with the manufacturer's age, height and weight restrictions, and be sure your baby is developmentally ready before putting her in a walker – she should have a strong back and be able to hold her own head up well, so four to five months is the earliest age at which they become suitable. You should stop using both walkers and door bouncers as soon as your baby is showing signs of walking in case they interfere with her progress in doing so.
- Be wary of taking on second-hand equipment of this kind. Only accept an item from someone you know and trust, so you can be certain it's not damaged, and check that it was made recently enough to comply with current safety standards. The standard number should be marked on the product – for walkers, BS EN 1273:2005; for bouncers, BS EN 14036: 2003.
- Don't leave your baby unsupervised in a walker. Although a walker may give you brief moments of freedom to carry out tasks, it can only ever be in the same room. They are not 'babysitters'.
- Don't let your baby use a walker near stairs, steps or thresholds. Avoid their use upstairs at all, unless you have a *very* securely fixed stairgate – the sort that's screwed into the wall.
- Check there is nothing in the area that she could reach and pull on, such as hot drinks, electrical cables or anything heavy or sharp. Be extra vigilant in the kitchen – better still, avoid using a walker in there at all.
- When fixing a bouncer to a door, be scrupulous about applying the manufacturer's instructions and recommendations, and check that the frame is sturdy and solid enough to take your baby's weight. Avoid using narrow doorways, as your baby could bounce sideways and hurt herself on the frame, and make sure the bouncer will not slide sideways for the same reason.
- Limit her use of bouncers and walkers to very short bursts – no more than about 15 minutes at a time, once or twice per day, is a good guideline.
- Try before you buy, especially when something's pricey. Items such as these may not be in use long and some babies just don't like them, so find a friend with one who'll let your baby give it a whirl before you fork out. Consider, too, whether you've got enough room and, in the case of a bouncer, your doorframes are suitable.

- Look at some safer alternative ways to keep your baby safe and stimulated. For example, consider a stationary activity centre, which she can sit in; a soft baby nest, or doughnut, which supports her while she sits and offers her the chance to explore different textures and colours on its sides; or a playpen or cot (if you've got the room) with a selection of her favourite toys in it. In the end, though, nothing is safer or more stimulating for her than your full attention! (For more advice on how to make your home a safe zone for your baby, see p. 218.)

What the netmums say

Walkers and bouncers

My advice is try before you buy. My eldest hated anything with straps (including his car seat and pram!) so bouncy chairs and door bouncers were a waste of money. The one thing he did love was one of those static entertainment centres. But they do cost a fortune so if you want one, check out the Netmums Nearly New pages or local free ads, or buy second-hand. They're not in them that long and take a lot of room up in the house!
Debra from Rotherham, mum to Finn, four and Louis, two

All three of mine have had bouncy chairs, door bouncers, play gyms and baby walkers and the youngest has also had a stationary play centre, and a Bumbo [a type of seat, designed to keep the baby in an upright position from around three months old]. Me and my friends pass this sort of equipment round between us, with the exception of walkers, which we always buy new. All three have especially loved their walkers and we have never had an accident, unless you count us having our ankles rammed into on occasion! I've always bought the ones that are really chunky and weighty, and supervised them whenever they are in them. I allow a maximum of 20 minutes in whatever item Katie's playing in and then it's back to good old floor play, cuddles and songs.
Sarah from Oldham, mum to Andrew, 13, Jennifer, two and Katie, nine months

When it comes to all this gear I think the best thing to do is either test it in the store with your baby if possible, or ask one of your friends if you can try theirs before you buy. I spent £60 on a baby swing for my eldest and she loathed it! Think hard about longevity, too. I bought a freestanding jumper for my youngest (an alternative to the traditional doorway bouncer), which she loved at first, but she's hardly made the best use out of it. Just a month after purchase she figured out how to crawl, and now thinks it's a prison! I didn't even consider a baby walker, having heard so many horror stories about accidents. My kids can get into enough trouble without any assistance. I've learnt the expensive way that the thing that really makes my children happy is following me about the house and playing with anything and everything they can get their hands on. They have always been more interested in everyday things than toys.

Sara from Stafford, mum to Noor, three and Jasmine, 11 months

The doorway bouncer was a huge hit for both my little ones from around four months until they were more mobile. They loved sitting and having a good bounce. I would not have been without it. It made it possible for me to cook dinner, tidy the kitchen, or have a coffee without feeling I was neglecting them. My daughter loved her walker – she scooted all over the place at quite a pace – but my son hated it. I think the safety risks are to do with parents not thinking it through, like the new height of baby, and reach. You need to put yourself at that height and go round the house and look at curtain pulls, hot drinks, cables, TVs on stands, etc, to ensure there's nothing they can get at that they should not have. And never, never use upstairs!

Heather from Sheffield, mum to Jasmine, four and Jack, two

We didn't get a walker for our first daughter because our health visitor warned they were bad for the child's posture. I think a bouncer is a good idea, though, but just get a plain, simple, easy-wipe one. I wouldn't recommend the vibrating sort, as Isabel hated it. Carys loves the bouncer, too. I also got an inflatable ring thing, which she loved up to six months, but she can now tip herself out of it! To be honest, I think most (apart from the bouncer) equipment is just a way for new mothers to spend money, and raising kids is expensive enough as it is. With my first, we bought a pink blanket, put it on the floor, put toys on it and she was happy!

Ffion from Aberystwyth, mum to Isabel, four and Carys, seven months

All About You

Going back to work

If you haven't already, you may now be thinking about, or actively planning, a return to work. Although new mums are legally entitled to take up to a year away from their jobs, regardless of when they were employed, few will get paid for the whole period, which means thinking carefully about how much time you can afford to take off in your baby's first year.

Of course, it's not just about finances. Being at home all the time with a baby isn't everyone's ideal, and lots of mums return to work because they need the social or mental stimulation. Either way, the return to work can be an emotional and practical minefield. You'll need to give yourself plenty of time to prepare for it.

Time for a change?

Perhaps you'll be returning to your old job – same place, same role, same hours. By law, your employers must keep your old role open for you if you return to work after maternity leave of six months or less, and must offer you a suitable alternative if you can't return to your old role after taking maternity leave of six to 12 months. On the other hand, maybe for you it's always been a no-brainer – you knew from the start that your choice was to stay at home, for the foreseeable future, with your baby.

Many parents find themselves reassessing their lives after having a baby, and decide that it's time for a change. Some women discover they don't want to return to work as planned, or at least, they don't want to commit the same proportion of their time to work as they once did. Others decide to look for a different job altogether, or begin working for themselves. Dads, too, are more likely to make changes to their working lives these days when they have a family – although, even now, the onus to do so is still more likely to fall on the person who carried and gave birth to the baby!

Working out whether you can afford to stay at home, change your hours or switch jobs altogether will probably require a careful audit. In fact, having a baby will probably force you to get the calculator out, because even if you return to the same job and your income remains the same, you'll have childcare costs to consider, not to mention lots of other expenses. For some mums, the cost of childcare means that a return to work isn't always financially worthwhile.

You'll need to sit down with a pen and paper and do some sums, looking at the areas – mortgage, bills, food, holidays, cars – where you might be able to cut back substantially and reduce your outgoings. If you're not sure where to begin, you could use the budget planner on Netmums to give you a headstart – and don't forget to make sure you are getting all the benefits you are entitled to, such as tax credits. (A number of organisations can help you to understand this complex system of benefits, and details are included in the back of the book.)

Asking for flexible working hours

Returning to work part-time, or on a more flexible basis than before, is a compromise that suits many new mums. If you are an employee, although you do not have an absolute right to flexible working, you have a legal right to request it. Your employer must by law give it consideration and, if they turn you down, they must give you a good reason. Flexible work doesn't just mean part-time hours. It could be a change in the start or end time of your working day, a different shift pattern, compressing your hours into a timeframe that suits, a change of workplace, or the chance to jobshare, or work from home. You've got nothing to lose by asking!

Working it out: Your employment rights and responsibilities after having a baby

- You are entitled, by law, to take up to 12 months maternity leave from your job regardless of how many hours you work or how long you have worked there. The first 26 weeks of this leave is known as ordinary maternity leave (OML), and the second 26 weeks is additional maternity leave (AML).

- You should qualify for statutory maternity pay (SMP) for the first 39 weeks of your leave if you have worked for your employer since you became pregnant and if you earn more than £90 per week. SMP is 90 per cent of your average pay for the first six weeks and then the basic rate of £117.18 per week for a further 33 weeks, or 90 per cent of your average pay if it's less than this (figures for the tax year 2008/09). That means that if you decide to take your full year of maternity leave, the last three months or so will be unpaid. You may also have rights to maternity leave and pay beyond the legal minimum under your contract of employment. Not all employers offer enhanced maternity benefits, but it is worth checking to see if yours does. If you leave your job while on maternity leave, or do not return at the end of your leave, you do not have to pay back any statutory maternity pay, but some enhanced benefit schemes may require you to return to work for a certain period to qualify – or to pay it back if you leave.

- If you don't qualify for SMP, are unemployed, self-employed, work casually or are on low wages, you may be able to claim maternity allowance (MA), which is (again, for 2008/09) £117.18 per week for 39 weeks, or 90 per cent of your average pay if it's less than this.

- Your employer should assume you are taking your full entitlement of 12 months maternity leave, but it's worth letting them know anyway. If you want to return before then, you must give them at least eight weeks notice, or they can postpone your return date.

- If you return from ordinary maternity leave, you are entitled to go back to exactly the same job. If you return from additional maternity leave, you are entitled to go back to the same job if at all possible and, if not, you must be offered a suitable alternative with terms and conditions that are at least as good.

- While on maternity leave, you are entitled to go into work for up to ten days, if you think it will help you keep up with what's going on in your workplace – known as 'keeping in touch' or KIT days. This can be useful for training days, for example, or for easing yourself back into work gently. You should agree in advance with your employer when you will take these days and how much you will be paid. Your employer cannot force you to return to work for KIT days but they are entitled to make 'reasonable contact' with you during your maternity leave.

- If your job becomes redundant while you are on maternity leave, you have special rights to be given any alternative role that is suitable for you. You can't be asked to go through an interview or other competitive process – if the job is suitable, you should be given it.

- If you want to negotiate fewer working hours or other forms of flexible working, you can put this request to your employer and it *must* by law be given consideration. From a practical point of view, and to allow you time to make necessary arrangements, you should make this application as soon as possible, outlining exactly how you would like things to change. (This continues to be a right for all parents with a child under the age of six or, if the child has a disability, under 18). Once your employer receives your application, there is a set procedure that must be followed. Your employer must meet you within 28 days of receiving your application to discuss your request. You are allowed to be accompanied at this meeting by a trade union representative or a work colleague. After that, your employer has 14 days to give you a written response. If your request is refused, your employer has to make the reason clear, and you have 14 days to appeal against the decision. Your employer should then arrange another meeting within 14 days of receiving your appeal to discuss it, and write to you within 14 days of the appeal meeting to advise you of the decision.

- If they haven't followed correct procedure or if their decision is based on incorrect facts, you can appeal against it and make a complaint to an employment tribunal, which you must do within three months less one day of the refusal of your appeal. Employment tribunal claims and time limits are complex, so it's always advisable to seek advice from a solicitor, law centre or Citizens Advice Bureau.

- Dads are also entitled to request flexible work, and this applies for as long as they have a child under six, or if they have a disabled child under 18.

- If you decide you don't want to go back to work at all, you must give whatever notice period is set out in your contract – obviously, it makes more sense to do this at the end of your maternity leave, so you get your maximum entitlements.

- You are entitled to build up holiday leave during your maternity leave but there is no automatic right to carry over holiday from one year to the next. This means you should plan carefully when to take your holiday leave, especially as your maternity leave may span two holiday years. You may choose to take some or all of your leave before, or at the end of, your maternity leave period to extend it. In some cases, you may be financially better off having a shorter period of maternity leave and taking holiday leave instead. Your employer should not refuse your request for holiday leave because you have been on maternity leave, and if they do, this may give rise to a claim for discrimination.

- If you go back to work and you want to keep breastfeeding, or express so that you can do so, your employers must provide you with the time, space and facilities you need. (There's more on this on p. 146.)

- If you think you've been treated unfairly by your employers, you may have a discrimination claim and you should seek advice from your local Citizens Advice Bureau, or from a specialist law firm, such as Russell Jones & Walker. You can also get help and advice from Working Families, a campaigning charity that supports working parents (details for all these organisations are at the back of the book).

Going it alone

There is a huge range of opportunities out there for mums who'd like to work for themselves on a flexible, at-home basis, such as taking on a franchise, or setting up your own business from scratch. So if you don't want to return to your old job but you want or need to get back to work, this could be the option for you. There are lots of general ideas for ways you might go about this, as well as lists of companies who employ people on this basis, on www.netmums.com.

If you want to keep on breastfeeding

It is possible to return to work, for periods of more than a few hours at a time, and to carry on exclusively breastfeeding your baby. It takes a fair bit of commitment, though, and will usually mean you have to express your milk, and store the results, at work. Your employer is required by law to provide you with the space, time – and fridge – that you'll need to do this, so it should certainly be possible. You're also entitled to take a break to breastfeed your baby, if you can arrange for someone to bring her in to your workplace.

Many mums find a very happy compromise in mixed feeding at this point. Their baby's carer gives them formula or expressed feeds while they are at work, but they continue to breastfeed in the morning and/or evening.

Leaving your baby behind

If you're going back to work, give yourself plenty of time to get used to the idea – don't be in denial about it until the last moment or you'll have an even harder task getting back into the swing of things. For some mums, it can feel devastating to leave their baby for the first time, and this is often compounded by a feeling of guilt, a fairly inevitable factor in the working mum's life. The fact is, your baby will be fine without you, even if it takes her a little while to get used to it. And most mums find that, when the time comes, they cope much better than they thought they would.

Don't make your first day back at work the first time you leave your baby. It's always a good idea to get her used to other people, so make sure she's spent time without you, being cared for by her dad, gran, auntie, a close friend or any other trustworthy and familiar person who'll have her. Even if you're not going back to work, you'll need to leave her some day. Make sure she's spent at least some time with whoever is going to look after her. All good childminders, nurseries and nannies should be happy to offer a couple of short 'taster' sessions before taking her on permanently.

When the time comes to leave your baby with a carer, make the parting brief, and don't look back. You may feel terrible, perhaps even spending most of the day in tears, but as time goes by and you come to realise that your baby is fine without you around, it will get easier. She'll be fine, and so will you. (For more information about this issue, see p. 232.)

Getting the best care you can for your baby

Of all the practical arrangements you'll need to make before a return to work, the right childcare is paramount. There's no evidence that leaving your baby with a reliable second party while you go to work will harm her, and you certainly shouldn't feel guilty about doing so, but naturally, you do need to be certain that your little one is in *very* good hands. It's important to get it right first time, if possible, because babies (and all children) need consistency in childcare – you don't want to have to change care providers if you can help it. Not only that, but getting the best childcare you can secure will give you peace of mind and help keep the dreaded guilt at bay.

Start looking for a childcare provider as soon as you know you'll need one (you may have done so long before reaching this point). The Children's Information Service (also sometimes known as Families Information Service) at your local council will be able to help you find the right childcare and answer any questions you have – you'll find them in the telephone book or online. You can also get all the information you need, including a comprehensive database of local nurseries and childminders, at www.childcarelink.gov.uk. And there are lists of childcare providers on the local boards on www.netmums.com, which in some cases include comments and opinions from members based on their personal experiences. You could ask all the other parents you know – a personal recommendation from someone you trust is always valuable.

Who's looking after your baby?

Your basic choice in paid care for your baby is between day nursery, childminder or nanny. Some people are also fortunate enough to have a reliable family member on hand who is prepared to help. There are pros and cons to each one of these.

The next best thing to you: Your childcare options

Childminder:

- Childminders must be registered, which means that they must undergo regular inspections and meet vigorous standards to prove that their home is a safe environment, the food they give is nutritious, and they provide appropriate, stimulating play. They will have secured some basic training (and many will have achieved higher qualifications), be insured, have had a Criminal Records Bureau (CRB) check and have knowledge of first aid.

- Childminding fees vary according to area but on average you can expect to pay between £2.50 and £6.00 an hour.

- Childminders offer an environment that's more like home, and your child will always be looked after by the same person. Numbers of other children will always be limited. Childminders can care for up to six children aged under eight at any one time, their own included, of whom no more than three must be aged under five, and only one of those may be under one year – although occasionally a childminder may be registered to care for two babies under one.

- If you're considering a childminder in the UK, make sure he or she is registered with Ofsted (in Scotland, the registering body for childminders is the Care Commission; in Northern Ireland it is DENI, the Department of Education; and in Wales it is the CSSIW, Care and Social Services Inspectorate Wales). You should check that your prospective childminder's registration is up-to-date and read his or her last inspection report, either by asking the childminder to show it to you, or at the website of the relevant registering body (addresses and contact details are at the back of the book).

- Before making up your mind, interview a childminder carefully. The National Childminding Association of England and Wales (NCMA – details given in the appendix) recommends asking the following questions. Why did you decide to become a childminder? What do you enjoy most about the job? How long do you intend to continue in childminding? Are you a member of NCMA? What training have you done? Do you have any relevant qualifications? Other than children, is there anyone else regularly at home during the day and, if so, are they also registered to look after children? Do you belong to a childminding group or network? Are you taking part in a quality assurance scheme? Can I see your registration and insurance certificates? Can I see your Ofsted (or equivalent) inspection report? Could I see any references from other parents? How many other children do you currently look after, how old are they, and how long have you been looking after them? Do you have any children of your own and, if so, how old are they? Can you describe a typical childminding day or week? What arrangements do you have for meals or snacks? What do you consider to be unacceptable behaviour and how do you deal with this? Which festivals and special occasions do you celebrate and how do you celebrate them? What would you do in an emergency involving yourself or one of the children? Do you ever take the children out in the car and, if so, do you have suitable insurance cover, seat belts and car seats for this? Do you and the children go on outings or on special trips out? If so, what arrangements do you have if these involve extra costs and extra hours of care?

- Be guided by your instinct. Does the childminder seem like a nice person, and does his or her home seem like one that your baby will be happy in?

Day nursery:
- Nurseries must be registered and inspected, yearly, by Ofsted. At least half the staff must hold a relevant childcare qualification and, as of September 2008, all nurseries (and childminders) must follow the statutory government-set Early Years Foundation Stage (EYFS) learning framework – so you know your baby will be getting appropriate stimulation.

- Again, it varies hugely, but according to the Daycare Trust the typical cost of a full-time nursery place for a child under two is £159 a week in England, which works out at more than £8,000 a year. Nurseries may also charge fees if you are late.
- Unlike childminders, who will take (paid) holiday time and may have sick days, nurseries will provide full-time care throughout the year.
- They won't take your child if she is ill, though, (as a childminder may) and she is very likely to be, since being in a nursery exposes babies to lots of bugs.
- Mixing with large numbers of other children early on will make her more confident and sociable, and means you probably won't have difficulty settling your little one at pre-school or school, later on.
- Since they're staffed by a number of childcare professionals, you're not putting your trust in a single person.
- Before enrolling your child with a nursery, check it is registered with the appropriate body (these are the same as for childminders, see above) and make sure it has a current certificate of insurance. Ask to see a copy of their most recent inspection report (or check it online). According to the National Day Nurseries Association (NDNA – details are included in the appendix), you should ask the staff – or yourself! – the following questions when you visit a potential nursery for your child. Is there a safe and clean outside play area? Is the interior bright, warm, clean and welcoming? Is the equipment good quality, clean, safe and appropriate? Do the children in the nursery look happy and well occupied? Are they using a variety of equipment and are staff involved with their play? Are the staff happy, relaxed, well presented, calm and confident? What are the staff to children ratios (there should be a minimum of one member of staff for every three babies)? Will your child be attached to a key worker? What does the fee include – nappies, meals, holiday charges, for example? Finally, does it seem like a friendly and relaxed place to be, and did your child enjoy the visit?

Nanny:

- Nannies work from your home, perhaps even living in, if you have the space to accommodate them. They'll often be prepared to work longer hours than a childminder and be more flexible about them.

- They will usually be happy to take on extra responsibilities, such as cleaning and cooking for your child.

- As they provide one-to-one care, in your own home, having a nanny may be the closest thing to being with you. Your baby will never have to get used to new surroundings and can form a close bond with her carer, who may even become 'one of the family'.

- There is no formal system in place for nannies to be registered, although Ofsted runs a voluntary register, so you are reliant on references and personal recommendations for reassurance about them. You may wish to arrange for your own police check through the Criminal Records Bureau (CRB).

- They are usually costly – expect to pay anything between £150 to £400 a week, as well as tax and National Insurance contributions (for which you must also take on the responsibility of the paperwork, or pay someone to do so for you). If you find a nanny through an agency, you will have to pay an agency fee. Although this all sounds rather expensive, a nanny may be cost-effective if you have more than one child, or make an arrangement to nanny-share with another family. Bear in mind that, unless your nanny has voluntarily registered with Ofsted, you will not be able to claim any financial help towards childcare costs in the form of tax credits.

- Before you take on a nanny, make sure you draw up a contract that outlines the roles and responsibilities you expect him or her to take. Questions to ask a potential nanny include the following: What qualifications do you hold? Are you registered with Ofsted's Voluntary Register? What experience do you have in childcare? What are your views on play, food, discipline and education? Will you be willing to take my child/children swimming, to the library, to local groups or other types of trips or activities? Do you have any knowledge of first aid? Will you be willing to work extra hours if needed? If so, will I have to pay you for overtime? If so, at what rate? Which household duties would you be prepared to take on? Do you drive and, if so, do you have a clean driving licence? Do you smoke?

- Make sure you and your baby have a chance to get to know a new nanny before leaving your little one alone in his or her care. The same goes for a childminder and staff at a nursery.

Relative:
- If your little one already has a close relationship with a relative, it won't be nearly so hard for either of you to be separated, and if it's your mum/mum-in-law/dad/auntie, you can have total trust in them. Do bear in mind that if the person is getting on in years, he or she may find it hard going, caring for a demanding baby.
- A relative may be prepared to be flexible for you. On the other hand, this may not be the case, and you may not reasonably be able to demand a regular schedule – especially if you're not paying. It may be a good idea to draw up an informal 'contract', so that it's clear what's expected by both parties.
- The savings can be great, as some relatives are happy to look after your baby for little or no cost. Never assume that's the case, though – find out first if he or she expects payment, or payment in kind. If you do pay for the care, you will not be able to get any financial help via the tax credit system, unless your relative goes through the motions of registering as a childminder – and taking on all the responsibilities incumbent to that process.
- Grandmothers and other close relatives may have different views and attitudes to childrearing from you – and may feel they have a right to practise them! If you can't handle this, it's probably not going to work.

What the netmums say

Going back to work

After having my son I was offered part-time, hours to suit, in my old department on the same pay scale as before and with the same fringe benefits. I started to think about childminders and worried about whether they'd look after my rather expensive pram, which brought me up short and made me realise there was no way I'd be able leave a real live child with someone if I was worried about a pram! I thanked my boss for the job offer and said no – I would have earned £60,000 over the next four years, but would never have got my son's childhood back. Since then, I've been involved in all sorts of things – running toddler groups, writing, peer-supporting, parent volunteering at school – and loved every minute of it. I began working again, part-time, when my son had settled at school.

The one thing that makes me laugh out loud is when people say they go to work for the 'adult conversation'. In virtually every workplace I've been, the conversations are about last night's TV, tonight's dinner, who's dating who at work, celebrity gossip and holidays. Since being a Stay-At-Home-Mum, I've had more more 'adult' conversations – politics, philosophy, emotions – than I ever had at work.

I'd never condemn anyone who chooses to work, though, and I do understand there is often a financial imperative that overrules all other considerations.

Jo from Lowestoft, mum to Alex, five

I'm old-fashioned, I suppose, and think that on the whole the best place for babies and young children is at home with their mums. We are by no means financially secure, but we just decided to go without a lot of stuff, and so I stopped working when I was due to have Jasmine. I couldn't have imagined trusting anyone enough to look after her! Anyway, there was no way I would earn enough to make it worthwhile working and paying for childcare. That first year at home with my little girl was one of the best, the hardest and most wonderful of my life. But I should add that this was what was best for us and in no way would I judge another mum who chooses to, or has to, go back to work.

Heather from Sheffield, mum to Jasmine, four and Jack, two

I would love to return to work, but I have looked into childcare costs and I'd be paying more than £1500 a month. I also think I would miss out on so much with my girls, even if I could find a job that paid enough to cover it. So I've decided to stay home for the moment.

Nikki from Middlesex, mum to twins Jessica and Isabel, two

I worked full time before having my daughter, and after it was time to go back I went part-time and my employer was very good with this. After having my second daughter, I changed my hours from four days to three. I'm glad I go to work because mentally I couldn't have taken staying at home. Being on maternity leave for nine months with my daughter was long enough! I suffered with PND, too, so getting back to work really helped me out. I also had to go back to work as we needed the money. I'm very lucky because my mum has the girls – although she has said if we have any more children she won't be able to look after that one, too, which is fair enough.

Sara from Norfolk, mum to Georgie, four and Hollie, one

I've recently returned to work three days a week as a relief pharmacist. My job means I go to different shops each day – a particularly fun experience when I have to ask each day where the best place to breast pump at lunchtime is! It's a bit stressful, making sure there's always enough breast milk in the fridge and freezer, but worth it. I have to express every morning and night as well as lunchtime and when I get home on my workdays. We have an entire freezer shelf at home dedicated to my milk, and it seems to work for us.

Sarah from Newcastle, mum to Ewan, five months

The company I was working for when I was pregnant closed down so I had to look for a new job, for financial reasons, but also for my own sanity. I started working again part-time when Lara was six months old. She's looked after by my mother-in-law, which saves on

childcare costs. I work for two and a half days a week, and it's absolutely perfect.
Ruth from Greenock, mum to Lara, two

Because I was earning more, we decided it would be me who returned to work full-time while my husband took on the childcare. I didn't find it too hard going back as I knew they were with my husband and were really happy with him. It did put me off continuing breastfeeding, though, as I couldn't cope with the thought of expressing at work! This time round I won't be going back until my daughter is eight months old. I love having the time with her, and the others, but I'm ready to go back. My husband relishes his role as stay-at-home dad and happily takes the kids to everything from ballet to mother and toddler group, even if he is the only bloke! It seems a shame to have kids and then get someone else to look after them. We have had to sacrifice a lot to live on one wage – foreign holidays, new cars. But it's worth it.
Clair from Falkirk, mum to Lottie, four, Lexie, three and Minnie, five months

It was always the plan for me to go back to work as I'm the biggest earner and we've struggled a bit with bills in the later stages of my leave. But I missed my little one something terrible. I was petrified about going back to my job as a nurse, as I thought I wasn't going to know what I was doing, but I actually enjoyed myself – then I felt guilty about enjoying myself! I rushed home 12 hours later to get a cuddle, and give him his bedtime bottle. He goes to nursery, and does seem to be thriving being around other babies. It makes me glad I put him in there, and lessens my guilt about going back.
Angela from Edinburgh, mum to Andrew, eight months

I went back to work when my son was nine months old, initially for three days a week and later, when he was one, full-time. My parents look after him three days a week and he goes to nursery two days a week. My husband also takes time off to look after him if necessary, and does the drop-off and pick-up from nursery. Frankie didn't like nursery at first and it's taken him a good six months to settle, but now he's fine. I was relieved to be going back to work, to be honest, as I found being at home all day every day with a baby who didn't sleep at night very hard. I think being a full-time mum, and staying sane, is the hardest job in the world! I enjoy being part of the career world again and feeling that I am making a contribution – but also feel the strain of trying to make everything balance sometimes. I miss Frankie when I'm at work but I know he is happy, healthy and well cared for, and that I'm doing all I can to give him a good life and better future.

Roberta from Cheam, mum to Frankie, one

I went back to work when my son was six months old once my maternity leave had finished as I needed the reassurance of a regular income. I felt my son missed out on quality time with me and the guilt and sadness I felt every time I was away at work was horrible. Even though he was in a lovely nursery, nothing compares to Mum or Dad. The other major problem was the expense – I look back over the past five years and realise I was working just to pay childcare fees! I plan to be a stay-at-home mum for my daughter.

Laura from Mexborough, mum to Thomas, five and Hollie, two months

I had to go back to work when my maternity leave was up, having had 25 weeks at home with Matt. I'm the main earner, so there was no other option for me. At first I was devastated about going back and I cried myself to sleep the night before! Once I was there it was like I had never been away and now it's just part of normal life. Matthew gets time with me, his dad (we both work shifts), his childminder – who is a gem – and my mum and dad and sister, who all look after him sometimes. He doesn't even notice I'm gone.

Joanne from Stockport, mum to Matthew, two

The Sixth Month

Welcome to your sixth month of motherhood

Your baby's fast approaching the middle of her first year! Not so long ago she was a tiny, fragile and completely dependent bundle in your arms – it's amazing just how much she's changed in the short time since birth, not least in terms of size. By now, most babies have doubled their birth weight.

You'll probably be planning the move to solid food, if you haven't already. It's a big turning point, and something to take at a gradual pace. It could be a little while before she gets to grips with the notion of food being delivered via a spoon. But it's an exciting milestone, too, as she begins to explore the wonderful world of nosh – sitting up at the table in her own chair and eating meals with you, or perhaps even joining you in a restaurant. Not all establishments are baby-friendly, though, so choose your venue with care!

And as for you, how are things with your other half? Important relationships can go by the wayside sometimes in the months after a baby's arrival, not surprisingly. Now could be a good time to take stock and remind yourself of what it is to be a couple, and not just a mum and dad.

Health, Growth and Development

Baby milestones

Now that she is five months old, your baby will typically:

- Be reaching out for objects.
- Explore objects by putting them to her mouth.
- Try to bear weight on her legs when supported.

And she might also:

- Be rolling over.
- Be able to sit up if well supported by cushions, or even on her own.
- Push up with her arms, lift up her back, neck and head and have a good look round while lying on her tummy.
- Be making make repetitive babbling noises.
- Enjoy blowing bubbles or raspberries!

Milestone focus: Rolling over

This exciting development may come as a surprise when your baby first attempts it successfully – to her, as well as to you! She'll soon realise it's an ability that can actually propel her from A to B – and a source of great enjoyment.

Rolling over usually comes once she's got strong neck and arm muscles and good head control – you'll be able to see her developing the strength she needs in the months beforehand as she lies on her tummy and practises her mini push-ups. Flipping from front to back usually comes first, from her fourth month onwards, because it requires a little less muscle power than the flip from back to front, which she's more likely to master during her sixth or seventh month.

Not all babies roll over, with some going straight from lying or sitting to crawling or bottom-shuffling, so there's no need to worry if your baby is showing no signs of doing so. As long as she's sitting up well with support, for which she needs the same group of muscles, and she finds some other way to get where she wants to go over the next few months, it doesn't matter!

You can encourage development of your baby's rolling-over skills by holding an object a little way away from her and giving her lots of smiles and claps when she flips. Once she discovers she can roll over, she'll probably do it lots, because it's so much fun – and it gets her places. There's an important safety warning to be heeded here, though. Never leave a baby who is in, or likely to be approaching, a rolling-over phase, particularly not on a raised surface. It takes a very brief moment for her to roll herself into trouble.

Feeding

The start of weaning

By the end of this month your baby will be six months old, so it's important to start thinking about the leap to solid food, if you haven't already. Most babies will be capable of getting to the recommended six month (26 weeks) point on breast or formula alone, by which time they should be physiologically and developmentally ready to begin the weaning process. However, you may need to get cracking sooner if you have a particularly big, hungry baby, or you might want to start a bit earlier because weaning is a gradual process.

Bear in mind that all babies are individual. What they need, and when, can vary enormously, and they may not conform to the averages that official guidelines are based on.

Whether or not you make it to six months, the Department of Health and other authorities on child nutrition, such as ESPGHAN (the European Society for Paediatric Gastroenterology, Hepatology and Nutrition), advise that the start of weaning shouldn't be left any *longer* than that because babies are starting to need more iron and other nutrients than milk can provide. It's also a widely held view among experts that introducing a good variety of foods early in a baby's life encourages her to eat well later on. Another important factor is that babies should ideally be accustomed to lumpier textures and having some finger foods by the time they are eight months old, because they need to be practising their biting and chewing skills by then – vital for speech development – and also because, if you leave it much later, they might reject solids altogether. So if you *do* begin at six months, you shouldn't linger over the introduction of solids and should move on to the second stage of weaning (introducing finger foods) fairly swiftly. Your baby should be quite ready to do so. (For more information about progressing to the second stage of weaning, see p. 191.)

Before you begin weaning, you might want to try giving your baby a plastic spoon to play with so she becomes accustomed to the whole concept. She may well put it in her mouth – all very useful practice! It's also a good idea to make sure she sees you eating and enjoying your food. That way, she'll know what to do when her turn comes round. So sit her on your lap sometimes for meals, or if she's ready, strap her in her highchair and pull her up to the table so she can have a look, and maybe a little poke at, or taste of, anything appropriate that you're eating.

Keep cool

The business of feeding our children is something that stirs strong emotions in mums (and dads, too, but mainly in mums!). It's in our very instincts as mothers to nourish our offspring, so it's not really surprising that we are so desperate to get it right, and feel anxious or even miserable if we feel we're failing. These feelings usually begin in the early days of breast or formula feeding – and only accelerate when the time comes to wean!

Try not to worry about weaning. It's a gradual process and one that should be enjoyable and exciting for you and your baby. This is your chance to start giving her positive messages about food from the start. Take things slowly, and never force it – if your baby isn't that keen, wait a few days and try again. If it's obvious she's had enough, leave it there – she'll soon let you know by turning her head, clamping her mouth shut or simply by spitting it out! Don't try to push any more down her or press her into 'another few mouthfuls' if she doesn't want it.

Kicking off

The very first foods your baby eats should be very smooth, thin purées, the consistency of yoghurt. This is what conventional wisdom dictates, although there is another theory, baby-led weaning, which takes a different view (see p. 170). Most parents try baby rice mixed with a little breast or formula milk for the very first few attempts, because the texture offers a natural halfway house between liquid and solids, so it's a good way to get her used to a different consistency. It's very bland, though, and doesn't always prove a popular offering. A flavourful possibility is puréed fruit or vegetable, with or without a little added milk – there are more specific ideas on p. 163.

If your baby doesn't seem sure about taking food from the spoon, you could try offering a little from your finger at first.

When to offer the food

Offer her first solids after, or in the middle of, a milk feed, because she might not respond well if she's really hungry. Once she's more used to the idea, you can begin to give the solids first. Pick a time when you're both feeling relaxed, but avoid teatime, in case something disagrees with her that then causes problems at bedtime or during the night. In fact, it's a good idea to avoid new foods at teatime generally in the first few months, for the same reason.

At first, try her with no more than a couple of spoonfuls – you may get an enthusiastic response, or you may not! Remember, this is a whole new ballgame for your baby, and it might take her a while to get her head round the idea. At first you should just try giving her solids once a day to get her used to the idea, but once she seems to be eating and enjoying a single meal, and is obviously ready for more, there's no reason why you can't expand it to two, then three meals a day.

After a couple of weeks you can include a nutritious second course with each meal, either based around fruit, (stewed apple or pear, for example) or milk (rice pudding or a yoghurt), or some combination of both. It's fine to offer a pudding such as these, even if she hasn't finished her savoury course. Be guided by her appetite – never try to force her to eat more often, or larger amounts, than she really seems to want.

To cook or not to cook?

If you cook your baby's food yourself, it will be probably be more nutritious and, let's face it, will probably taste better, too. You know exactly what the ingredients are and it won't have been heat-blasted to sterilise it, as baby food from a jar usually has, which inevitably affects the flavour. Plus, the taste and texture of home-made fare is more likely to resemble the sort of adult foods you'll want her to eat later, after the age of one.

That said, not many mums have got the time or inclination to pain-stakingly cook and purée every morsel that passes their baby's lips (and even if you do it for your first, you probably won't for any that come afterwards!)

The answer is probably some kind of compromise. Cook as much as is feasible (and cook in large quantities, freezing what you don't need in ice-cube trays, so you can de-frost just the amount you need when required) and try not to rely on jars and packets frequently. When you do buy commercially prepared food, go for the good quality, fresh brands as often as you can afford them, and check the labels for added ingredients, such as sugar and starch, which are best avoided.

It's true that all that sterilising, cooking, puréeing and freezing can seem like hard work. So make life easy on yourself whenever possible, and remember that you don't necessarily have to reach for a jar to dish up fast first foods – after all, it takes only a minute to peel and mash a banana, or an avocado. A good timesaver is to get into the habit of setting aside a little veg (or whatever else you're making, when it becomes appropriate) as you're cooking for yourself. Just make sure it doesn't have salt in it. (For more on salt and other foods to avoid, see p. 133.)

Hygiene and safety matters

When you're weaning, it's really important to be careful about hygiene because young babies are so prone to infections. There's no need to sterilise feeding equipment such as spoons, bowls and anything else you use to prepare her food, as long as you make sure they are always scrupulously clean, washing them thoroughly in very hot, soapy water, or the dishwasher. You should avoid drying with a tea towel, though, because these can become germ-ridden, so use a paper towel instead. And you should continue to sterilise bottles and teats – old milk tends to harbour bacteria – until she is a year old.

Heat food up thoroughly, allowing it to cool before serving (room temperature will probably go down best) and always throw away any leftovers – never be tempted to serve again later, because bacteria may have developed in the meantime. It's not safe to reheat previously warmed food, or to refreeze food that's been defrosted or warmed, for the same reason.

Always stay close to your baby when she's eating, to make sure she doesn't choke. There's more advice on choking in the Health and First Aid A–Z on p. 330.

Mess

Weaning's a messy business. In fact, you can expect mealtimes to be fairly chaotic from here onwards for a while. Be prepared for food to go everywhere – she may want to play with it or even try to feed herself, and it's really important to let her have free rein to do so, because it will help her to develop a relaxed and positive attitude to eating. Cover the floor with a sheet of plastic and your baby with the biggest bib you can find – one of the plastic variety with a crumb-catcher is good, and so is one that covers most of her upper body and arms. Then get ready to duck!

What's on the menu, Mum? Good first foods – and the bad ones

When you begin weaning, you can try:

- Suitable cereals, such as baby rice, mixed with a little formula or breast milk. You can also use small quantities of full-fat cow's milk when weaning, although this is not suitable as a drink for babies until they are one.
- Thoroughly mashed or puréed cooked veg, such as potato, parsnip, yam, sweet potato, courgettes, squash, swede or carrots. At first, you may want to mix in a little milk or made-up baby rice, so the flavour's not so strong and the consistency nice and runny.
- Fruit purées made with ripe banana, avocado or peach. You don't need to cook any of these first – just mash with a fork, and add a little formula or breast milk (or cow's milk if you like. You can also purée cooked apple or pear. To cook fruit or veg for babies' meals, peel, slice, cover with a little water and simmer until just tender in a saucepan or cook in a microwave.
- Rotating different flavours regularly. Once she's tried them all and seems keen, you can experiment a bit with combinations. Sweet and savoury can work well together – carrot and pear, for example.

Good enough to eat: Some tried and tested weaning recipes from www.netmums.com

Potato and parsnip with carrot (suitable for freezing)

Makes 4 portions
Ingredients:
1 potato
1 parsnip
1 carrot
Fresh or dried thyme

- Peel and dice the vegetables.
- Place the vegetables and a small sprinkle of thyme in a steamer or cover with water and bring to the boil. Cook for 15 minutes or until the vegetables are soft.
- Purée with a masher or mouli (not a blender because this will release the potato's starch and create a glutinous consistency), adding some of the reserved cooking water to loosen the mixture.

Plums and pears with bananas (not suitable for freezing)

Makes 2 portions
Ingredients:
½ a banana, mashed
1 plum, peeled, stoned and cut in halves
½ a pear, peeled, cored and cut in quarters
1 tablespoon of baby rice

- Place the plum and pear in a steamer and cook for 4 minutes until soft.
- Purée or mash the fruit until smooth, then add the mashed banana, the baby rice and two tablespoons of the cooking water and mix together until smooth.
- Alternatively, use two tablespoons of breast/formula milk to make it creamier.

Carrot, swede and peach (suitable for freezing)

Makes [2–3] portions
Ingredients:
100g (4oz) of diced carrots and swede
Handful of tinned peach halves in fruit juice

- Boil the diced carrots and swede for 14–16 minutes or until tender.
- Remove the carrots and swede from the heat, and strain.
- Purée the carrots and swede, using a blender.
- Strain the peaches and add them to the carrot and swede. Purée again until fully mixed.

Weaning rice pud (suitable for freezing)

Makes 4 portions
Ingredients:
1 cup of whole milk
¼ cup of pudding rice
½ a cup of apple juice (unsweetened)
½ a banana mashed (optional)
1 peach, peeled, stoned and chopped
Pinch of cinnamon

- Add the rice, apple juice, cinnamon and milk to a saucepan. Cover and simmer for 30 minutes. Add the peach and cover, simmering for a further 10 minutes.
- Blend to the consistency that you want.
- Divide into four portions, and add the mashed banana (if using) to the portion you are about to serve. Don't add the banana to the entire quantity because it will make the purée turn brown.

Memory box

This is a big one! Don't forget to make a note of when your baby first tried solid food, and what it was she had. You might want to record the moment on camera, too.

food allergies

Food allergy – an adverse immune system response to certain food proteins – affects up to 6 per cent of young children. Allergic responses usually occur within two hours of eating (or touching) the food and may result in a variety of symptoms, such as an itchy, blotchy rash, sneezing, red eyes, vomiting, diarrhoea, wheezing, and swelling around the mouth. Although they can be worrying for parents, most allergic reactions are mild and can be treated with simple antihistamines – you should always seek a diagnosis and treatment from your doctor if you suspect one, however mild. There's no cure for food allergy at the moment and the only way to prevent reactions is to avoid the problem food, until a doctor tells you it's safe to reintroduce it to the diet. More severe allergic reactions are called anaphylaxis, and are most commonly caused by a nut allergy, although occasionally one of the other common allergens may trigger them. They are life-threatening, but very rare. Symptoms include a widespread rash, facial swelling, breathing difficulties with severe wheezing or noisy breathing, pale complexion and collapse. If you suspect your baby is having an anaphylactic attack, you should dial 999 immediately. After a diagnosis of anaphylaxis, you'll be given a pre-loaded syringe containing medicine that can be given urgently, should the reaction occur again. You'll need to learn how to use it and will usually be provided with several so you can keep one at home, carry one with you, and leave one with any regular caregiver or at school.

A bad reaction: The basic facts about food allergies

- Allergies are on the increase, but no one really knows why, although there are plenty of theories. However, it *is* known that family history is a risk factor, so if an immediate family member, such as a parent or sibling, has an allergy or suffers from an atopic disease, such as eczema, asthma or hay fever, then your baby is also at risk of developing one – and that risk increases the more family members have problems.
- Cow's milk is the most common cause of food allergy. It may cause a reaction in formula-fed babies before weaning, and even in breastfed babies, if a mum has cow's milk in her diet.

However, once weaned, a child with a cow's milk allergy may be able to tolerate food made with milk products that have been heated during the cooking process, since this changes the structure of the culprit proteins and so removes the problem. The same principle applies to egg white, which is the next most common type of food to cause allergy – some children have reactions to scrambled eggs but are OK with cakes where the eggs have been fully cooked.

- Other foods that cause allergies are peanuts, wheat, soy, tree nuts (such as hazel or brazil nuts) and fish. Some fruit and vegetables, such as strawberries, tomatoes and citrus fruits, can trigger allergy, but these will usually be small, localised reactions in the mouth.

- Many children grow out of their allergy by around the age of seven, although some allergies, particularly those to peanuts, tree nuts and fish, are more likely to be lifelong. A baby or child with an allergy will be monitored regularly and, if tests show an improvement, the doctor may suggest 'challenging' your child when she's older to see if the allergy really has improved by introducing a small amount of the allergen into her diet. This should only ever be done under medical supervision.

- For babies born into high-risk families, it's a good idea to wait until the recommended six months (three years for peanuts and peanut products – although, again, this advice is under review) before beginning solid food and then introducing new foods one at a time – waiting a couple of days in between – and in small amounts, to check for any reactions. If your baby does have an allergic reaction to a particular food, it may be advisable to avoid other foods that are also likely to cause a reaction until she is older and better able to cope with any adverse reaction that may occur.

- Food intolerances are very different from food allergies. They can cause unpleasant reactions to certain foods but are never life-threatening and will take hours or days to occur rather than minutes, as with an allergy. Symptoms include weight loss, abdominal pain, diarrhoea and bloated tummy. Often there are no useful blood tests and the best way to make a diagnosis is to remove the suspected food product from the diet to see if symptoms go away. Children may often tolerate a certain amount of the food before symptoms occur. For example, they may not be able to tolerate drinking full-fat cow's milk but be OK with occasional yoghurts or cheese.

- If you think your baby has an allergy, it's important to see your GP. If necessary, the doctor will refer you to your local allergy clinic for tests, and it will be helpful if you can go with a written description of exactly what happened. Your doctor will advise on treatment and give dietary advice, perhaps involving a dietitian. Always seek medical help in pinpointing the culprit and making the right amendments to your baby's diet, and once an allergy is diagnosed, liaise with your doctors every step of the way.

- Allergies are a complex subject and if they affect your family, you'll need more information than there is space to include here. Details of a couple of useful organisations and websites may be found at the back of the book.

What the netmums say

Allergies

I didn't start weaning until six months, but the first couple of times my son had strawberry yoghurt he came out in a rash and had a temperature, and once I realised that it was connected I then cut out everything strawberry related. My daughter is breastfed still and seems fine with strawberries, although I was really nervous about trying her with them, and initially said that I wasn't going to give her them, but one day I gave her strawberry yoghurt without realising and she was fine. My husband's allergic to strawberries, too.

Margaret from Newhaven, mum to Cameron, four and Pippa, one

Finley was sick from the start. When he was still being sick all over the place at 12 months he was booked in for an allergy test for dairy as that seemed to be the culprit. We found out that he doesn't have an actual allergy, but that some (although not all) dairy products make him ill. We had to see a dietitian to talk about some dairy-free alternatives and he now has soya milk formula every night instead.
Emma from Radstock, mum to Jayden, two and Finley, one

When James was seven months and just starting on solids, I tried him with a tiny bit of the yoghurt I was eating: within minutes he was bright red and blotchy. I took him to the GP the following day – having sat with him all night, as I was worried his breathing would be affected. We were referred to hospital, where an allergy test showed he had a very high response to peanuts and milk, and a high response to egg and wheat. It was terrifying. I didn't know what I should or shouldn't feed him. Due to the severe reactions, combined with his asthma, James is a high risk for anaphylaxis. He has an EPI-pen [a pre-loaded syringe, which allows the user to administer urgent treatment] which we have to carry everywhere. He has had allergic reactions from sitting in a shopping trolley and highchair when out, so now we avoid these situations and most friends come to our house as it's safer for James. Unfortunately, there are no allergy specialists in Scotland, and we're in the process of requesting a referral to a specialist in London.
Nicola from Grantown on Spey, mum to James, two

When my daughter was around five months old we started to wean her, mainly using fruit purées. However, a couple of weeks later a rash appeared overnight, so I got in contact with my doctor who diagnosed eczema and suggested we take her off solids and continue with just breastfeeding. Unfortunately, the rash just got worse. It was horrible to see her covered from head to toe in eczema and not being able to help. Finally, after several months of trying different creams, we were referred to our local hospital, where she had a scratch test done, which was really horrible. We were then told our baby girl was allergic to dairy, eggs and peanuts. I couldn't believe it. So straight away we cut all these things from her diet and as I was still breastfeeding her, I had to cut them out as well (which was not good!) She had her first birthday last week and I had to make her a special cake without milk or egg in it. Her eczema is all gone apart from a tiny bit on her ankle, and our dietitian is going to try her with a little bit of milk near Christmas to see if she's grown out of it.

Sarah from Lowestoft, mum to Freya, one

Hold the purée: All about baby-led weaning

The theory of baby-led weaning (BLW) is based on the principle that, at six months – the current recommended age for weaning – most babies will be physically capable of sitting up strongly in a highchair and able to reach out for, grab and put food into their mouths for themselves, and that their chewing and swallowing skills, and digestive systems, should be mature enough to cope with a good range of solid food. In other words, you can miss out the purées and spoon-feeding altogether.

Fans of baby-led weaning say it's a good way to introduce your baby to the positive habit of eating round the table with the rest of the family early on, and means you are far less likely to end up with a fussy eater. They point out that it's a lot less work for mum, since it dispenses with the need for cooking individual meals – in theory, baby just eats an appropriate selection from whatever the rest of the family's eating. Suitable BLW foods from six months include pieces of bread or toast, chunks of cooked or raw fruit and vegetables and cooked pasta shapes, with pieces of meat or boneless fish introduced once she's got the hang of it.

Critics of baby-led weaning question whether a baby of six months can derive all she needs nutritionally from a fairly limited ranged of finger foods (and point out that there have been no studies carried out to prove this either way). They also have concerns about the risk of choking. Fans counter that it is perfectly possible to feed a baby a nutritious range of foods this way, and that the risk of choking is no higher than it is with ordinary weaning.

If you do decide to give baby-led weaning a go, do bear the following advice in mind:

- Be sure to do your research (links to sources of more information are in the appendix) and chat to your health visitor before attempting BLW.
- As the name suggests, let your baby lead the way, taking whatever she wants from what's in front of her, at a pace that suits her. Make sure everything within reach is appropriate for her age (the same guidelines as for ordinary weaning apply) and of a size and shape that she can get to grips with easily – BLW advocates recommend 'fist-sized' or 'chip-shape' foods. Offer as wide a variety as possible. If you're starting before six months and you have a history of allergies in your family, avoid any potential allergens.
- Always make sure your baby is sitting in an upright position, preferably in a highchair, and supervise her carefully when she's eating. Be prepared for her to gag or choke at first – it's fairly common as babies begin to experiment with solids. This advice stands whether or not you are trying the baby-led weaning approach, since it's recommended that all babies are introduced to appropriate finger foods from about six months. Never be tempted to put your fingers into a baby's mouth to retrieve something that's causing a blockage, because you could push it farther down. If she seems to be gagging or choking on something she's eaten, give her a few seconds to see if she coughs it up for herself, which is most likely. (For more information on choking, see First Aid at the back of the book.)
- Consider a flexible approach rather than trying to be purist about the theory – a compromise, including at least some mashed foods, spoon-fed, might be your best bet.

What the netmums say

Baby-led weaning

It could be because I'm lazy and didn't want to spend my time puréeing up food, but I think BLW is the stress-free way of feeding your child. I had planned on trying it (after much reading and research), and expected not to give solids until six months. However, by four months my daughter was really interested in food. As she was reaching out for what we were eating, I offered her slices of cucumber and banana and she'd hold this to her mouth, or lick it, but generally play with it and have fun as she learned about different tastes and textures. She didn't properly eat anything until she was 24 weeks. Her first food was banana, which she devoured greedily. After that, she quickly went up to three meals a day. BLW has been great fun, if a bit messy, although I haven't abandoned the spoon either. Mashed banana or mashed potato, as long as it's lumpy, was fine, along with soft vegetables, fish, or anything she could hold. Toast was quickly a favourite. Now she's eating just the same as us: a mini Sunday roast, lasagne, soup, pasta, sandwiches. Baby-led weaning, to me, was the most natural way of weaning her on to solids and it's meant I haven't taken a lot of effort to purée and freeze everything like most of my friends do. Everything I cook is low salt, low sugar and high fat anyway (to the detriment of my waistline) and she now eats everything we do.
Liz from Swindon, mum to Daniella, aged 11 months

I didn't know baby-led weaning existed when my first child was a baby so I went down the traditional route of purées – unfortunately, she loved them so much that she refused to eat anything even vaguely lumpy and we didn't get her to eat properly until she was well over a year old. After finding out about BLW, I vowed I'd never go down the purée route again. Jonah's been on solids for about six weeks now, and it's fantastic. Initially I started him on one small meal a day but he made it very clear he loves his food so much we quickly progressed to three meals plus snacks every day. He still drinks tons of breast milk. He fed himself fruits and vegetables, and

we've already moved on to just about most things we eat as a family. He loves it, I love it. We are definitely a no-purée household.
Meg from Swansea, mum to Eden, three and Jonah, seven months

I used BLW with my second child, who has reflux and hated being fed via a spoon as she associated it with pain. I gave her toast at five months and she ate it without question, which was a huge step for us. Since then I've tried a mixture, but she does prefer BLW. She eats almost anything you give her to eat in her hand – spaghetti bolognaise, jacket potatoes and toppings, pasta – she's much happier feeding herself foods than when I try to do it. I still feed her myself things like yoghurt and cereal. I was initially worried about choking, and she has got things caught in her throat a few times. But I've read up on it, and the best thing you can do if a baby gets something stuck in their throat is leave them for a second to see if they can get it back up on their own. It's very messy, but the way I see it, she's happy, she's eating a variety of foods, and she's putting on weight. A little bit of mess is well worth it.
Laura from Stoke, mum to Benjamin, three and Jasmine, 11 months

I think to be evangelical about one particular method of feeding is wrong. I'm using a mixture, doing whatever suits me at the time when it comes to feeding my son. Finger foods and breast milk alone don't satisfy his hunger and I want to be able to feed him a healthy balance, including iron-rich foods, such as lentil casserole, which can only be fed to him on a spoon. Some BLW advocates are totally anti-purée, which is mad when even adults love to eat mushy, comfort foods, like cottage pie and rice pudding, sometimes. Babies just can't get that sort of thing into their mouths unaided, and why should they miss out? The term 'baby-led weaning' is a misnomer because it suggests that all other methods are not what the baby wants. But my baby leans forwards for his 'mush', and opens his mouth. I think that offering the whole range of options, and being tuned in to what your child's communicating, is much more baby-led than following one particular method, irrespective of your baby's preferences.
Helen from St Asaph, mum to Ceridwen, two and Ceirion, nine months

Don't cancel the milk

Although solid food becomes an increasingly important element of your baby's diet, her milk feeds should continue. Breast or formula milk is still the only suitable milk for babies at this stage, although during weaning, you can begin to use small quantities of cow's milk in cooking or with cereals. Your baby may well drop a milk feed once she's eating three meals a day, but she still needs 500–600ml (17½–21fl oz) of formula or two to three breastfeeds a day, regardless of how much solid food she is eating, until she's a year old.

Introducing a cup

It's a good idea to introduce your baby to the concept of drinking from a cup at around the same time you start weaning, whether she's breastfed or bottlefed, because drinking from a cup is an essential life skill, and water becomes an important supplementary drink from now onwards. It's particularly important if you're bottlefeeding, because experts recommend that babies drop bottle use altogether by around the age of one, due to dental and speech and language concerns.

At first, stick to giving her plain water in her cup with meals. After she's six months old, the water no longer needs to be boiled and cooled, and this is the healthiest drink you can give her at this stage. (Don't give her bottled mineral water because it has a high sodium content.) You can also give her extra drinks of water in a cup if she seems thirsty between meals.

Don't be tempted to give your baby anything else to drink in either a bottle or cup – squashes or flavoured milks, even those specially marketed for babies, will just encourage a sweet tooth, and tea and coffee are not to be recommended because caffeine isn't suitable for babies and children, and the tannins they contain stop iron from being absorbed. Although fresh fruit juices do have some nutritional value because of the vitamins they contain, which can aid the absorption of iron, they're also very high in sugar and will encourage a sweet tooth, so are best avoided altogether during the first year. If you *do* give fresh fruit juice, make sure you give it very well diluted – ten parts water to one part juice – and only ever at mealtimes. Offering it at other times may spoil her appetite, and increase her risk of tooth decay. (For more on the pros and cons of fruit juice, see p. 257.)

If your baby's bottlefed, you could try gradually introducing her to the idea of taking her milk from a cup, once she's got to grips with one, with a view to making a permanent switch by the time she's one, as recommended by dentists and speech therapists. Of course, most babies love their bottle because of the comfort factor, and it can take a fair bit of persistence to convince them – which is why it's a good idea to begin the process early!

When it comes to choosing a beaker, the best sort are *not* those with the valve, which the non-spill sorts usually have and which bottlefed babies tend to favour because they're accustomed to *sucking* their drinks (breastfed babies don't have to work as hard to draw milk from a boob because it's more free-flowing). Those beakers aren't recommended by health professionals for that reason and also because they encourage longer drinking times – they can easily be carried around by the child – and are a risk to teeth. Although spills are inevitable, it's better to get your baby used to a lidded free-flow cup with a few fairly large holes in the spout, from which she can learn to sip. Alternatively, you might want to bypass the beaker entirely and try a Doidy cup, which is a specially designed lidless beaker that's angled to make drinking easier and is suitable for babies as young as four months. Make sure your baby is sitting down when she drinks, to minimise spills and to discourage her from trailing her beaker (or bottle) around with her and sucking away at her leisure – a habit that's particularly frowned upon by dentists and speech therapists because it prolongs the teeth's exposure to the sugars in milk, and reduces or restricts her opportunities to practise talking.

Does she really have to give up the bottle?

All babies love their last bottle of the day, and not surprisingly, few will be keen to give it up. If it's an established part of your baby's night-time routine and helps to settle her at this time of day, there's really no harm in letting her continue – as long as she's also learning how to drink from a cup during the day. Just be sure that she drinks her milk before she goes into her cot (allowing her to lie down with a bottle means the milk bathes her teeth and increases the risk of tooth decay), and be strict about cleaning her teeth afterwards. At this age, a little comfort goes a long way. (For tips on getting your baby 'off the bottle', see p. 285.)

What the netmums say

Introducing a cup

I started Matthew with a Tommee Tippee Easiflow® cup when he was about five months old and he really took to it. At first he had it during meals with water and he soon mastered feeding himself with it. By eight to nine months he was off the bottles totally and was using the beaker all the time.
Joanne from Stockport, mum to Matthew, two

Harrison had a basic beaker from about six months but he wouldn't drink water, only very dilute juice. A while later, I tried his milk in the beaker – no way! As soon as he realised it wasn't his juice he spat it out and threw the cup down! Now he's 12 months and I've tried just about every beaker on the market for his milk, to no avail. He will happily drink water now, though, out of any of them!
Kelly from Birmingham, mum to Harrison, one

I couldn't get my daughter to drink any water and really didn't want to give her juice. It was a hot time of year so I was worried she wasn't getting enough fluids. When she was five months old I tried her with a Doidy cup with water in it and she instantly knew what to do (although she did make a mess at first!) I then tried her on a sip cup and she took a while to adjust but then after a week or so she loved it.
Bethan from Basingstoke, mum to Willow, seven months

I got both my little ones on to a soft spouted beaker at around five months. I thought as soon as they can grasp something accurately then they are ready to hold the handles of a beaker. They managed fine once they got the idea of tilting it. I then managed to get them off a bottle for night-time feeds by swapping the teat on their Avent bottle for a beaker spout. It worked wonders.
Alicia from south London, mum to Kyrus, two and Demiyah, one

Is she sitting comfortably?

Babies are all different, but as a general rule she'll be ready to use her own highchair once she's confidently able to sit up on her own, generally from about six months. Since it's a good idea to get your baby used to eating at the table (experts reckon it's one of the best ways of fostering a good attitude towards food and eating) and sharing mealtimes with you whenever possible, consider buying a highchair without a tray that simply pulls up to the table – if you've got a nice table, you'll have to invest in a large mat or wipe-clean tablecloth, too!

There's a bewildering range of highchairs available. Before you buy one, you might want to think about the following points:

- How sturdy is it? (Look for a wide base.)
- Will it fit comfortably where we need it?
- Is it easy to fold up and down?
- How many years' use will we get out of it? (Some are multi-functional and can be converted later, so they're suitable for toddlerdom and beyond, which makes them more cost-effective.)
- How easy to clean is it?
- Will it look OK in our dining room or kitchen? (Trivial, perhaps, but worth considering – highchairs often come in bulky, bright designs that you may live to resent! Plenty of stylish looking versions are available these days.)
- Don't forget that a portable feeding chair of some sort, which can be safely strapped to a normal chair, or fixed to a table, is also a very worthwhile investment for occasions when you're visiting or eating out.

Seat safety

For safety's sake, always make sure your baby is well strapped in, and never leave her unattended. When buying a highchair, make sure it conforms to the current safety standard: the number to check for is BS EN 14988. If you're buying second-hand, before handing your money over be sure to check there are no sharp projections or loose bits, that the seat cover is not split or torn, and that the collapsing mechanism, if it has one, is working properly.

You should also be sure to give it a good clean after every meal – and don't forget to check under covers and in corners where food can gather, making a happy home for bacteria.

Leisure and Learning

A helping hand

About now, your baby's skills are blossoming and you can help. Here are some ideas.

Gross motor skills: These are major movements, such as sitting, rolling, crawling and walking. Change her position regularly to encourage them. Put her on her tummy sometimes, for instance, to familiarise her with the starting point for crawling – place a favourite toy just in front of her as motivation. Try propping her up with lots of cushions, so she can practise sitting, and help her to develop her back and leg muscles by gently pulling her up by her hands to a sitting or standing position – most babies of this age love to bounce up and down on a lap or the floor, with support from an adult they trust.

Fine motor skills: These are smaller movements, of the fingers and hands for instance, which will eventually help her to master vital life skills, such as feeding, writing, tying shoelaces and many other things. To encourage their development, provide her with appropriate toys – activity centres, perhaps, and blocks – or just ordinary household items, such as pots and pans and empty boxes. Also, play finger games with her, such as pat-a-cake, and itsy-bitsy spider. Be careful not to let her have anything with very small parts, and always be vigilant – once she can pick up small items, she can put them in her mouth!

Social skills: Much to the delight of her doting relatives, your baby is probably becoming quite a 'people person' by now – she's not reached the stage where strangers are a bit scary (this typically comes a bit later, from around eight months) and will usually smile, laugh and generally charm most of those around her with her cute attempts at communication. It's not too early to start encouraging friendliness and good manners – try repeating hello and goodbye to her and teaching her to wave or blow a kiss. Her early attempts at these things will melt your heart – guaranteed!

Language and intellectual skills: Words and language are beginning to make more sense to your baby now, so keep on talking away to her to help boost her understanding and, eventually, her own ability to talk right back. (For more about talking to your baby, see p. 271.) Even now, your baby's intellectual development is beginning, and you can help to stimulate it through play. Be wary of flashcards, educational DVDs and electronic toys that promise you a baby genius, though – the very best stimulation is the sort that you give her yourself. Play peek-a-boo, sing nursery rhymes and just be with her as much as possible as she explores and experiments with the amazing world of colours, textures, sounds, shapes, noises that's opening up in front of her. To a nearly six-month-old, these simple things are lots of fun!

Making a splash

Most babies enjoy a bath by now – splashing around in the water is yet another chance to have lots of fun and, in any case, it's a good idea to get her used to water, and to the often disliked, but necessary, routine of having her hair washed.

Your little one may have already outgrown her baby bath, or soon will – that is if you bothered with one in the first place. So it's time to consider a change to the big bath, which opens up yet more opportunities for bathtime fun. If she can sit up well on her own by now, she'll probably be fine if you put her on a non-stick mat (a small towel or flannel serves the same purpose) but you'll still need to hold on to her as well, or at least stay very, very close by. You can buy special seats to provide support. They are stabilised on the bottom of the bath by suction, but you should still never leave her, even for a moment. These seats are usually inexpensive, and can double up as normal seats, although they may need a blanket or something soft for padding.

Not all babies like water or being in the bath. Never push it. It's by no means necessary to bath her daily. In fact, it's better not to, because it can be drying for the skin – don't let that put you off, though, if your baby's evening bath is a much-loved part of her bedtime routine. Babies who don't like baths can get by on one or two a week, as long as you wash her face, neck, hands and bottom every day.

Wet, wet, wet: How to have a safe, and comfortable, bathtime

- Be sure to hold on tight, and never leave her unattended in the bath – even for a moment.
- Cover the taps with a towel, so there's no risk your baby could be hurt or burned by one.

- Run the bath and check the water temperature before you put her in the water. Always put the cold in first and add hot rather than the other way round, so that the water is never scalding, just in case she slips in. Test the temperature with your elbow – it should be comfortably warm, never hot. Better still, use a bath thermometer – no hotter than about about 38°C/100.4°F.

- Until she's six months old, about five inches of water is enough. After that, it should be waist height.

- Make sure the bathroom's warm and there are no draughts. Have a soft towel ready – the sort that has a hood will help to keep her head warm.

- Have everything you need ready and within easy reach, so you don't have to stand up or leave the room to fetch anything.

- Use skin and hair products sparingly and stick to mild, unscented ranges formulated especially for babies, particularly if she suffers from eczema or has very dry or sensitive skin. You may have to experiment to find a product that suits her. If your baby has eczema, your GP may prescribe a moisturising emollient for use at bathtime.

- Encourage splashing games, but don't splash her in the face.

- Don't pull the plug while she's in the bath – some babies are, quite reasonably, a bit freaked out by this!

- Hair washing is often unpopular, even if most baby shampoos are made from non-sting formulas these days. If your baby hates it, consider investing in a shampoo shield or a special shampoo rinse cup which has a flat surface and a watertight seal to help keep water and suds out of the eyes. You could also try making a game of it, or offering some sort of distraction, such as a loudly sung song. And bear in mind that you don't need to wash a baby's hair more than once or twice a week, depending on how much hair she has.

- Share a bath with your baby sometimes, or get your partner to – especially if she's not keen on being in the water. It's a lovely thing to do together.

What the netmums say

Bathtime with baby

We moved Sophia into the big bath as soon as she was sitting up by herself, and we got an Aqua Pod [a non-slip mat with back support and handle] from Mothercare, which was good. She's been swimming since she was three months, so I think she's just happy in water. She's fine with hair washing, and we make a point of pouring water over her head, so she gets used to the feeling.
Karla from London, mum to Sophia, seven months

Charlotte screamed on contact with water for the first 18 months. As a result we bathed her twice a week only, but it was not fun. She screamed as soon as she'd touch the water. It was OK when she was little as I would just hold her and wash her while she was wriggling about, but it got harder when she could sit down herself – I had to buy a bath seat that she couldn't get out of. She's fine with baths now. She goes in with her baby brother and likes to wash him.
Carmen from Catterick, mum to Charlotte, two and Leo, one month

Noor hated going in the bath until she was able to sit up properly at around seven months. She used to scream her head off throughout every bath and went so red she looked like an angry lobster! As a result she got a lot of 'top and tails' as a young baby, instead. Once she could sit up and play with bath toys she changed her mind about the whole thing and then would start screaming when I took her out of the bath! I eased the transition into the big tub by putting her baby bath into it a couple of times before trying her on her own in there. Jasmine, on the other hand, adored her baths and looked instantly relaxed every time she went into the water. I had expected to dread the daily bath again, so it was a pleasant surprise! Now they bath together and seeing them splash about and giggle is one of my favourite moments of the day.
Sara from Stafford, mum to Noor, three and Jasmine, 11 months

All About You

You and your man

There's no doubt that having a baby together can have a massive impact on a couple's relationship – let's face it, life changes for good once the two of you invite a third party in. And, although in many ways, it can bring you closer, becoming parents can sometimes cause problems, too.

It's hardly surprising if a new member of the family puts pressure on a couple. Exhaustion, anxiety, stress and fluctuating emotions are all par for the course when you're feeling your way around parenthood for the first time – naturally, these things can't be taken out on the baby, so who's next in the firing line? Lack of sleep is a particularly relevant factor, as fatigue can make small problems seem like big ones.

Adjusting to your new roles and lifestyles can take a while. The loss of freedom and the dramatic dip in couple time can come as a shock – whatever happened to Saturday nights out? Sunday mornings in bed? Weekends away?

It's also common for jealousy to arise. Men – and it's usually this way round, although it can sometimes work the other way – feel pushed out, because their partner has become so wrapped up in the baby. Women who've opted to stay at home may feel resentful of the freedom their men have in going to work every day – particularly if they don't feel they're getting enough help when Daddy *is* around. You may also have very different views about how to bring up your baby and, considering this is probably the most important job you've ever had to undertake, it's going to be a problem if you cannot agree.

Then of course, there's the scarcity of hot sex. Most new parents know all about this. (For more on this specific issue, see p. 124.)

Baby love: How to be partners as well as parents

- Make your relationship a priority – and make sure he does, too. Of course, your baby is the main focus at the moment, but don't let her be an excuse for neglecting each other. If you've spent the last five months lavishing all your time, attention and affection on the new love of your life, maybe you need to redress the balance a little.

- Talk about it. Relationships can founder when communication goes down the pan, so make an effort to talk to each other. It doesn't have to be about anything profound – but make it about something other than your baby sometimes! If something's bothering you, don't let festering resentment build up inside. Get it out there!
- Give some consideration to how *he* feels. Maybe he's also tired, and equally anxious. He may feel under pressure to be a breadwinner and a good dad, and be struggling to do both, for example. If you're not sure what he's thinking, ask.
- Try to agree on how to bring up your baby. If you're not thinking along the same lines, talk about it and agree to compromise if necessary. Remember that your partner's views count – it's easy for mums to assume they know best, but dads are just as qualified! Whatever your views may be, try not to criticise – you'll probably know yourself how much it hurts when someone questions your decisions as a parent.
- Schedule some together time. Grab moments for a chat and a spot of affection or intimacy whenever you get a chance – even if it's just a snatched cuddle while your baby naps – and ditch less important tasks, such as housework, in order to fit it in. Book a reliable babysitter once in a while, so you can go out on a date, just like you used to (for hints on finding the right babysitter, see p. 184). Never feel bad about leaving your baby for this reason! It's good for someone else to look after her sometimes, because it will help foster her independence. If you can't find a babysitter or can't afford one, or if you're just not ready to leave her yet, lay the table, light the candles and have that date at home.
- Do whatever it takes, sometimes, to remind yourself – and your man – that you're a woman, and not just a mum. Swap the sick-stained baggy t-shirt for something more slinky, go to the hairdresser's, get your nails done or have a bikini wax.
- If your partner goes out to work, and you're at home with the baby, make sure he spends plenty of his spare time doing what

you do – let's face it, that's probably harder than any day he'll ever have in the office. Maybe he is the main breadwinner at the moment, but that doesn't mean he's the only one 'at work', and it doesn't let him off the hook when he's at home.

- Seek comfort in the fact that things *will* get better with time, as you gradually adjust to all the changes, and your baby takes up less of your time and attention. Try booking a night away for a couple of months down the line – it will give you something to look forward to, and you'll have plenty of time to prepare yourself and your baby for a short period of separation.

- Seek help, if things seem really serious. This is particularly important if you have PND and it's affecting your relationships. (For details of Relate and some other useful organisations and websites, see the Useful Addresses appendix at the back of the book, p. 333.)

Finding the right babysitter

If you're heading off for a night out, you need to be certain that you're leaving your baby in very good hands, for obvious reasons. (Apart from anything else, you won't enjoy yourself much if you're worrying!) Many couples are lucky enough to have a willing relative or close family friend to help out, but if not, you'll need to find someone you can trust. One of the best ways to do it is to form a babysitting circle with a few close friends, which works on a reciprocal basis.

Don't ask anyone you don't know to sit for your baby, unless a close friend or relative can vouch for them. If you do take on someone your baby hasn't met before, make sure she has several opportunities to get to know her beforehand.

Here are some other golden rules for finding and using a babysitter:

- Try to find someone who has first-aid skills or, at the very least, children of their own or experience in caring for children. If your baby has a childminder, it's worth asking if he or she would be interested. Nursery staff are often keen to earn a bit of extra money, too, so if your baby attends one, do ask.
- Never ask someone under 16 to babysit for you.
- Don't leave your baby with a sitter if that person is ill or unsettled for any reason.
- Don't leave your sleeping baby with a sitter she doesn't know well. If she wakes up, she'll be very distressed.
- Always take a fully charged mobile phone with you, and make sure your sitter has your number, and that he or she knows where you are going. Leave the number of at least one other reliable local person, just in case you can't be reached.
- Make sure your sitter knows exactly what to do should they be called on to feed, change or comfort your little one.
- Establish any important rules for your sitter before you go, such as 'no smoking'.
- Treat your sitter well, and hopefully he or she will become someone you can rely on regularly. If you're paying, make sure it's the going rate, leave refreshments, and make arrangements for the sitter to get home safely.

What the netmums say

Being partners, as well as parents

I remember finding my love for my daughter so all consuming, I worried that I wouldn't love my husband enough any more, but gradually things re-balanced and I found space for my husband again, which was a relief to us both. For a while I think we felt almost resentful of each other and it took a little while to learn how to work together as parents.

Maggie, from Glasgow, mum to Maddie, six months

Having a baby had a huge impact on our relationship in many ways, and it took well over a year for things to settle down. Our eldest was extremely hard work. He had colic, and screamed almost non-stop for the first 13 weeks. We had no idea what had hit us, and I can remember nights when we sat at the table, shell-shocked and on the edge of tears, while the baby screamed and we had no idea what to do. I felt guilty that I had brought this little person into the world to tip everything upside down, and then guilty for thinking that. My hubby loved our baby, but I think he felt I'd conned him into thinking it was a good idea. You can imagine the pressure it put on us. Luckily, we both felt strongly about working at marriage, and in time, it did get easier. By the time our baby was 18 months old, all was well. And when our second baby was born, my hubby said it suddenly made sense. He knew who he was – himself, as well as 'Daddy'.

Jen from Chorleywood, mum to Jack, four and Theo, one

I was 37 and recently married when I fell pregnant. It was a much-wanted baby, but I had had a life with variety and partying and just being! Then my daughter came along after a long, arduous labour and all hell broke loose. There was this bundle of joy that took my breath away – and my sleep! As to our relationship, it suffered. I was diagnosed with PND after returning to work, and then we just got on the treadmill of life and lost sight of each other. But then we realised that we loved each other immensely and that our daughter would survive if we left her with someone else and we found the time to spend with each other doing non-baby related things. We now have one weekend a month together to spend quality time rekindling the love, which only helps to make a good family unit. Being a parent is hard but it does get better if you talk to each other, make time for each other and – if you're lucky! – have sex now and again. But a hug, kisses and laughter are just as important. And communication is key.

Sarah from Manchester, mum to Milly, two

Having a baby and me giving up paid employment changed our relationship on every level. I think he felt more pressure to be the

breadwinner and this affected his stress levels, as he didn't feel he was doing enough no matter how often I assured him he was a good provider. Fact is, though, I wanted more than a good provider. I wanted a partner and someone to share the weight of caring for our baby and looking after the house. Organisation is not my strong point and having a baby, the emotional impact, the sleep deprivation and not having the time for me any more hit me like a sledgehammer. My other half had more traditional views – he works, I sort the children and house – and it took a long time for him to see I could not do it all. My way of thinking was when he was at work I looked after the baby and the house, but when he came home our baby and our house was our responsibility jointly. I got hardly any support for the first three months, but after that things began to improve. He started having our daughter for an hour every day, so I could have a bath, or whatever. Then it got easier as she started settling in the evening better, and he would occasionally bath her, and give her her last feed from a bottle. It took about a year for things to settle and things have continued to improve ever since. He helps more and understands how stressful and unrelenting looking after the kids is and that when he comes home from work (after a cup of tea!) I need him to be hands on and helpful. When I look back I have no idea how I coped and how we survived as a couple, but we did and I'm glad.
Heather from Sheffield, mum to Jasmine, four and Jack, two

It's brought me and my husband closer together. Sure it's been hard, we're both tired, there's so much to do, we're under stress financially as I was made redundant while on maternity leave and he is the sole breadwinner, and I have mood swings! But I could not have wished for a better husband. He helps around the house, he takes Holly to his parents on Saturday afternoons, which gives me a chance to have some me-time (though in fact I usually do the ironing, but at least I get to watch a DVD at the same time!) and he has been very supportive about my breastfeeding. We talk, we check in with each other and recently we've decided to have a cuddle-DVD-and-wine evening every Saturday. We also try every six weeks to go out for a drink or meal, or occasionally go out shopping together. And we still have sex, too – not as much as before, but still just as fun!

Sarah from Ledbury, mum to Holly, nine months

The Seventh Month

Welcome to your seventh month of motherhood

By the end of this month your baby should be eating solid foods, perhaps even enjoying three good meals a day. As weaning progresses, her culinary options become much more interesting and varied – and most babies of this age are surprisingly open to new tastes, once they're used to the novelty of proper grub. They usually love the social aspect of eating, too, so make sure your baby is pulled up to the table and that you're eating alongside her whenever possible – it's a really healthy habit to foster.

One of the benefits of her expanding diet is that her tummy gets fuller and that means she is more likely to sleep through the night – or, at least, that she's capable of it. If a continuing lack of sleep has been affecting you badly, now's your chance to do something about it, by teaching your baby how to get through the night without you. It may not be as hard as you think – although you do need to be committed. Some effective sleep-training techniques are outlined on p. 200.

Health, Growth and Development

Baby milestones

Now that she is six months old, your baby will typically:

- Be able to see across a room.
- Have begun to babble.
- Sit up, if well supported with cushions.

And she might also:

- Reach for objects, usually with both hands, and grasp them.
- Show pleasure or annoyance with squeals or screams.
- Raise her arms when she wants you to pick her up.
- Sit up unsupported.
- Drink from a cup.
- Get into a crawling position, or have begun to try crawling or bottom shuffling (either forwards or backwards!).

Milestone focus: Grasping and grabbing

These are the skills that will eventually help your little one to master a great many everyday tasks, from building a brick tower, to feeding herself. Although born with a grasping reflex (she'll instinctively curl her fingers round one of yours in the early weeks), babies soon forget this and spend the following months re-learning it. The early stages of grasping and grabbing begin during the first few months, when she'll spend time opening and closing her hands, peering at them and trying to make sense of how they work. Her grasping and grabbing skills become more finely honed as her hand-eye coordination improves – in other words, when her physical ability to get hold of an object catches up with her ability to see it!

By her fourth month she'll be batting and swiping at tempting objects, and by her seventh, grasping hold of them with two hands and a firm hold. You may find that she is able to hold and control her own feeding bottle fairly well – even so, it's best not to leave her unsupervised during feeds, just in case of choking.

This increasing efficiency at getting what she wants means you'll need to keep an eye on her and, if you haven't already done so, make your home as safe a place as possible (see p. 218). Do bear in mind that once a baby can grab, she soon learns to let go – some babies develop pretty skilful fast-bowling techniques around now, so watch out for low-flying toys! In a few months' time, her grasping skills will become even more dexterous and she should be attempting to grasp very small objects between her finger and thumb – known as a pincer grip.

You can help to stimulate your baby's grasping and grabbing skills by offering her opportunities to practise. Place bright, appealing items within her reach so she can grab at them, or dangle them over her when she's lying on her back. Make sure she's got appropriate playthings, such as soft toys and bricks, or anything else you've got lying around that's easy for her to get hold of and won't cause a problem if she puts in her mouth. Instigate games that involve giving and taking objects from one another. If she wants to hold her own bottle, cup or spoon, let her (in spite of the mess!) and, of course, give her lots of suitable finger foods with meals and as snacks.

Generally speaking – and always bear in mind that developmental milestones may occur at different times for babies who were born prematurely – your baby should be grabbing and grasping by the time she's nine months old. If she's showing no signs, have a chat with your health visitor or GP about it.

Feeding

The second stage of weaning

If you haven't introduced solids in some way, shape or form by now, then it's time to get cracking – milk still provides the *main* source of nourishment between now and her first birthday, but by six months, her growing body starts to require other and more varied sources of nutrients, too. Babies of this age also need to start becoming familiar with the concepts of thicker textures and lumps in their food, and to practise chewing and swallowing skills. Postponing the introduction of solids much beyond this point could make it harder to interest your baby in making the effort when you do begin.

If your baby doesn't seem that keen on the solids you're offering, it may be because she's not hungry enough – always wait a while after her usual breast or formula feed before trying – late morning, a couple of hours after a milk feed, is ideal. Be persistent, but don't allow yourself to get stressed about it. You could try something different if she's refusing whatever you're offering – a little puréed fruit or sweet vegetable, such as carrot, for example, if she's turning her nose up at baby rice. Chat to your health visitor if you're concerned.

You'll probably find, though, that your baby responds well to your offerings if you're beginning solids around now, and you can move on to the second stage of weaning fairly quickly. This involves two to three meals a day and a much wider choice of tastes and textures. Equally, if you're already well into the weaning process by now and your baby is enjoying regular meals based mainly on fruit or vegetable purées, it's time to broaden her horizons by offering meat, fish or their veggie equivalent.

A healthy habit

Don't forget to pull your baby up to the table in her highchair and eat as a family whenever possible – it's an excellent way to encourage good eating habits, even at this early stage. Aim to eat breakfast and lunch together, and even if your baby needs an earlier tea than you and your partner are ready for, sit down and enjoy a drink or snack with her while she tucks in.

Next on the menu

Once she's got to grips with basic combinations of puréed fruit and vegetables, you can begin to offer different sorts of food – but don't blend it to a fine purée any more. Aim for a thicker, lumpier texture. (She may well gag at first, but persevere – she'll soon get used to it.) Try introducing meals that offer a good balance, so that she's getting something from all the main food groups – not necessarily in one meal, but over the course of a week or so. Dish up plenty of protein, in the form of mashed or finely minced meat, fish (checking very carefully for any bones first) or pulses, along with some carbohydrates, such as potatoes, rice or pasta. Continue to offer her lots of fruit and veg with her meals and as snacks, and increase the variety you give her – the more she tastes early in life, the more receptive she'll be to them later. And don't be permanently put off if she rejects something – babies often need to taste some foods several times before they decide they like them.

Include plenty of dairy products, as it's vital for her to get enough calcium, which builds strong bones, so try her with mild cheese and homemade cheesy sauces, yoghurts, fromage frais and milk-based desserts, such as rice pudding and custard (cow's milk is now OK to use in cooking). Do bear in mind that reduced-fat versions aren't suitable for babies because they need a full complement of calories for energy, and the extra vitamin A.

Making a meal of it: Second stage grub she'll love

- Fish pie made with flakes of soft white fish, mashed potato and cheese sauce
- Beef, lamb or lentil and veg casserole
- Cauliflower cheese
- Shepherd's pie
- Pasta with tomato and vegetable sauce, and a handful of grated cheese for protein
- Chicken or veggie gratin
- Rice pudding, or stewed fruit with custard, for afters

Finger foods

From six months onwards, you can give your baby appropriate finger foods as part of a meal, or as snacks, gradually increasing the variety you give her as she becomes more proficient at picking them up and eating them. Stay close by at all times – it may take her a while to get used to eating foods like these and she may gag or choke a little at first. If this happens, give her a few moments to sort the problem out for herself, which, in most cases, she will. There's advice on how to cope with more serious choking episodes in the First Aid appendix at the back of the book.

Self-service: Finger foods to offer from six months

- Peeled and sliced soft, ripe fresh fruits, such as peach, banana, melon, mango and pear. Avoid whole grapes or berries because of the risk of choking – you can give her these halved or quartered, though. You could also try soft dried fruits, such as apricot and prune. Harder raw fruits, such as apple, are better grated at first.

- Bread and butter, crumpets or muffins; mini sandwiches with soft cheese or egg filling; toast, chapatti or pitta fingers. Don't offer only wholemeal varieties of bread – although it's a healthier option for older children and adults, babies' stomachs can't cope with too much fibre, so give them plenty of the white stuff, too. The same goes for rice and pasta.
- Breadsticks and rice cakes – look for baby and child versions, which are unsalted.
- Lightly cooked veg – steaming is best because it helps to retain flavour and nutrients: green beans, broccoli or cauliflower florets, carrot or courgette sticks. From about nine months, try sticks of raw carrots and cucumber, which are harder – especially helpful at teething times. You could also try offering a dip, such as hummus, to go with them – she may not get the hang of this concept for a while, but she'll have fun trying, and some goodness may go down! Courgettes, peppers and carrots, roasted with a little oil, make a soft and tasty offering.
- Cubes of cheese, such as Cheddar or Edam.
- Chunks of omelette; pieces of well-cooked scrambled or hard-boiled egg; strips of eggy bread.
- Cooked pasta shapes.

Still OFF the menu after six months

Salt: Official guidelines are no more than 1g of salt per day, which means that babies (and this goes for toddlers and older kids, too) shouldn't have any *added* to their food, because there's already plenty in ordinary products, such as bread, cereals and cheese, for example. For the same reason, you should aim to steer clear – for the whole of their first year – of highly processed adult foods, such as pasta sauce from a jar, and bacon. These are very high in salt, so at the very least be careful to give them infrequently. Your best bet for avoiding salty products is to cook from scratch, although the one nutritional advantage that shop-bought baby-food has is that, by law, it cannot contain salt. If you give your baby food that you've made for yourself – and you should do this as much as possible to save on work – make sure you cook it without salt. You'll just have to add yours later!

Added sugar: Babies don't *need* sugar and if you give her much at this stage, she'll get a taste for it, which could eventually lead to tooth decay and even, later in life, obesity. Avoid (or strictly limit) biscuits, chocolate and other sweet treats for at least her first year – what she doesn't know about, she won't hanker for! Quite a lot of foods that are suitable for babies of this age and a useful source of other nutrients, such as milk-based puddings, will have some sugar in them already, and that's fine. But you shouldn't *add* sugar, for instance to stewed fruit or cereal, and if you're making puds from scratch, keep quantities of sugar down, or better still add something else to sweeten them, such as fruit. Don't give your baby anything made with artificial sweeteners, either, because other health risks are associated with them. Drinks containing sugar are a bad idea full-stop, so stick to water and milk. Fresh fruit juice should be given very diluted, and only at mealtimes.

Honey: This should be avoided altogether for the first year because, in rare cases, it may contain bacteria that causes a serious illness called infant botulism.

Whole nuts: Best avoided altogether before the age of five because of the risk of choking.

Shellfish, raw eggs and unpasteurised soft cheeses: All still to be avoided because of the risk of food poisoning.

Fiery flavourings: Chillies and hot spices are not suitable for babies.

Dropping a milk feed

You'll find your baby wants less milk the more solids she takes. Babies often drop a feed or two by the time they are well established on three meals a day, but they do still need some milk. As a general guideline, 500–600ml (17½–21fl oz) of formula or two to three breastfeeds a day, is about right. Milk used in cooking and on cereals counts, too, so you can boost the amount your baby's taking, if necessary, by including milky puddings and sauces, as well as cheese or yoghurts, in her daily diet.

Equally though, it's important that your baby isn't drinking too much milk around now because it may interfere with her appetitite for solid foods. Aim to allow her no more than 600ml (21fl oz) a day. (There's more about this on p. 257.)

What the netmums say

Second-stage weaning

Just when I thought I was getting the hang of things . . . along came weaning! A time of confusing, mixed advice; mess like I couldn't believe and hours spent puréeing, mashing and concocting weird and wonderful mixtures of fruit, veg and meat – sometimes all in the same meal! And then hours mopping it off the walls and out of my hair before binning half of it uneaten . . . happy days! My daughter was slow to take to solids and the fear of choking on lumps was a big one, not helped by a proper choking incident early on. Looking back, I know she wasn't ready and I shouldn't have felt pressured. They get there in the end. In her case, on a joyous Christmas Day, when little Miss Independence realised she could feed herself with her hand, banished the spoon . . . and smooth food was rejected in favour of lumpy solids and finger food. She never looked back! She's been eating pretty much what we eat for a while now, the more flavour the better.
Jo from Sheffield, mum to Alice, one

I was always a bit scared to give Harrison anything lumpy, but began to when he was about seven months, two months after we began weaning. He gagged a lot for a long while, and I thought we'd never get there. Then I tried finger foods – pasta spirals, bits of toast, lumps of cheese etc – and he was absolutely fine with those! He still gags occasionally, but it's usually because he's stuffed too much in! Now he eats a lot of what we do – chopped up, not mashed or blitzed to within an inch of its life!
Kelly from Birmingham, mum to Harrison, one

Holly's been eating the same as us from seven months – I don't blend, mash or purée her foods any more. Lumps she took to very quickly at six and a half months. I just slowly built up the consistency of foods to get her used to them. Choking, yep we've had a few scares, and twice I have had to get her out of the chair and bang her on her back to get the food out. It really doesn't bother her! The first time it happened I was so upset and scared. But I got great advice and support from the Netmums food and weaning board. Holly loves her food and is a very happy, healthy (if messy, independent and strong-willed!) baby.

Sarah from Ledbury, mum to Holly, nine months

Liquid refreshment

If you're still going strong with the breastfeeding now, that's fantastic! You've made it to the end of the recommended period and you can feel certain that you've given your baby the best possible start in life. Carry on by all means – the health benefits for your baby don't stop and many mums still find it an enjoyable experience well past the six-month point. You'll almost certainly find your baby demands fewer breastfeeds once she's eating solid food, but as long as she's still getting a couple of feeds a day from you and the rest of her diet is varied, she'll be doing OK. It's normal for breastfed babies to self-wean (drop the feeds naturally) when they're ready, at some point between six months and two years, and some mums are very happy to wait until that point rather than going to some trouble to cut breastfeeds down or out.

If you do feel ready to stop now, or to cut back on breastfeeds (perhaps to just one in the morning and one at night), do so gradually to avoid having very full, painful breasts. You may find that your baby is reluctant to take a bottle at this late stage, in which case it may take patience and persistence to introduce one. (For some helpful hints, see p. 68.) If you *are* trying to encourage your baby off the boob, you'll do better if you have a partner to help by offering a feed from a bottle, or some other distraction, such as play.

Many breastfeeding mums don't bother with bottles at all, though, and get their baby used to a beaker. Babies often make a fairly natural changeover when they're around one year old, once it's OK to give them cow's milk.

What the netmums say

Extended breastfeeding

I breastfed both of mine until just over a year. I went back to work part-time when my second was seven months so I expressed for a while, but that was very hard work so I switched to formula for nursery, and breast at home. Challenges to feeding after six months include the fact that my babies often woke in the night and nothing but a breastfeed would get them back off again. Also, feeding in public can be harder (I felt more self-conscious, particularly as older babies tend to want to see what's going on around them and leave mum exposed). Also teeth can be an issue – I was once bitten so hard in public that I screamed and was left bleeding. On the other hand, after six months, feeding gets a lot easier – less frequent, and no problems with latching on, leaky breasts, engorgement or colic. It can be a cuddly treat for both of you after a day at work and nursery. In fact, I'd go so far as to say that if you stop feeding at six months, you miss out on the best bits. I stopped at around 13 months because from that point they could have cow's milk, their sleep patterns had matured and I wanted to be able to go out or have a night away sometimes. I also felt that, in order to convince others that breastfeeding is a normal and OK thing to do, I didn't want to be seen as extreme or a lactivist.
Clare from Sheffield, mum to Hannah, three, and Sophia, one

I loved breastfeeding, but my daughter was a very hungry baby and so I supplemented with formula last thing at night from early on. By six months she was having a feed in the morning only, and one day she just didn't seem to want it and so I stopped altogether, bought a bottle of wine, had a hair cut and went out and bought new bras. I was ready to stop, and for me it was symbolic. I was getting my body back. My son never took a bottle, even though I wanted him to, and fed frequently through the night even at six months. I just kept offering him a bottle every few days and not making an issue of whether he took it or not. Then he did! So I brought in the bottles during the day and gradually stopped breastfeeding through the night. I didn't want to be feeding still when they were walking – just something I was not comfy with. I also wanted my body back – and some sleep!

Heather from Sheffield, mum to Jasmine, four and Jack, two

I planned to stop breastfeeding at six months and change to formula. However, my son had different ideas, so I've gone with the flow and I'm still breastfeeding at eight months. I've had such fantastic support from my peers and from midwives at the Baby Café [a national charity devoted to supporting breastfeeding mums at local drop-in sessions – details are given in the appendix] in Manchester, and I feel able to continue breastfeeding for a while longer.

Michelle from Manchester, mum to Elliot, eight months

My daughter was a very efficient, pain-free feeder and we both enjoyed breastfeeding. I also had an abundance of milk, which helped. She had just breast milk until she was seven months, when I had to go back to work. I had romantic ideas of expressing in my lunch break so she would never need formula, but soon realised the practical issues with that! I continued to breastfeed her in the evening and on weekends, and she had formula at nursery. The last feed to go at ten months was the evening feed – when Alice ditched me of her own choice, I'm afraid!

Adilla from Bideford, mum to Alice, three

Vitamin drops

The Department of Health now recommends that breastfed babies, or babies drinking less than 500ml (17½fl oz) of formula, should be given supplementary drops of vitamins A, C and D from six months. You may qualify for free vitamin drops under the government's Healthy Start scheme if you are claiming benefits. Ask your health visitor for details, or visit the Healthy Start website to find out more (see Useful Addresses at the back of the book).

Follow-on milk

This commercially available product is meant for babies of six months plus. Follow-on milk has added iron in it but is considered by most health professionals to be an unnecessary invention of marketing men. Your baby really needs just one type of formula milk to see her through her first year. After six months, if she's having a variety of solid food, she won't need follow-on milk.

Sleep

Time for some sleep training?

It's very common for babies of six months to be waking in the night for a feed or some other comfort provided by mum. Your baby may have slipped back into a night-waking habit, having slept through before, perhaps because of hunger, teething pains or just the growing excitement of life. It may also be that she no longer settles easily at bedtime – or maybe you have only ever been able to settle her at bedtime by feeding or rocking her to sleep. If any of these scenarios are the case, you may be feeling fairly desperate for a good night's sleep, particularly if you've returned to work. The good news is that, at this stage, you can do something about it, if you want to, by encouraging her to go to sleep on her own, and to make it through the night without the need for you to get out of bed and tend to her! Her seventh month is a good time to attempt some kind of sleep training. By now, with a bigger stomach and a daytime diet that includes solids, she is definitely quite capable of sleeping all through the night. So you can be pretty certain that when she wakes, it's not through hunger, but habit. All you need to do is break that habit by teaching her to 'self-soothe' when she wakes – and it's better to do this sooner rather than later, because habits such as this one get harder to break the longer they are allowed to continue.

Whatever you decide to do to help both your baby and yourself get a whole night's sleep, the single most important thing is to ensure she has a consistent bedtime routine. This is best put in place early on, but if you haven't already done so by now, don't fret – it's never too late to start one. Consistency is key, so make sure you begin bedtime at the same time each evening and follow the same pattern every single day. All babies are different, so there's no right time. Whenever she's calm and beginning to get sleepy is good. A warm, quiet bath, pyjamas on, milk, a story and cuddle, perhaps a song, and then lights-out is a pretty typical routine, but whatever you do, the aim is to do the same thing every night and make it a relaxing and loving experience for your little one, so that she sees bedtime as something pleasurable. It's also helpful if the rest of her day has a fairly consistent pattern to it, so her naps and mealtimes fall at around the same time, which means she's likely to become sleepy at the same time every night.

The other important thing is to make sure your baby has finished her feed and is still awake when you lay her down to sleep. That way, she'll learn how to fall asleep on her own and, in theory, how to resettle herself when she wakes in the night, which she will usually do several times in any case, because of the natural cycles of deep and light sleep that we all move through during the night.

If you've kept your baby in your room with you for the recommended six months and are moving her into her own room about now, allow her whatever time she needs to get used to this arrangement before starting any kind of sleep training.

And don't forget that many babies have at least a little grumble on being put into their cot, or if they wake in the night – she might well cry or whine for a while before settling back to sleep on her own, so it's always worth waiting for a short time before dashing in to tend to her.

Leaving your baby to cry

The methods of sleep training that tend to be effective most quickly involve leaving your baby alone to cry it out, so that she eventually learns you're not coming, and there's no point in calling for you. These techniques – variously known as controlled crying, crying-down, timed settling or Ferberizing (after Dr Richard Ferber, the paediatric sleep specialist who pioneered it) – can, unsurprisingly, be extremely tough to see through. However, they usually work, and fairly fast, and as most hollow-eyed parents are pretty desperate for an uninterrupted night's sleep by now, it's often a case of needs must.

Once you've successfully sleep-trained your baby, you probably won't look back – although it's worth bearing in mind that illness or a dramatic change in routine can unsettle her again and you may have to go through the process once more (although, fortunately, it's likely to take less time).

Is it cruel to let her cry?

A handful of child psychologists have spoken out against methods that involve leaving a baby to cry, because they believe it could be damaging. One theory is that when a baby's stress levels are allowed to rise, brain cells may be killed off, resulting in potential emotional or psychological damage later in life.

However, controlled-crying techniques *are* advocated by a great many other experts, who stress that leaving a baby to cry for very short bursts will not harm her. They also point out that good sleep patterns are vital for a child's health, but rarely happen on their own – and that tired parents need a good night's sleep for the sake of their own wellbeing.

There are a few golden rules. You need to be sure your baby is crying out of habit rather than genuine hunger, thirst, pain, discomfort or fear before you attempt one of these techniques. If she's waking at the same time every night, that's a pretty good indication that it's habit. And as most mums are pretty tuned in to their babies' different cries, it will usually be obvious if she's in pain or has some other urgent need you should attend to. The other important rule is that you should only ever leave your baby crying for short periods of time – a maximum of ten minutes once training is well underway – before going to offer her reassurance.

Sleep tight: How to make a success of controlled crying

Controlled crying means leaving your baby to cry in her cot for a short time, whether that's at bedtime or if she wakes in the night. Before you start, bear in mind that the process can last a week or two, so pick a time when you know you're not going anywhere for a while. You may also need to warn your neighbours, if your walls are thin!

When your baby cries, wait for three to five minutes before returning briefly to her room to check she's OK. Don't touch her or pick her up – although in some variations of this technique you can lay a hand on her back, give her a little stroke or adjust her bedding – but say something quiet and soothing like, 'Night-night, it's time to sleep.' Then leave the room again and this time, if she's still crying or begins to cry again, wait for another three to five minutes before returning. The next time, and subsequently, you can wait for ten minutes – but not longer – before returning to comfort her. You may prefer to limit the periods you leave her to five minutes when you first try it. It's also a good idea not to hang around outside her room, listening to her cry, because this is inevitably upsetting. Find a useful task to do – within earshot – while you wait. Repeat until she falls asleep, and then repeat the following night and for however many nights are necessary. It will usually be one to two weeks only before you get results, and sometimes a matter of days.

For this technique to work, you have to be committed to it and very persistent – if you give in one night, you can fully expect to be back to square one the following night. It's vital that your partner is in agreement, and equally committed, because you'll need emotional and practical support to see it through. You're particularly likely to need your partner's help if you're still breastfeeding and trying to ease your baby off night-time feeds. She's less likely to settle if she gets a whiff of your milk. You may also need to express a little at this point if your boobs are uncomfortably full, although you can help yourself by wearing a firmly fitting bra.

A gentler approach

If you find controlled-crying methods too hard to put into practice, a gentler approach to sleep training may be a better bet for you and your baby, such as gradual retreat, also known sometimes as the 'disappearing chair' method. With this, you allow your baby to cry but you don't leave the room. At the start, you sit right by her cot and make soothing noises, although you still shouldn't pick her up. The following night you place your chair a little farther away from her cot, and a little farther still the night after that. Eventually, you sit by the door and, finally, you should be able to leave the room and she will settle on her own without you there. It will take longer than controlled crying, and so calls for even more patience and commitment – but probably not quite so much heartache. A variation on this theme is the 'elastic-band' method, which involves moving around the room but never leaving it while she's crying, coming back to her side periodically to comfort her. The method recommended by the late babycare guru Tracy Hogg (also known as The Baby Whisperer) advises picking her up and holding her every time she cries, and putting her back down as soon as she is settled, the theory being that if you keep going – and it may take many, many pick-ups and put-downs per night before she gets the idea, so it's a pretty wearing technique – you'll gradually be able to reduce the number of times you pick her up per night until, eventually, you don't have to pick her up at all. (For recommended reading on sleep training, see the appendix at the back of the book.)

Why daytime naps are still important

By now babies have generally settled into a regular pattern of two naps a day, one in the morning and one in the afternoon. It's a good idea not to let her nap for longer than two and a half hours at a time, or later than 4p.m. in the day, if you want her to be tired enough to settle at bedtime. But equally, she does need to have a full complement of daytime sleep if she's to sleep well at night because overtiredness, ironically, can often disrupt sleep later. (For more information on daytime napping, see p. 236.)

Different strokes for different folks

Some parents are happy not to bother with sleep-training techniques, choosing instead to go with the flow, content in the knowledge that all children sleep through, eventually! There's absolutely nothing wrong with that if it fits in with your lifestyle – and as long as you're prepared for the possibility that she may still be waking you for many months and even years ahead.

What the netmums say

To sleep train, or not?

When I had Noor I was determined never to let her cry, and read the Baby Whisperer book religiously. It was great, but I just couldn't get her to sleep without her screaming for sometimes up to two hours. All the recommended pick up, put down stuff was just exhausting for both of us and I was so stressed about bedtimes. Then I heard about a version of controlled crying where you keep checking on them even when they've quietened down. The idea is that they realise that they will get your attention and that you are still around whether or not they are crying, so they don't feel that the only way to make sure you are there is by sobbing their hearts out. I was desperate and this made me feel a bit better about the idea of controlled crying. It really worked for me. Noor and I were much happier as there was less screaming and pretty soon bedtimes were lovely relaxed affairs.

As soon as Jasmine turned six months I did the same with her and now I have my evenings back to myself and I'm able to make plans that don't have to take unlimited screaming and being held hostage in a baby's room into account. As a result, we're all happy.
Sara from Stafford, mum to Noor, three, and Jasmine, 11 months

Controlled crying works! With Sophie I started when she was about six months old. I always made sure she was not teething or had a temperature, then I would start with leaving her for three minutes, then six, then 12, going into her room at these intervals and putting my hand on her chest. She would settle straight away and if she didn't, I knew there was something else wrong, a dirty nappy for instance. It was was heart-wrenching leaving her to cry. Sometimes it's best to do something while you're waiting for the time to pass, for example, cleaning bottles, or even phoning a friend. But it worked. Now when I put her to bed, I tuck her in and leave the room and she just falls asleep without a noise. Together with a good night-time routine, it works perfectly. But I also think all children are different.
Kerry from Southport, mum to Sophie, one

I hate the phrase 'controlled crying' – it's self-soothing, teaching them to go to sleep on their own. I had to do this with my younger one after 12 months of no sleep, and it was incredibly hard, sitting downstairs listening to my poor baby cry and then crying and getting upset myself. But I knew it was the only way to help her go to sleep. I think people think it's a cruel thing to do – I can even remember being called a bad mum by somebody for doing it, which made me feel like rubbish. After a week of crying, though, she

stopped and, after that, she could always get back to sleep or go to sleep without crying. I wished we'd done it sooner.
Dawn from Maidstone, mum to Genevieve, two and Millie, one

With my first child I listened to all the different opinions that were forced on me from health professionals, friends, family and did what I was told. I remember letting my son cry for a bit, until he fell asleep. When my daughter came along six years later, I'd learnt to trust my instincts and not be swayed by books and well-meaning advice. So I picked her up when she cried and rocked her to sleep, without a thought as to whether it was making a rod for my own back. As far as I'm concerned, I was responding to my baby's needs. She's now grown into a very independent little girl, so it certainly hasn't caused a problem. I'm doing the same with my second son, following my instincts. Sometimes it take hours of rocking, cuddling and nursing to get him to sleep, but I don't put pressure on myself to get him sleeping through. I think parents too often believe that babies should be doing things by a certain age, and if not, then action should be taken. Some children just take longer than others to sleep through, walk, talk, etc, and parents should take it in their stride.
Claire from Leigh, mum to Owen, eight, Monica, two, and Peter, six months

My daughter was not sleeping through at six months and we both needed more sleep. She had a dummy and was waking because when she came out of a deep sleep she needed her dummy to get back off again, and it was not there. So I took her dummy away and taught her to go to sleep without it. I stayed with her, picking her up and laying her back down as needed, telling her, 'It's all right, it's time to go to sleep.' I stroked her check and patted her bum a bit, just to let her know I was there and she was safe. Gradually, she needed this less and I moved away to the chair and then the door. It took about ten days but then she had got it and although sometimes she woke and needed a cuddle, it was less often and not every night. She is four now, and still needs me sometimes in the night but I am OK with that. I did the same with my

son and it took a few months to get him to the point where he was settling well on his own, because I took it slowly to ensure he felt safe and secure at all times.
Heather from Sheffield, mum to Jasmine, four and Jack, two

Leisure and Learning

Language lessons

It's never too early to talk to your baby, but you may also want to try out a slightly different method of communication – baby signing, a system for teaching your little one to express herself with a 'vocabulary' of hand gestures. Six to seven months is an appropriate time to start, although it may well be a good few months before your baby responds well to it. You can join a class (and enjoy the social benefits, too), most of which are run by parents who've tried and enjoyed signing with their own babies. Otherwise, there are a number of books, websites, DVDs and home courses devoted to baby signing, so you could teach yourself and your baby the basics at home – even learning a handful of common signs and their meanings can be useful. (For more details, see the appendix at the back of the book.)

Why sign?

Babies can control their hand and arm muscles, and their own understanding, before they master speech, so signing can be a way to help them communicate before they can talk, which reduces frustration for them. It's also said to help later development of their language, vocabulary, understanding and literacy, and to strengthen the bond between baby and parent. It can take them a while to pick it up, though, so you need to be patient.

Show me what you mean: Top tips for baby signing

- Begin with basics, such as more, eat, drink, milk. Follow your baby's lead, and at first use signs for whatever you think will be most useful and interesting for her.
- Always say the word as you sign – this is vital for encouraging spoken language.

- Speak slowly, but in a natural way.
- Keep it simple, using just one sign per sentence.
- Use lots of repetition and always emphasise the key word along with the sign, so your baby can clearly understand the connection.
- Happily accept any of her signing attempts, even if she hasn't got it quite right. Be consistent in how you show a sign, though, however your baby adapts it.
- Be patient and relaxed about baby signing. Praise her when she gets it right – and keep it fun.

What the netmums say

Baby signing

I signed with my children, which inspired me to get qualified, and I also run weekly classes in my area. How many 11-month-olds do you know who can say 'strawberry' or 'hamster'? Yet my daughter could sign these words and it meant that I could respond to her requests without having to say 'pardon' over and over again and watch her get increasingly frustrated with my lack of understanding. My children are ten, eight and two now and we still sign to each other when shouting isn't an option! Like this morning, across the playground my daughter signed 'book, bag, car' to let me know she'd left her book bag in the car! And if in the excitement of getting a party bag at the end of a party, they forget to say thank you, I can prompt them with a sign.

Daniella from Pinner, mum to Phoebe, ten, Isabel, eight, and Sophie, two

I started baby-signing classes with my middle daughter when she was about eight months old. I was a bit sceptical but, being a teacher, I was open to anything that could help with language and communication. I was completely blown away by it. Evelyn did her first sign at ten months and they were pretty free-flowing after that.

Babies understand so much more than we realise and she was able to demonstrate this through the use of signs. It also saved a lot of tantrums. Another great use was when she was just starting to talk and I couldn't always understand what she was saying – she would give it a few tries and then do the sign if she knew it. She was able to let me know if she was hungry, cold and even if she was tired. Her speech has always been very advanced for her age, which I'm sure is no coincidence. I now teach my own baby-signing classes and I still get very excited when parents and carers share their signing stories with me and are obviously finding it as helpful as I did.

Vicki from Twickenham, mum to Amy, 13, Evelyn, four and Bethany, nine months

I started taking Harrison to baby-signing classes when he was about three and a half months old. I desperately wanted to get out and meet people, but wanted us to do something more than the usual mother and baby groups. The classes are a lovely mix of singing and signing, then musical instruments and finally toys for the babies and chat for the parents. Harrison seemed to enjoy it from the start and definitely understood a couple of signs after a few weeks. Now he's started signing a few words – 'milk', 'bird', 'duck'. He really enjoys the classes and I think we've both found the signs useful and will do so for some time to come!

Kelly from Birmingham, mum to Harrison, one

I take my daughter to signing classes. We started when she was seven months old after my best friend recommended it. I wrote a list the other day of the signs she can do – I've counted 51! I believe it's assisted her greatly with development. It's fantastic to be able to communicate with Mia and understand what she's trying to tell me. Her speech is also developing fast now. She knows quite a number of words and is trying to say a lot more. I cannot recommend it enough.

Vicky from Worcester, mum to Mia, one

We go to a baby-sign group. My younger daughter is six months old and already recognises the sign for 'milk'. In fact, she gets really

excited when I do it to her. We're also convinced she moves her hand to sign it back, but maybe I'm just getting carried away!
Lu from Sheffield, mum to Freya-Grace, three, and Piper, six months

All About You

Getting some me-time

Opportunities for a spot of me-time can be scarce, to say the least, when you're a mum with a baby under one. But it's really important to grab whatever spare moments you can to devote just to yourself – rather than to your baby, your other half or the mess that your kitchen's in. Getting a bit of me-time is even more important than you might imagine – and not just for purely selfish reasons. Even short bursts of time spent on yourself can give you a much-needed rest – physical and mental – from the considerable strain of caring for a young baby, and that will help you enjoy your baby all the more when you *are* on duty. If it helps, think of your me-time as like servicing a car – a little care and attention over the course of time should prevent any major breakdowns further down the line!

Negotiate with your partner so that he's available to take charge when you take time off – offer to return the favour when he's next in need of a break, if need be – as me-time is best enjoyed when you know you're not going to be disturbed. If you're a lone mum, your me-time is probably even more important, so lean on a relative or close friend when you need them to do the honours.

Me, me, me! Ideas for me-time moments

- Ten minutes devoted to a sit-down, a cup of tea and a bar of chocolate.
- Fifteen minutes devoted to some long, slow, deep-breathing exercises.
- Twenty minutes devoted to a flick through a glossy or celebrity magazine (or the next chapter of a good book, if you're more discerning about your reading material!).
- Half an hour devoted to a hot, deep bath.

- One hour devoted to a swim, power-walk, bike ride or aerobics session.
- Two hours devoted to a viewing of your absolute favourite movie ever, on DVD.
- Three hours devoted to a major DIY pamper session, including a leg and bikini wax, eyebrow shape, face pack, deep-conditioning hair treatment and a manicure.
- A whole afternoon devoted to clothes shopping, including lunch or a coffee out.
- A whole evening devoted to a new hobby or night class.

What the netmums say

Me-time

My brother bought me some posh bath bombs when my second son was born. They were bought with the intention of me having a luxurious soak and some me-time. Yeah, right! They were on the bathroom shelf for well over a year before I got round to using them! Personally, my favourite bit of time-out was at the end of the day when the baby was about to have his last feed. I would go up to bed early and have a nice relax and read while hubby did the last feed with my expressed milk. It also meant he got some dedicated baby-time, too (and a guaranteed stinky nappy!!). Another bit of me-time was during brisk walks around the park. Yes, I had to push the pram/buggy, but I was pretty much guaranteed a quiet half-hour or more just to myself and my thoughts.

Helen from Poole, mum to Thomas, four and Samuel, two

My partner used to work six days a week and long hours, leaving me on my own with my babies. I got my me-time when my little ones slept. I rested, put on some TV, read a magazine with a coffee, had a nap, whatever I wanted. In the evenings, a glass of wine and a good book was (and still is) bliss. And the chance to have my hair done in a salon was a wonderful treat. These days I like to go for long walks – the peace, quiet and solitude is such a contrast to my normal day. You've just got to put yourself first sometimes.

Heather from Sheffield, mum to Jasmine, four and Jack, two

I like nipping out to the shops by myself while my other half watches Oscar. Just being in the car, driving on my own, with my music on loud, is great.

Iona from Leeds, mum to Oscar, two months

Every Monday as soon as hubby gets home I go straight to the gym and I just sit in the sauna. It's lovely and quiet, I empty my mind of my worries and thoughts of my daughter and just relax . . . bliss! Also, if my husband is popping out, to the shops for example, he always takes Amelia with him in the carrier, which he loves. I usually use this time to do some housework – not strictly me-time, but it's surprising how appealing it can be compared to the constant breastfeeding, nappy changing, weaning and playing!

Julia from Northampton, mum to Amelia, five months

I go horse riding for a day at the weekend, from 9a.m. to 5.30p.m. My husband has the children. He doesn't have a choice, they're his children. He's not 'having the children for me', it's his duty. He's doing it for them, and for himself. The children and the hubby benefit from the time together, and he says I'm a nicer person to live with if I get a horse ride in. And of course, I am happier for all the fresh air, exercise, relaxation, social chitchat, rest from the children and countryside views that I get! I have to live with the fact that the house may be untidy, the children may not have eaten tea or got to bed on time. But it doesn't harm them – and my husband certainly won't get better at it if I don't let him practise!

Helen from St Asaph, mum to Ceridwen, two and Ceirion, nine months

The Eighth Month

Welcome to your eighth month of motherhood

Watch out! Your baby may be properly on the move now – or she could be soon. And once she knows how to get from one side of the room to the other, there'll be no stopping her. Apart from this being an exciting move forward in her development, the main implications are safety. If you haven't done so already, it's time to pay some careful attention to what the potential hazards around your home could be, and what you can do to negate them.

She's also due a second major routine review some time around now, and it's a great chance to reassure yourself about any health, growth or developmental issues that have been worrying you, or just to ask advice about everyday matters, such as feeding and sleeping.

If you're feeling a little pinned down by the drudgery of domestic life, maybe it's time to get your glad rags on and get out for the night. A healthy seven-month-old baby is more than capable of coping without mum around for an evening, so why not make the most of this freedom and crank up your social life again? Leave your baby with your partner, or some other reliable babysitter, and have a night out (or in) with the girls. It could be just the thing you need.

Health, Growth and Development

Baby milestones

Now that she is seven months old, your baby will typically:

- Be able to grasp larger objects, and pass them from hand to hand.
- Turn immediately in response to your voice from across the room, or to very quiet noises on either side of her if she's not too distracted by something else.
- Be babbling loudly and tunefully.
- Bear her own weight on her legs for a while, when supported.

And she might also:

- Sit unsupported.
- Enjoy a game of peek-a-boo.
- Have made attempts to progress along the floor, either by rolling, wriggling, crawling, bottom-shuffling or by bear walking on her hands and feet.
- Be able to pull up to a standing position, with support from you or a solid object.

Milestone focus: Crawling

As the precursor to walking, crawling is a key milestone. However, it's important to remember that crawling is a very individualised skill and the time frame in which babies do it is very broad – some may begin to crawl in their seventh or eighth month, some when they're closer to a year. Others don't do it at all, relying on altogether different ways of covering distances, such as bottom-shuffling, commando-style tummy-wriggling, or walking like a bear cub on hands and feet. A small number of babies bypass these methods of locomotion altogether and go straight to cruising and walking. ('Locomotion' is the term used by some experts to describe the ways in which babies move around.)

Babies will only crawl once they've got strong head control, and once their arms and legs are strong enough to support themselves. For some time, your baby may crouch on her hands and knees, rocking backwards and forwards, before she finally works out how to push off with her knees and propel herself forwards by moving opposite legs and arms at the same time – however, don't be surprised if she masters backwards crawling before she goes forwards, as this is very common.

Encourage your baby to crawl right from the start by giving her lots of tummy time, and later, when she's coming close, try a little carrot-dangling – place appealing toys, or yourself, just out of reach. You can put her in pole position for crawling by placing her on her front regularly. Give her lots of verbal encouragement when she's making all the right moves, and once she's on the go, make sure she has a good, clear, safe space in which to practise – or scatter cushions around to make a mini-obstacle course, for a little added challenge!

Some babies simply aren't inclined to take up crawling, so you shouldn't fret if yours is showing no signs of doing so. You don't have to worry about *how* she moves about, as long as she's doing so somehow or other, before she reaches her first birthday. (Some pre-term babies may well take longer than that.)

The second general review

You can usually expect your baby to receive a second routine review of her health, growth and general developmental progress some time between her sixth month and her first birthday. Exactly when, and what it involves, varies a great deal across the country. Sadly, in some areas these days, a second review is not routinely offered at all. Spending cuts have put health visitors under increasing pressure. However, according to the government's Child Health Promotion Programme guidelines, *all* babies should undergo a second major health review before their first birthday – parents are urged to take a proactive approach, so if your baby hasn't been invited to attend a second health review by her first birthday, do contact your health visitor, local clinic or GP's surgery to request a check.

The review may be carried out in your home or in a clinic or surgery, and its aim is to make sure your baby is growing and developing normally. It's also a chance for health professionals to check on other matters, such as sleeping and feeding, and for you to ask any questions. There's no need to feel nervous – it's not a test of your baby's abilities that she will either pass or fail, just a routine check to see if she's developing at a normal rate, as well as a chance for your health visitor to check that her immunisations are up to date, pass on some information and for you to ask questions. Don't forget to take your red book so her progress can be recorded.

The content of the review is as variable, according to area, as the timing, but the checks your health visitor makes, and questions she asks, could include:

- Weighing your baby, and measuring her height and head circumference, to make sure her growth is steady and she's a healthy size for her age.
- Checking her gross motor skills are developing well for her age – for example, by asking to see if she can sit up with little in the way of support.
- Observing her use of her hands, perhaps by passing her a toy, or – if she's nine months or more – by asking to see if she can pick up a small item with her fingers yet.
- Making sure her hearing and communication skills are developing normally by asking whether she is babbling, and discussing the importance of reading to her and using descriptive conversation and repetition when you talk to her.
- Checking for any sight problems, for example a squint (and asking whether there is a family history of such problems).
- Asking if she's progressing well on solids, getting plenty of iron-rich foods and still having sufficient milk feeds.
- Asking if she's sleeping OK.
- Advising on other issues, such as accident prevention and dental care.
- Checking that her immunisations are up to date.
- Asking whether *you* are healthy and happy – in fact, this may be the first question you are asked because it's considered such an important part of the check.

What the netmums say

The second health review

Jamie had a check when he was seven months old. Our health visitor came to our house and did the usual checks: sight, hearing, crawling, his speech, weight, testes [it's not commonplace for testes to be checked at this time; if testes are undescended at their six to eight week review, you should get a much earlier referral], passing items from one hand to another, clapping. She also discussed how weaning had gone, and safety around the house. Neither of us had any concerns and it was reassuring to know that I was doing everything OK!
Ruth from Lancaster, mum to Jamie, three

The health visitor rang to say she needed to do this check on Grace, just before her first birthday. She came round to the house and wanted to know when she'd been weaned, how much milk she was taking, what her weight was, was she walking (which she had just started do) and if I knew how to make sure the house was babyproofed, at which point Grace fell over and banged her head on the table! We had a chat about myself and a couple of issues of my own, which was nice. She told me I wouldn't see a health visitor again until Grace was about three, unless I specifically requested to see one. I thought it would have been useful earlier than that, but that's how it goes, I suppose.
Jennifer from Manchester, mum to Grace, one

When I asked my health visitor at a routine weighing clinic about when my daughter would have this check I was told that they no longer carry them out for all babies – if I had any concerns, I could request a check, but they only targeted certain families and children now due to a shortage of health visitors. I am not sure how they get to know which children and families to target! It seems a shame that the system is different, depending on where you live. I guess that's the case with everything now.
Kathryn from west London, mum to Ava, two

How to babyproof your home

Newly mobile babies are all over the place and into everything – so much so, it can be quite stressful trying to keep tabs on them. Keep tabs on them we must, however, because at this age they don't have the understanding required to steer clear of danger themselves. And because babies need lots of freedom to move around and explore, for the sake of their development, it's no answer to be permanently picking them up or imprisoning them in playpens for long periods. So once they're showing signs of shifting, you'll need to babyproof your home properly – and any other places where they regularly spend time – to make sure they can't run into (too much) trouble! It's also a good idea to look out for any risks when you visit other people's homes.

The main safety checks to make around the home are included here, and ways in which you can safeguard against the most obvious risks. Good advice on this subject is available from the Child Accident Prevention Trust (CAPT) and the Royal Society for the Prevention of Accidents (RoSPA). (For contact details, see Useful Addresses at the back of the book.)

Safe as houses: How to reduce the risks for your baby at home

The Risk: Burns and scalds

- If you have an open fireplace, make sure you use a securely fixed fireguard. If you have a fire or heater that a fireguard will not fit, you will just have to be extra vigilant when your baby is in the room.
- Don't forget that radiators can be very hot, so keep your baby away from them.
- Take care with hot drinks. Never leave one near your baby, and avoid drinking one while you're holding her.
- Put cold water into her bath first, when filling it, so that the water is never scalding (just in case you drop her), and test with your elbow before you put her in. Consider having a thermostating mixing valve fixed to your bath taps.

- Keep your baby out of the kitchen whenever possible. If you do need to let her in there because you're preparing a meal, don't let her anywhere near the cooker – put her in her highchair or playpen, well away from any dangers. Keep pans with the handles turned backwards as a matter of course, or consider fitting a hob guard.
- Keep appliances, such as hair straighteners, hairdryers and kettles, well out of her reach.
- Make sure you have a working smoke alarm (and don't forget to check the batteries regularly). These should conform to BS EN 14604 or BS 5446.
- Plastic socket covers may not be the necessity you imagine. All modern British sockets already have an in-built safety shutter mechanism, which makes it almost impossible to be electrocuted by poking something into the socket, and neither RoSPA nor CAPT specifically recommend the use of socket covers.

The Risk: Falls

- Fix safety gates at the top and bottom of the stairs, and across the doorway to any room you want to keep her out of. Make sure gates are extremely securely fixed – the sort that screw to the wall are safer than pressure-fixed varieties, which can slip. Don't forget to let her have some stair-climbing practice, though, once she's capable; otherwise she'll never be able to negotiate this very normal obstacle without risk. Just make sure you're right behind her. Safety gates should comply with BS EN 1930:2000.
- Fix locks or 'restricters' to windows if they don't already have them – but make sure you're able to open them quickly in the event of a fire. Keep chairs or anything she could climb on to access a window out of the way.
- Check that your bannisters are safe, with none that are loose and no gaps that are large enough for your baby's body (rather than

her head – she could wriggle in backwards) to fit through. Fit netting or boards if necessary.

- When going downstairs with your baby, hold tight to the handrail. Make sure stairs are always clear of clutter.
- Don't leave your baby alone on a bed, sofa or other high surface from which she could fall. Get into the habit of changing her nappy on the floor.

The Risk: Cuts and bumps

- Fit corner protectors to the sharp corners of furniture or fireplaces – improvise with sponges and sticky tape, if necessary.
- Check for anything on a low surface or on the floor that she could pull over on herself, such as lamps, ornaments or pot plants. Make sure electrical cables are well tucked away and remove dangling tablecloths.
- Make sure freestanding units are securely fixed to the wall so she cannot pull them down on herself.
- Prevent curious little fingers from getting stuck by putting guards on video machines and DVD players.
- Fit safety glass or safety film to internal windows or glass doors.
- Keep scissors, knives, cutlery, pens and anything sharp, or easily broken, well out of her reach in cupboards or drawers fitted with suitable locks.
- Fit door-jammer devices to prevent doors from shutting hard on small fingers (but take them off at night so that doors can be kept shut, in case of fire).

The Risk: Choking, suffocation and strangulation

- Make sure dangling cords from blinds and curtains are tied up out of her reach.
- Check floors, shelves and any other accessible area for very small objects she could put in her mouth and choke on.

- Keep anything with string or ribbons well away from your baby.
- Store plastic and polythene bags well out of her reach or in a locked cupboard.

The Risk: Poisoning

- Make sure all household and garden products, medicines, alcohol and toiletries are stored well out of her reach or, better still, behind locked cupboard doors.
- Be vigilant when she is in the garden and don't let her put plants, berries or fungi in her mouth. Remove flowers or plants that are known to be poisonous (the CAPT website has identification information).

The Risk: Drowning

- Never leave your baby unattended, even for a second, in a bath or paddling pool.
- If you have a garden pond, cover it or fence it off securely. Better still, fill it in altogether. If any of your close neighbours has one, make sure there is no way she could access it.

Low-income families could qualify for financial help to buy safety equipment for the home as part of a recently introduced government-run scheme. Contact your local authority for more information.

Making your baby risk-aware

In truth, there's no such thing as a totally babyproof environment – and even if there was, you couldn't keep your baby in it permanently. There'll always be risks, and minor accidents are a normal part of babyhood (and beyond). So, as well as doing everything you can to make her stomping ground a safer place, you should do everything you can to teach your baby about risk and danger by using words such as 'hot', 'dangerous' and 'ouch', with accompanying actions, whenever relevant – eventually, she will make the right associations in her mind whenever you repeat such a warning, although you should never *assume* she will. A loud, sharp 'no' if she does come close to a risky situation should be enough to pull her up. Don't be tempted to issue a slap or smack, though, however frightened you may feel.

What the netmums say

Babyproofing your home

With my daughter I didn't do much babyproofing at first as I thought 'no' would be enough, but after she'd emptied and tried to eat the fake coal out of the fire for the sixth time I removed it, along with everything else she might break or hurt herself on, and put locks on the cupboard doors. My tip would be to keep CD or DVD players out of reach, as they love to open them and insert food or drink inside. (Admittedly, this is more for the sake of your equipment than their safety!) And use a bath mat – my son broke his tooth badly on our bath when he slipped and fell in it. Oh, and get plastic covers for hot pipes on radiators. My son burned his hand on ours, resulting in another trip to the hospital. I think that whatever you do, though, they will hurt themselves and break stuff somehow!
Heather from Sheffield, mum to Jasmine, four and Jack, two

We babyproofed (as much as you can) when our daughter started to crawl. All the usual – stairgates, sponges taped on to the edges of sharp corners, etc. I've got animals so we've always been careful not to leave small things lying around. We moved the dangerous cleaning stuff to the top cupboards and gave Daisy her own cupboard in the kitchen with plastic/non-dangerous stuff in, so she could play nearby when I was in there. I did forget one thing, though – I came into the kitchen one day to find my vegetarian baby with dog food dribbling out of her mouth. I was horrified! In both houses we've lived in with her, we've not been able to put the stairgate at the bottom of the stairs – so we've put it across the hall,

which has had the bonus of stopping her from getting to the front door, too.
Kath from Nottingham, mum to Daisy, three

We haven't gone too mad with the babyproofing at the moment, as a little risk can be a good thing! We can't attach a gate at the bottom of our stairs, which is problematic as I sometimes find Harrison halfway up. At the moment we have the parcel shelf from my car wedged in the bannisters, instead. Harrison's very curious and we've had to fit cupboard locks in the kitchen, and never let him in there unless we're with him. We've covered our fake-coal fire with netting – it's set into the wall so a fireguard is no good, but those coals looked mighty tasty! One thing we did forget was that the radiators would get hot when we finally turned the heating on. We quickly remembered when Harrison cried out after touching one. Oh yes, and we've had to tape the Sky card into place in the receiver, as it kept disappearing!
Kelly from Birmingham, mum to Harrison, one

Make sure your stairgates are properly fixed to the wall – or be very careful not to lean on them. We had the pressure-fixed sort and there was a horrible accident one morning when my husband leaned over it to kiss our daughter goodbye. He put his weight on it without thinking and both he and the gate fell forwards on to her. She wasn't badly hurt, thankfully, but she was pretty traumatised, as were we. It could have been absolutely horrendous.
Katie from Milton Keynes, mum to Betty, two

Leisure and Learning
Hands, knees and bumps-a-daisy
Now she's in the second half of her first year, your baby will respond more than ever to fun and interaction with you. Simple games based on actions and words, rhymes or a song, will keep her enthralled for short periods, and not only will they pass the time and raise squeals of delight, they will help boost her gross and fine motor skills, language and understanding and

intellectual development, too, and promote bonding between the two of you. All that, from a simple game of pat-a-cake!

Play away: Six little games your baby will love

- Peek-a-boo
- Incy-wincy spider
- This little piggy went to market
- Round and round the garden
- Heads, shoulders, knees and toes
- This is the way the farmer rides

What the netmums say

Interacting with your baby

Logan loves peek-a-boo, either with me hiding, or when I hide one of his toys, then pop it back up again. He likes round and round the garden, with a big tickle at the end! His favourite song is 'Old Macdonald' at the moment, and he finds the pig noise very funny. His daddy plays the more rough and tumble games, throwing him up in the air. I'm always scared I will drop him.
Claire from Blackwood, mum to Caitlin, seven, Abbie, five and Logan, seven months

A favourite game of Tabitha's when she was a bit younger was, 'Where's my nose?' She'd sit on my lap and I'd say, 'Where's my nose?' or 'Where's my ears?' and she'd point to whichever bit of my face I was talking about. We'd play it for ages before she got bored.
Julia from Hastings, mum to Tabitha, one and Louis, two months

I don't think they mind what you play with them as long as you do. It's your time that makes the difference, not the activity or the toy.
Heather from Sheffield, mum to Jasmine, four and Jack, two

All About You

Getting out with the girls

You might already be back into the swing of a social life, but lots of new mums find it takes a while before they've got the time, energy and opportunity to paint the town red again. Things may be a bit different by now, though – perhaps your baby sleeps through the night, you're no longer breastfeeding, or you're just not as tired as you have been. Don't feel bad about wanting a night away from home life, or leaving your baby in someone else's capable hands while you let your hair down.

Maybe it's hard getting out for a night on the tiles, perhaps because you're short of cash or you're a lone parent with babysitting issues. How about hosting a night in, instead? All you need is a little imagination (see the box below for some ideas) and a handful of guests. If your old, pre-baby friends have been a bit elusive lately, make a point of rounding them up; or call on your new ones, instead. Fellow mums will always be glad of the invitation – just try not to talk about your babies *all* night.

A word of warning about booze. If it's been a while since you had a few, take care because you may find you can't take it quite like you used to. Don't get plastered while you're the only one around to look after your baby. And don't get so drunk you won't be able to care for her the next day (unless you know your partner or another reliable adult will be around to take over).

If you're still breastfeeding, you don't have to avoid alcohol altogether, but don't have more than two or three units, unless you know you can 'pump and dump' and offer your baby an alternative, instead.

Big night in: Eight ways to have an evening with the girls, without leaving home

Movie night: Rent a classic chick-flick, pop some corn and dim the lights.

Come and buy: Host a sales party, such as those offered by Virgin Vie, Chocoholics or (dare we say it) Ann Summers. Serve chips 'n' dips and wine.

Dinner party: Ask everyone to bring a contribution, so you're not lumbered with the cost and effort involved in hosting alone. Assign responsibility for appetisers, pud, main course, side dishes and wine to different guests. Make the table look lovely and ask everyone to wear something nice. Don't forget to put your baby's highchair in a different room or it might cramp your style!

Book group: Make a date with all the literature lovers you know, pick an easy-to-read classic or recent bestseller (bear in mind that baby-brain may still be at large) and then talk it over. A glass of wine or two should liven up proceedings and may even stimulate the old brain cells.

Pamper party: Devote a whole evening to hair, hands, feet and faces and catch up on some of those beauty treatments that went by the wayside after having your baby. Create a spa-like ambience with candles, soft music, fluffy towels and glossy mags. Serve up white wine spritzers (lower in calories than some other drinks!) and healthy crudités with dips.

Dining-room disco: Push back the furniture, whack up the stereo and get grooving. Handbags optional. (NB: this is only good if your little one is a very sound sleeper!)

Wine tasting: Get everyone to bring a bottle from a different region, and see if you can work out the difference. Creating cocktails can also be fun (but mix your drinks with extreme caution).

Games night: Gather round a board game, such as Trivial Pursuit, or gamble your chances on a game of poker – you can up the ante by playing for Monopoly money or copper coins.

What the netmums say

Nights out with the girls

I found I was pretty much housebound for the first few months. My elder son was so hard in the evenings that I just couldn't leave him, even for an hour. After a few months, I became much closer to a group of friends I met through antenatal classes. We used to meet with the babies during the day but, when they were around six

months old, someone suggested we met on our own for dinner, leaving the dads to babysit. We took it steady that night (a lot were still breastfeeding, and we were all exhausted), but we all had so much fun, and found we could talk about things other than the babies. We've been going out regularly ever since, around once a month. Needless to say, our nights out have become a lot more lively!
Jen from Chorleywood, mum to Jack, four and Theo, one

I've been out a couple of times already since my son was born. Luckily, my husband doesn't mind. He even looked after my friend's daughter one night, too. We don't really talk about kids or babies when we go out. That's the time to get away from it for a few hours. And it's nice not to smell of baby milk for a bit.
Carmen from Catterick Garrison, mum to Charlotte, two and Leo, two months

I had my first night out in more than two years recently! Lots of baby talk, yes, and I didn't drink, mainly because it's been that long now it just gives me a headache – and I still have to deal with the kids the next day! I don't miss going out. I used to go out once a week at least, whereas now I'm happy enough to stay in with my babies.
Vix from Lymm, mum to Stacey, 15, Ethan, two and Molly, three months

To be honest, I was almost relieved to stop breastfeeding both my babies after four months, because it meant my nights out with the girls would be a possibility again. I've always seen them as a huge release from the many stresses of life at home. All my local friends are mums, too, and because we only go out every couple of months, we really let out hair down when we do.
Helen from Berkhamsted, mum to Amy, seven and Holly, four

As soon as I found out I was pregnant with my first I stopped going out straight away. Then after I'd given birth to my son I realised there was no other place I'd rather be than watching over his cot and looking at him with awe. I was more than happy to leave the nights out until he got much bigger: he was my child and I wanted always to be there. These days I get out of the house more, but it's usually with the kids in tow! I also invite people over here more. But that's just how I like it. I'm always there for my kids, and that makes me thoroughly enjoy myself when I do venture out.

Alicia from south London, mum to Kyrus, two and Demiyah, one

The Ninth Month

Welcome to your ninth month of motherhood

Your baby's almost three-quarters of the way through her first year now and you may find she's growing fiercely independent in some ways – keen to hold on to her own spoon or bottle, for example. On the other hand though, she might be letting you know just how much she still needs you by demonstrating 'separation anxiety', dissolving into tears if you so much as leave the room. It's a totally normal phase and one that the majority of babies go through to one extent or another – heartbreaking (and at times a little grating), it's just one of those periods you both need to get through as best you can.

Do you look down at your baby belly and wonder if it's ever going to slip away of its own accord? For some lucky women it will already have done just that. For most of us, though, a little extra effort is required. If it's a matter of importance to you, now might be the time to turn your thoughts to some belly-busting exercises. As the saying goes: 'nine months on, nine months off' . . .

Health, Growth and Development

Baby milestones

Now that she is eight months old, your baby will typically:

- Recognise familiar people and objects from across a room.
- Stretch out to grasp a small object when offered, and manipulate a toy with great interest.
- Be babbling loudly and tunefully.

She might also:

- Point at or poke small objects with her index finger, and perhaps even pick them up.
- Make her first (messy) attempts at feeding herself with cutlery.
- Be able to hold her own bottle.
- Be moving across the room in some way, by rolling, wriggling, crawling, bottom-shuffling, or by bear walking on her hands and feet – sometimes getting around at quite a pace!

Milestone focus: Vision

Your baby's vision has been gradually developing since she was born. In her first few weeks, she could see things clearly only when they were very close to her face – everything else would have been a blur. Within a month or so, things were becoming clearer to her and by six weeks she was able to follow a brightly coloured toy moved in an arc up to 20cm away from her eyes.

Initially, babies aren't able to coordinate both eyes, so they can't focus both at the same time, which is why squints are common in the early months, but by her fourth or fifth month, your baby had learned to control both eyes simultaneously. Once that happened, she started to acquire some 'depth perception', which means she could see things beyond her immediate vicinity. That helped her to hone her 'tracking' skills, so that by six or seven months she was able to follow a fast-moving ball with her eyes.

By the ninth or tenth month your baby's vision will be good enough for her to recognise familiar people or objects across a room. She should look in the right direction for a falling or fallen toy, and carefully watch activities of people or animals within a three or four metre radius. She'll also be able to focus on very small items directly in front of her, which combined with her ever-developing grasping skills, means her hand-eye coordination is improving, and she'll soon be able to zoom in on and gather up even tiny little objects.

Although health professionals will be on the alert for eyesight problems during her routine checks, it's important to seek help if you suspect anything is wrong with your baby's vision – such as a squint (known medically as strabismus) where the eyes look in different directions – particularly if there is a history of eyesight problems in the family. Although squints are quite normal in the first few months as the muscles round the eyes strengthen, a persistent squint at this stage should certainly be checked. Talk to your health visitor or GP about it as soon as possible. In many cases, early treatment of eyesight problems is all-important. Squints, for example, can go on to cause a condition called amblyopia (commonly known as lazy eye), which can affect the vision permanently. And the earlier treatment is given – by wearing an eyepatch, or even surgery – the more effective it can be.

You don't need to do anything special to stimulate your baby's vision – just make sure she has lots of interesting things to look at and play with, and provide her with plenty of opportunities to make eye contact with you.

Separation anxiety

You may notice around now that your baby seems clingy or shy, and may begin to cry if you leave her – even just by walking out of the room. This is separation anxiety, and it's a very normal phase in her development – in fact, almost all babies experience it to one extent or another. Also, just as with adults, babies' personalities vary – some are simply clingier than others.

Separation anxiety typically kicks in some time between six months and a year, but around eight to nine months is a particularly common time for it to start, because this is when your baby begins to understand the concept of a world outside her immediate vicinity but won't necessarily have grasped that you are always going to return from that other place. It may also strike – quite understandably – whenever the time comes for you to leave her with someone she doesn't know very well. It's an unfortunate coincidence that the period when separation anxiety tends to kick in is also the time that many mums make a return to work.

It can be both heartbreaking and frustrating if your baby is hanging on to you like a limpet. It may help you to cope if you think of it in terms of a positive developmental phase – and a sign that your baby has developed such a loving attachment to you!

Easing her anxiety

There are some things you can do to ease her fears at times when she's experiencing separation anxiety. Practise short bursts of separation at home by leaving the room for increasing periods of time, and playing games such as peek-a-boo and hide-and-seek, which will help her to understand the concept of object permanence – in other words, teaching her that just because she can't see something, it doesn't mean it doesn't exist.

Leaving her with others

If you're leaving your baby with a new carer, make sure she has plenty of opportunities to get to know him or her first. When the time comes to leave her, don't prolong the agony by hanging around – give her a big hug, say goodbye and that you'll see her later, then make sure she sees you leaving. Never be tempted to sneak off when she's not looking because that could make her even more anxious. Try to stay positive and don't show her that you're also upset by the separation. Almost always, she will stop crying soon after you've gone, and you should be able to get reassurance of that later on from the carer. Although it may be days or weeks before the phase is over and she settles without tears, it will be temporary, but she may well suffer from periods of it again, later on – typically at around 18 months, and when the time comes for her to start school.

Separation anxiety can also occur at night-time. If your baby is going through a clingy phase, it may not be a good period to try sleep training. If you do, one of the gentler methods that involves offering her lots of reassurance that you're still around (see p. 203) would be best.

Blanket love

A comfort object, such as a blanket or favourite toy, may offer your little one reassurance when she's suffering from separation anxiety, with the added bonus that it can help her settle to sleep without you. A comforter does have drawbacks, though. It can become very grubby, and you may be unpopular if you try to put it through a wash cycle – babies can become very attached to the smell of an unwashed comforter! It is easily lost, often resulting in a fair bit of trauma, and you may end up being woken at night if she loses it in her cot and can't find it again.

If your baby has a comfort object, you may want to think about trying gently to restrict her access to it to times when she really needs it, such as when she is going to sleep or if you're not around. Although at this age there's no harm in having a comforter around on a permanent basis, it can be a habit that's very hard to break, and later, when she's older and a rigid attachment to a blanket or toy might restrict her playing and learning opportunities – not to mention the possibility of teasing from their peers – you might be keener to get rid of it.

If your child's comfort object is something she sucks, such as a dummy, there are some good reasons why you might want to start discouraging its use, or at least imposing limits, by the end of this year. The main one is the risk to her speech and language development that too much dummy use can pose. (For more information about this, see p. 268.)

What the netmums say

Separation anxiety

Paige will start to cry if I go to the loo at the moment – it's the same at night, too. I have found that I can leave her and Morgan in the same room together and she'll be fine as she has him to entertain her, which comes in really handy when I'm having to do the dishes and get breakfast ready first thing in the morning. She also seems OK when I leave her in the room with the television on.

Julie from Leeds, mum to Morgan, one and Paige, six months

My son started this early, at four or five months. He'd cry if I wasn't looking at him! Then at about nine months he started again, not wanting either of us to leave the room. Sometimes now if we put him down on the floor, or you move slightly, he'll murmur as he thinks we're getting up to leave! He'd even cry if I stopped pushing the pram and I wasn't in his immediate view for a second, as he thought I'd gone! If I have to go into another room and shut the safety gate to stop him coming in, he stands there and cries. He also cries at night when I walk out of his room. I found it helped to tell him where I was going or what I was doing in a reassuring voice and then to get on with it rather than popping back every few seconds. Distracting him with a favourite toy also helped.
Tracy from Liverpool, mum to Jem, ten months

When Luke was eight months I went back to work and he went to nursery for two days a week. He cried terribly when I left him, but settled after a few weeks, then started it all again! He still cries when I leave him sometimes with hubby and still cries at nursery. I have always made sure I go through the procedure of telling him what's happening, and kiss him goodbye and wave and have never just disappeared through the door. I'm sure it will get better but it's always been hard to leave him because he is such a mummy's boy. I wouldn't have it any other way though!
Sharon from Nantwich, mum to Luke, one

My elder daughter has never suffered from separation anxiety and is quite happy being left with anyone. My second was a clingy baby from the start, though, and I've always had trouble leaving her, even with my husband or close friends. Because she's been so bad I have not returned to work as I felt that it would be a waste of time if I kept getting calls to pick her up. I've had some experience of this when I've tried putting her in a crèche!
Tracy from Plymouth, mum to Emily, two and Isabelle, one

I used to work as a nursery nurse and I can always remember the children crying when the parents left and me telling them they'd be fine, that it was just a phase, and that they would be all right after a few minutes. My own daughter is ten months old and I now know how awful all those parents felt. It's horrible leaving her behind and going to work wondering if she's OK.

Amanda from Peterborough, mum to Rebekkah, ten months

Self-feeding

Trying to use a spoon

Your baby should be getting to grips with lumpy textures and finger foods by now. (If she's still showing no interest or is flatly refusing these things, carry on gently persevering and have a chat with your health visitor about it.) She may even be making her first attempts at using cutlery. Although it's messy and can be frustrating watching as she makes her early attempts to hit the target, try to let your baby have free rein when she's intent on feeding herself. As her hand–eye coordination develops, she'll get more and more skilful at it from now on. Protect the floor and table with wipe-clean coverings and ensure she's wearing a good bib. A bowl with a non-slip or suction base can be a real boon, and a wide-cupped plastic feeding spoon or fork, which will enable her to get a decent sized mouthful, may also help. Some mums find a two-tier feeding system works well – give her a spoon to hold and experiment with, and have one yourself, so that you can be sure at least some food is going down the hatch! Don't forget that the best way to teach your baby how to feed herself is to show her how it's done, so make sure you share as many mealtimes with her as you possibly can. Don't expect much more than messy experimentation at this stage, however.

Your baby may not start trying to feed herself using cutlery for quite a while yet, though, and even if she does, it could be many months before she actually masters it!

What the netmums say

Self-feeding

Charlie started feeding herself at five months and she will rarely let anyone feed her. She only uses her hands but it gets from bowl to

mouth, which is all that matters at the moment. She loves it and yes, it's messy, but very funny to see. We put a shower curtain under her highchair to catch the spills.
Laura from Northampton, mum to Charlie, eight months

At the moment, she's trying to feed herself by holding Mummy's hand with the spoon in and shoving it in the general direction of her mouth. This often involves the food ending up on her cheek or the spoon going too far in. I'm thinking about switching to smaller spoons!
Ruth from Exeter, mum to Ellie, six months

The first thing Elijah fed himself was steamed broccoli, which he picked up and mushed all over his face! Weetabix was a favourite, scooped out of the bowl with both hands and used as an art material. The bowl made a fetching hat! He started using cutlery at about ten months – and ate in the nude, mainly!
Gail from London, mum to Elijah, three

My son didn't start eating finger food until he was about nine months and even now is not showing much interest in feeding himself with a spoon. He's done it on a couple of occasions and we've made a big fuss of him but now he's reverted to being fed. When he has done it, he's hit his mouth OK, but seems to have trouble collecting the food on to his spoon. He's also really messy as he likes flicking the spoon. And he doesn't like holding his beaker much, preferring us to do it for him!
Sarah from Poole, mum to Arthur, one

Sleep

Naps

It's pretty exhausting being a baby. At this age they still need 12 to 14 hours of sleep a day to aid the development of their growing brains and bodies, so a couple of daytime sleeps are still necessary to make up the full quota. It varies, but typically at this age your baby will have two naps, one in the morning and one in the afternoon; or perhaps three, made up with a shorter burst at either end of the day and a longer one in the middle. Regular naps help her to function well until bedtime, as any parent of a grumpy, inconsolable baby who's missed out on her usual scheduled kip will tell you, and they aid night sleep. Overtired babies are often harder to settle and more likely to wake. They also provide some vital time for you to catch up on whatever needs doing, including having a rest yourself, if necessary!

It's a good idea to put your baby down for her nap in the same place every time, preferably her cot, in a darkened room, and just as with night-time sleep, it's better if she's able to go happily into her cot and soothe herself to sleep. But of course, naps often have to fit in with other things you need to do that day, and there's no reason why she shouldn't get her forty winks in the pram or buggy.

At home, a little pre-nap ritual consisting of a cuddle and a story, perhaps, will help her to build positive associations with napping in her mind. It's helpful if you can instigate nap time when she's beginning to get tired, rather than leaving it until she's so exhausted, she fights you. Look out for yawns, crankiness, drooping eyelids and rubbing of eyes and ears – by now, you will no doubt know the signs!

If she's fallen asleep in her car seat, don't forget that some safety experts advise against leaving your baby there unsupervised because there's a small risk that her air flow could be restricted if her head flops forward. It's also not advisable for her to be in a seat for more than a couple of hours at a time because of the strain placed on her spine. So, annoying though it may be, your best bet is to attempt to transfer her to her cot if she's still asleep when you arrive home.

You may well find your baby resists one or both of her naps around now, and puts up a show of displeasure if she's put into her cot during the day, even if she is clearly tired, and needs it. This may be because she needs less sleep as she gets older, or because life is just too exciting to be interrupted with sleeping. It's worth encouraging her to go into her cot, anyway, so she can get some quiet time and a rest (as can you). She may be happy to spend a few quiet moments there, at least, if you draw the curtains, and let her have some toys or books to play with. She may even drop off, anyway.

Your baby will probably dispense with one of her daytime sleeps by her first birthday, or at some point soon afterwards. It will eventually become obvious when she's ready to drop a nap (usually it's the morning one), because she just doesn't seem that tired any more!

What the netmums say

Naps

With both my babies I have them nap around me and what I'm doing. If I want to be out and about, I let them nap in the pushchair, or if I'm in someone's house and they fall asleep, then so be it. I don't believe in having set routines throughout the day. If a child is tired, then they should sleep when they want, not when you want them to. But that's just my opinion.

Julie from Leeds, mum to Morgan, one and Paige six months

Niamh has never been good at taking naps, so I just let her take whatever she needs when she wants in the day. I don't make any effort to reduce noise levels, and she naps wherever we happen to be at the time: front room, kitchen, out in the pram, car. I wanted her to realise that daytime is for napping, and that she has to fit in around us. It seems to have worked quite well, because I don't have to rely on being home at certain times or re-creating the scene anywhere I happen to be. Also, she sleeps for 12 hours a night without waking, so I figure I must be doing something right!

Laura from Gloucester, mum to Niamh, six months

Naps rule my life! When I had Noor I had real trouble getting her to go to sleep in the daytime. In fact, she could go all day without one and would then want constant eye contact or she would scream. As you can imagine, life was miserable for her and me! When I finally discovered the Baby Whisperer method [www.babywhisperer.com] of helping your child to sleep, everything was transformed and she started having two naps a day and sleeping through the night, too. But it pretty much chained me to the house for her naps – she refused to sleep anywhere else as I couldn't recreate the calm environment of her room while out and about. She would just get overtired and miserable. Various smug mums whose babies slept anywhere told me that it was my own fault for following a strict routine. So when I had Jasmine I tried my best to get her to sleep wherever and whenever – it didn't work! I now accept that my children just find the world too exciting to go to sleep when they are near stimulation of any kind. But there is a real benefit: although I may be a little chained by the routine, at least I know when I can go out and make arrangements around that. I never have to call someone up and say I can't make it because the baby has just gone to sleep – and she's always well rested.

Sara from Stafford, mum to Noor, three and Jasmine, 11 months

I plan my days around Jamie's naps. On the days when I have gone out and he has missed naps or had them at the wrong time, then I've really paid for it later on by having an extremely grumpy little boy! He still gets three naps a day, but they tend to be fairly short. If he skips the last one, at about 4.30p.m., then he becomes *really* grumpy and his dad is handed a screaming baby when he comes home from work! I don't find planning my day round them hinders me in any way. If I want to go out, I time it so we're driving when it's nap time because he would normally fall asleep in the car anyway. Or if I want to go out for a walk, I go at nap time because he would also normally fall asleep in his buggy. And I read somewhere that a well-napped baby will sleep better at night because they are not overtired and I really believe that. When he's missed a nap, he ends up screaming the house down at night, which makes feeding him dinner and putting him down for the night quite traumatic for everyone concerned. He'll get all sweaty and agitated. But when he's had all his naps, he eats his dinner happily, gets read a story before a bottle and goes quietly to bed . . . with no screaming! Also, when he sleeps during the day, I get an opportunity to do things round the house, or even just sit and eat lunch with a magazine, which is great.

Wendy from Edinburgh, mum to Jamie, seven months

All About You

Getting back into shape

It's often said that it takes nine months to gain your baby weight and you'll need nine months to take it off again – 'nine months on, nine months off', as the saying goes. So in theory, you should be back to your old shape by now.

Some lucky women find they can get back into their old clothes without too much effort. Some even find the weight drops off easily, perhaps because they're getting lots of incidental exercise chasing their baby around, or because they're too preoccupied to eat properly. Breastfeeding burns lots of calories, too. However, the truth is that for most of us, the remnants of baby-belly hang around unless we actively take pains to get rid of it.

Eating well

If you want to lose weight by dieting, choose a sensible programme that doesn't cut out any of the major food groups. Check with your doctor first, and then do it slowly, expecting to lose no more than a pound or two a week. If you're serious about dieting, it's a good idea to join a reputable club, such as WeightWatchers, where you can get peer support and the emphasis is on healthy eating and gradual weight loss. You don't have to follow a formal diet to lose weight, though. Sensible eating itself will do the trick, if you combine it with regular exercise – there are a few hints on how to do it below. Do bear in mind that while dieting alone may help you drop to the weight you want to be, it won't burn off all that excess belly flab – only exercise will do that.

Slim chance: How to lose weight by eating sensibly

Aim to make little changes to your diet rather than big ones: Cut out sugar in your tea, spread your butter thinly, grill rather than fry.

Cook your own food whenever possible: Ready meals and other pre-packaged foods are often loaded with hidden fats and sugars, so be label-aware. If you cook your own food, you'll know exactly what's in it, and you can make your own healthy amendments to recipes, such as cutting back on the fat or sugar content.

Eat three meals a day: Don't skip meals – you'll only end up hungry, and binge later. Breakfast is particularly important if you don't want to keel over mid-morning – something based around slow-release carbohydrates, such as porridge, which can be cooked in the microwave in minutes, is the perfect start to the day.

Drink lots of water: As well as being a great aid to general health, plenty of water can fill you up and help to stave off hunger pangs between meals. Bear in mind that some 'healthy' drinks, including fruit juices and smoothies, are still fattening because they've got so much sugar in them.

Stop snacking: Keep tempting food, such as chocolate, biscuits and crisps, out of the house – that way, they won't be there when you want them. If you need something to keep you going between meals, stick to nibbling on nutrient-packed fruit and raw vegetables. Don't forget that five-a-day is the recommended *minimum*!

Watch your portion sizes: It's easy to load up your plate when you're hungry. Try eating smaller portions than you're used to. Let it go down before reaching for seconds – you may find you're full, after all.

Treat yourself sometimes: Strict diets always fail because no one can live with deprivation for long. Enjoy your wine, chocolate or takeaway from time to time. Just enjoy it in moderation!

Exercise

It's not easy finding the time or energy to exercise when you've got a young baby, but it is a good thing to do. Whether or not you're concerned about getting your body in shape after birth, taking some regular exercise will not only make you fitter and healthier, it will improve your emotional health, and help you to cope better with life as a mum. That's because when you give your body a good workout, it releases endorphins, sometimes referred to as the 'feel-good' hormones. Not only that, but there's a huge psychological boost to be had from it, because managing to fit in some exercise can feel like a real achievement – better still if you've managed to get out in the fresh air in order to do so.

If it's a belly you specifically want to shed, you'll need to do a combination of aerobic exercise (the sort that raises your heartbeat and makes you a bit breathless) and some specific abdominal toning exercises, such as sit-ups and crunches – although do remember these are best avoided in the first six to nine months after birth (for more on that, see p. 79). It's probably best to try these kind of exercises – initially, at least – under the guidance of a qualified fitness instructor. Performing them incorrectly makes them worthless, and may even be harmful. But if you're going to try them at home, the main thing to remember is to pull your tummy in before you pull up, and be sure to use your stomach muscles to get you there rather than your head or elbows, which will put pressure on your neck. Make the movement slow and controlled – you don't have to come up a long way for the exercises to be effective, just far enough to raise your head and shoulders off the floor.

These days, fitness classes specifically for new mums are available, often offering you the chance to take your baby along and even involve her in the session. These classes are also a great social opportunity – but do check to make sure the instructor has a postnatal fitness qualification before signing up. (For details, including the website of the Guild of Pregnancy and Postnatal Exercise Instructors, where you can check to see what's available in your area, see the appendix at the back of the book.)

However, you don't need to leave home or go to the expense of joining a class. Instead, you could invest in an exercise video or DVD (charity shops are a great source), or try power walking with the buggy or sling.

To have any effect, you need to exercise for about an hour, three times a week. Always spend five to ten minutes warming up the muscles in preparation for their work-out, and be sure to do some stretches afterwards, which will help you to avoid stiffness and improve your mobility.

Do invest in, and be properly fitted for, a good sports bra and decent footwear if you're exercising regularly. A well-fitting bra can help reduce sagging boobs and poor upper body posture, and proper trainers will help guard against ankle or knee injury.

Excess skin

Some mums find they lose weight after having a baby, but retain lots of unwanted excess skin. This is generally down to genetics, although age and the extent of weight gain can be factors, and the strength of collagen in your tissues. Collagen is the name for the structural proteins that give the skin elasticity. Unfortunately, there aren't any solutions to this problem, other than surgery, or a good pair of control pants. Like stretchmarks, it's one of those physical prices that some of us have to pay for the privilege of becoming mothers!

Droopy boobs

Sagging boobs (the medical term is breast ptosis) are an unfortunate but very normal consequence of motherhood. As the breasts swell during pregnancy and breastfeeding, the ligaments and tissues that support them are stretched. How much they sag may be determined by a number of factors including genetics, age, your weight and how big your boobs were before, and even how supportive your pregnancy bra was. Recent research has found that smokers are much more likely to be affected by breast ptosis because of the break down of elastin, a protein that makes the skin stretchy.

You can't dramatically change the appearance of your post-baby boobs, but you can firm them up a bit with exercise – swimming is great for working the pectoral (chest) muscles, which support the boobs. You could also try this simple exercise at home: lie on the floor on your back, with your feet flat on the floor and your knees bent. Hold a can of beans in each hand, arms outstretched either side of you, then bring your arms together so they are both pointing up to the ceiling. Lower them slowly down to the floor, and repeat. Hold in your tummy muscles at the same time and you'll also be giving them a little exercise, while helping to keep your back stable and not straining it.

Of course, if you've a couple of thousand pounds to spare, you could always check in for mastopexy (breast uplift surgery) – but you'd be better off investing a few quid in a decent bra, instead. Be sure to get yourself measured properly if it's been a while since you bought a new one, because your breasts will very likely have changed in size and shape.

What the netmums say

Getting back in shape

By the time my daughter was nine months I was back to my pre-pregnancy weight, if not lighter, and just about back in my old jeans, but I'm definitely not the same shape. My tummy's really flabby and there's no doubt that my breasts have suffered. However, in some respects I'm more confident than I ever was because I'm so proud of what my body achieved in being pregnant and giving birth and breastfeeding – it makes me perceive my body as being a lot more

valuable than when I was mainly bothered about looking good. I'm not hugely keen on the belly, but it doesn't really bother me.
Margaret from Edinburgh, mum to Cora, ten months

My post-pregnancy body repulses me! I've been told I won't return back to the normal shape due to damage to my stomach muscles. My tummy is seriously bad, it looks and hangs like a bum and is full of stretchmarks.
Amanda from Nottingham, mum to Alex, three and Jake, ten months

When I had the twins I was surprised by how quickly everything popped back into place. But I wasn't all that big anyway and had continued with tap and ballet lessons until into the third trimester. Also I was young, so everything was a lot more elastic. One thing that made me laugh was when a gym-instructor friend asked me how I got my arms so toned – it was all down to carrying the girls around all day! You can't get that in the gym.
Natalie from King's Lynn, mum to twins Evie and Sophie, 13 and Amelia, 11 months

I consider myself to be quite fortunate. After having each of my boys I had a stone to lose, which I did within four to six weeks. I have a healthy diet, although I don't restrict myself, and I've always exercised, although having a shortage of babysitters I tend to exercise within my own home. My breasts have shrunk, from a D cup to a B, and definitely don't seem as 'full' as they were, but my nipples don't point south, so that's a bonus! I feel happy with my body.
Angela from Manchester, mum to Luke, nine, Joseph, four, Benjamin, three and Zachariah, two

I was a size 10 before having Ruby and exactly eight stone. Now I'm a size 10–12 and I can't seem to get my weight below nine stone. I have a nice rounded belly, which makes me looks like I'm a bit pregnant still. I also have lots of stretchmarks on my legs, hips, belly, boobs and arms. And my boobs have changed their shape as they are slightly saggier, not good when you have small ones! At first I was

unhappy and really hated myself, but now I'm not too bothered. Ruby loves me, and my partner loves me. I have changed my eating habits, though, and we eat really healthily now. For exercise, we go for long walks with Ruby in nature reserves and parks. It feels good, and I've definitely benefited.
Amanda from Bristol, mum to Ruby, one

Boy did I get a shock to see just how much your breasts really drop once you've finished breastfeeding for seven months. No worries, though, because there's a mums' life-saver called a push-up bra, thank goodness!
Alicia from London, mum to Kyrus, two and Demiyah, one

Aches and pains

Pain in the back – and elsewhere in the body – can be a lingering effect of pregnancy. This is partly because of the change in posture it forces on you, which puts pressure on the spine, and also because of the release of relaxin, the hormone that makes the body more flexible for birth. The effects of relaxin can hang around for up to six months afterwards, making your body vulnerable to aches, strains and injuries. Then of course there are all those different movements that a new mum can't avoid, which cause you to bend and twist your spine – constantly picking up and putting down your baby, moving her in and out of the car and cot, and hunching during breastfeeding.

In most cases, back pain can be relieved by careful self-management. However, if it's severe, your GP may prescribe you painkillers, or refer you to an osteopath, chiropractor or physiotherapist.

Mind your back: Tips for beating back pain

- Watch your posture. Bend your knees whenever you pick something up, and when you're sitting, especially for long periods, stay upright and don't slouch. Be particularly careful of heavy duty actions that may put pressure on or twist your spine, such as putting your baby in and taking her out of the car, or lifting her from her cot. Remember to draw your tummy in before you bend or lift, because this will help to give your back support.

- Keep active. Do some gentle exercise regularly. Swimming is good for back pain, as is yoga and pilates. Stick to low-impact activities and don't overdo it, especially in the first six to nine months, when your ligaments and joints are still unstable. Gentle stretching of the back and legs can help to relieve discomfort.
- Excess weight can aggravate back pain, so if you have some, make an effort to lose it.
- Wear low-heeled shoes or wedges. High heels will make it worse.
- Persuade your partner to give you a regular, relaxing back massage.

What the netmums say

Back pain after birth

The only consequence I had from giving birth was that I suffered with a terribly painful and weak back for many months afterwards. I couldn't even lift Jamie in his car seat into my car. Eventually, I went to see an osteopath privately and had about six sessions. It helped, but even now, three years on, if I lift something very heavy or lie in an awkward position, I still have some residual back pain.
Ruth from Lancaster, mum to Jamie, three

I started suffering from niggling lower back pain after having my first daughter. Recently I had some sessions with a chiropractor and a sports physiotherapist, and I also took up pilates. It's made me aware of how important posture is, and how strengthening my tummy muscles can ease the back pain. It's improved markedly since.
Helen from Berkhamsted, mum to Amy, seven and Holly, four

Dodgy bladders

Unfortunately, lack of bladder control (known as stress incontinence) after birth affects many women because of the weakening of the pelvic floor muscles caused by pregnancy, particularly after a difficult labour, or if you had a very big baby, and it can persist for months or even years. Leakage may occur whenever pressure is put on the muscles by simple actions, such as laughing, sneezing or coughing, or when you exercise and, inevitably, it can be unpleasant, inconvenient and embarrassing. Regular, simple pelvic floor exercises are reckoned to be the best way to reduce the problem. (For instructions on how to do them, see p. 43.)

Other methods of treatment include using vaginal weights – plastic cone-shaped weights, which are held inside the vagina to increase muscle strength. These are available from chemists or online. However, if self-help methods don't work, your doctor may prescribe medication or refer you to a specialist, such as a urologist or physiotherapist. In some cases, surgery may be the only solution.

If you do suffer from stress incontinence, don't be tempted to restrict your intake of fluids to reduce leakage – it won't solve the problem, and you need to drink to keep hydrated and healthy, particularly when exercising.

The Tenth Month

Welcome to your tenth month of motherhood

You're now more than three-quarters of the way through your baby's first year! The list of skills your nine-month-old may be acquiring grows ever longer and her physical abilities may surprise you – perhaps she can pull herself up to a standing position with support, and remain there for a few shaky seconds. She might even be cruising – able to work her way around the room by clinging on to anything solid she can find. Her language and understanding are also coming on, and by now she probably knows what you're talking about when you use some familiar words or simple phrases and instructions, such as 'give it to me'.

Now that the dust has settled on your first experience of motherhood, perhaps you're contemplating a second baby? For many it will still be early days, but lots of mums are keen for a shortish age gap between children, and there are certainly arguments in its favour. It's common to wonder how you would cope with another baby – or how you could possibly love them as much as your first. But while having two (or more) little ones to care for may seem like a daunting prospect, most mums find that with the benefit of experience, knowledge and confidence, motherhood is in many ways easier the second time around. As for your love – well, it stretches!

Health, Growth and Development

Baby milestones

Now that she is nine months old, your baby will typically:

- Be babbling loudly, combining syllables to make word-like sounds, such as 'ma-ma', although at this age she's still just experimenting with noises rather than calling you by your name.
- Be able to sit up unsupported.
- Poke at or pick up very small objects, such as crumbs, with her thumb and fingers.
- Be able to hold her own bottle.

And she might also:

- Have mastered the skill of letting go – deliberately releasing an object from her grasp, or handing something to you, if you ask for it.
- Be crawling or bottom-shuffling along the floor.
- Respond to her name, and understand basic words, such as 'no' and 'bye'.
- Bang objects together, or imitate hand clapping.
- Have fun putting objects inside a container – and taking them out again.
- Enjoy a game of hide-and-seek with a toy.
- Have begun pulling herself up to a standing position with support from you or a solid object.
- Stand alone for a few seconds.
- Cruise around the room, supporting herself on furniture.
- Climb up stairs and furniture. This is something she needs to learn, so do allow her to have a go, carefully supervised.

Milestone focus: Standing and cruising

Your baby's probably been practising her standing skills for a while now – from five or six months she'll have enjoyed bouncing up and down while you held her upright on your knees. All the while, she was strengthening the muscles in her legs in readiness for the next stage of mobility.

By her tenth month, she may be able to pull herself up to a standing position, perhaps even daring to let go of whatever she's holding and going handsfree for a few seconds before plopping down to the floor again. (It can take a while before she works out how to bend her knees and have some control over this movement.) She may even have acquired the strength and confidence required to take some wobbly steps round the room, clinging to the closest piece of furniture or pair of knees for support. This is known as cruising. It's still early days, though, so you shouldn't worry if your baby's showing no interest in doing any of these things yet. If she's able to bear her own weight when you hold her in a standing position on your lap and bounce her, then she's on the right track and will get there soon.

Bear in mind that a cruising baby can cover distance with surprising speed, so don't leave her alone unless you're confident there are no hazards in her path. It can be a slightly nerve-racking time, but give her time, space and encouragement to practise, despite the bumps, bruises and tears there's bound to be along the way.

You may notice your baby cruises on her tiptoes. There's no need to worry if she does this – it's fairly normal, and before long she should automatically begin to use the whole of her foot to support herself while moving around. If you're worried that her feet are turned either in or out to a great extent, mention it to your health visitor or GP.

Encourage your baby's standing and cruising skills by giving her physical support and praise while she gains confidence, strength and balance. Prop her up sometimes close to a sturdy chair or sofa – then give her lots of applause when she manages to stand there for a while. She'll probably look really chuffed about it! Once she's good at cruising, you can try moving furniture slightly further apart to give her more of a challenge – walking unsupported is only one step away.

First shoes

Your baby's adorable, delicate feet are made up of soft cartilage that gradually converts into bone as she grows. In fact, the bones in her feet won't be fully hardened until she's 18. This means they can be easily pushed out of shape or damaged, which is why it's vital to make sure your baby has the right footwear at the right times.

There's no need to put your baby in shoes *at all* until she's a well-established walker – before then, shoes are simply for keeping her feet warm or her socks on, and you should stick with very soft, flexible bootee-types of footwear made from fabric or very soft leather. Even these could cause damage if they're too tight, so always make sure they're the right size. Once she's moving around, going barefoot as much as possible indoors will help strengthen her arches and leg muscles, and makes it easier for her to spread her toes, which will give her optimum support, especially on a slippery floor.

Some manufacturers market cruising or pre-walking shoes, which are made of soft, flexible materials and are often washable. These are by no means necessary. They usually cost the same as proper shoes, and you might be better off saving your money. However, cruising shoes can be useful for short bursts of outdoor activity, when your baby does need some protection on her feet. As with proper shoes, you should make sure cruisers are properly fitted by trained staff in a reputable shoe shop. The Children's Foot Health Register has details of good shoe shops, as well as being a source of further information on this subject. (See the Useful Addresses appendix at the back of the book. p. 335.) It's absolutely vital that she still has plenty of barefoot opportunities, so take off her cruisers whenever she's indoors.

The exciting moment for those first proper shoes arrives when she's been walking steadily for at least six weeks – and even then, they're only necessary for getting around outdoors. The cost of shoes can be eyewatering, especially since she'll grow out of them so quickly – babies' feet double in size in their first year, and continue to grow rapidly after that, which is why it's important for you to get your child's feet measured every six to eight weeks. However, you're advised not to scrimp on shoes. Go to a decent shoe shop with trained staff who'll measure your little one for width as well as length. If you're concerned about costs, put off buying her shoes until sale time, or look for outlet branches of good chains, or discount shoe stores, such as Brantano, which sell quality brands at reduced prices, and still offer a proper fitting service.

When you're choosing a first shoe, pick something with lightweight, flexible, non-slip soles, a soft leather upper, padding around the ankle collar (the part of the shoe that sits just under the ankle) and strong, adjustable fastenings. Plump for the easy options, such as Velcro, if you can – even though your baby is too young to do up her own shoes at the moment, you'll be glad to have one less complication when you're getting ready to go out. It's worth remembering, though, that these may be easily removed by a dexterous little one, and therefore easily lost.

Don't forget to keep your baby's toenails trimmed regularly to avoid the risk of ingrowing, and remember to cut into a curved shape rather than straight across. Her socks also require some consideration – too small and they could be restrictive, too big and the excess wool could bunch up and cause blisters.

Memory box

A first shoe makes a wonderful keepsake – one day you'll never believe her feet were ever that tiny, and neither will she! Keep her first pair, or at least one of them, wrapped in tissue and stored in its tiny shoebox.

What the netmums say

First shoes

I proudly took my first son to a proper shoe shop and bought his first cruising shoes for a whopping £26. The first time I took him out in them, he took them off and lobbed one of them out of the buggy. I realised this when we were halfway home and had to re-trace my steps, asking in all the shops if anyone had found the lost shoe and handed it in. I never found it! He nonetheless learned to walk without them, mostly indoors as it was winter, and by the time summer came he was walking well enough to get a proper pair of shoes that stayed on his feet.

Beth from London, mum to Oliver, four and Harry, four months

As my son was born in the month of February we didn't want even more toys as presents from family so soon after Christmas. So for his first birthday we asked for Clarks vouchers.

It helped enormously with the cost of buying properly fitting shoes for him, as I believe this to be extremely important. I didn't buy cruiser shoes; my son just wore soft leather slip-ons whenever he wanted to stand up when we were out and about. At home, he just went barefoot.

Hilary from Romford, mum to Vaughan, one

Because I'd heard somewhere that it's best for their feet not to put shoes on until absolutely necessary, I didn't bother with cruising shoes. I just bought Noor some proper ones when she started wanting to walk outside. I loved putting on her shoes – it was one of those memories I'll treasure forever. To me there's just something so appealing about a tiny little person holding her foot out for a shoe to be put on. It's such a huge step forward for them and really draws the line between baby and toddler. Noor was delighted with hers.

Sara from Stafford, mum to Noor, three and Jasmine, 11 months

You get conflicting advice about shoes – people say don't put shoes on them, their feet need to spread, and they'll learn to walk better, while the shops (obviously, as they're trying to sell you a pair) say that shoes protect their feet, and encourage them to walk. My elder son had a pair of crawling shoes at six months and in my opinion they were a complete waste of money. He hated them and we kept losing them. We then got him cruising shoes, which were OK for outside, but inside I knew he was better off without them. My younger is an accomplished walker and we'll be taking him to get his first proper shoes soon. I don't agree with putting babies in shoes too early but I do agree with getting their feet measured properly, and having well-fitted shoes.

Katie from Cambridge, mum to Ethan, two and Oliver, 11 months

Head-banging

If your baby adopts a head-banging habit around now, rhythmically knocking her head against the side of her cot or the nearest hard surface, rest assured that it's not as alarming as it looks! Head-banging is surprisingly common, with up to a quarter of babies and toddlers likely to go through a phase.

Unlikely as it sounds, babies who head-bang usually do so as a means of self-comfort – similarly, rocking backwards and forwards is thought to be a comfort-seeking habit – although in some cases there may be an emotional problem or a physical pain that's driving her, which it's worth trying to rule out. Head-banging doesn't normally cause any damage, because she will stop when it starts to hurt!

Although the habit can persist for weeks or months, head-banging will usually stop without any intervention from you before your baby reaches the age of three. Ignore it, rather than fussing or urging her to stop. Try to find other, gentler ways to help her relax at the end of the day, such as a soothing bath or close cuddle. Meanwhile, you can reduce the impact by moving her cot away from the wall and putting a bumper or some other kind of padding round its sides – but be sure the padding is well fixed, and don't be tempted to put loose cushions or covers inside her cot, because they could be a suffocation risk.

Feeding

The third stage of weaning

Around now, or very soon, your baby should be at the third stage of weaning, which means she's eating three balanced meals a day, as well as snacks between meals. Purées are a thing of the past – aim to mince or finely chop her food, rather than blitzing it. Don't be surprised if she seems to want to eat more around now – her energy needs grow along with her activity levels. As long it's all good, healthy food, it's fine to let her eat as much as she wants – babies of this age are pretty good at regulating their food intake and are unlikely to eat more than they require. Equally, you should never force her to eat more than she seems to want.

It's a good idea to offer her a wide variety of flavours, colours and textures, because this will boost the likelihood of her being an open-minded eater when she's older. There's no reason, for example, not to let her sample a mild curry or chilli, with the proviso that, since taste buds and tummies are still sensitive at this point, you avoid anything too spicy. If you get her hooked on fish now, she might not turn up her nose at it later, which lots of kids do – a great shame because fish is a fantastic but lean source of protein and healthy fatty acids, especially oily fish, such as mackerel and salmon. Encouraging a preference for a good mix of fruit and veg is also essential, as research shows that getting her to 'eat her greens' now means she's more likely to be receptive to them later.

Although your baby's menu-choices are ever widening, don't be tempted to open up a world of adult temptations by letting her sample the joys of cakes, sweets, crisps and other forms of junk food – if she doesn't know about these things yet, why introduce them? The period between six to 12 months is a vital window for laying down healthy eating habits that will stand her in good stead throughout childhood and beyond. So if you can avoid these things now, you should. If you do give her sweet treats, make them few and far between. You'll be able to offer them a little more regularly after her first birthday – although you certainly don't have to!

Get the balance right

Aim for your baby to eat roughly the right balance of food over the course of a day. Ideally, a baby of nine to 12 months should be eating:

- Three to four servings of starchy food a day – for example, potato, bread, rice, pasta.
- A minimum of three to four servings of fruit and veg. Serve some with main meals because the vitamin C will help her to absorb iron, and also offer fruit and veg between meals as snacks.
- One to two portions of protein-rich foods, such as meat, fish, beans and pulses, or egg (well cooked). If your baby's veggie, make sure she gets plenty of healthy, protein-rich alternatives to meat and fish, such as eggs, lentils, chickpeas or tofu together with plenty of fruit and veg to boost her absorption of iron.
- One to two portions of cheese, yoghurt, fromage frais or milky puddings and sauces – essential for her calcium and vitamin D needs. If your baby has an allergy or intolerance to milk, you should always discuss alternatives with your doctor before attempting to cut any of these foods from her diet.

Drinks

With all the solid food she's eating, you may find your baby seems less interested in a daytime bottle or breastfeed now. She still needs around 500–600ml (17½–21fl oz) of breast or formula milk a day, which basically amounts to two bottle or breastfeeds a day, although you can include milk or milk products used in cooking in this quota. Give her a beaker of water to drink with meals and snacks, and continue to avoid other sorts of drinks. Diluted fresh fruit juices are better than squash or pop, but still best avoided altogether for the first year, or at least given only at mealtimes, in very dilute form. Ideally, you should continue to give diluted fruit juice at mealtimes throughout the whole of childhood. Although fruit juice does contain nutrients, it's extremely high in sugar, so it's not the healthy drink that many mums assume – in fact, many dentists and dietitians say excessive fruit juice habits contribute significantly to high levels of tooth decay and obesity in children.

Something to keep her going

As your baby is probably on the move, she'll be burning up lots of energy, and is likely to need regular snacks in between meals to keep her going. Try to make sure snacks are healthy, and not given too soon before a main meal, in case they interfere with her appetite.

It's a good idea to get into the habit of always having some easy, healthy snacks to hand whenever you're out and about, so you've got something available when it's needed. A bread stick or banana offered at just the right moment can mean the difference between a cross baby and a happy one!

Dried fruit is a popular offering and has lots of nutritional benefits, but it's very high in sugar and dentists advise that you keep careful tabs on how much you offer. They recommend giving it with meals, rather than as snacks.

Between-meals: Healthy snack foods for your baby

- Toast, pitta, bread fingers or mini sandwiches
- Bread sticks or rice cakes – go for low-salt or no-salt varieties if possible

- Sticks of cooked or raw fruit or vegetables – you can't beat a banana because you don't even need to prepare it
- Small cubes of cheese
- Oatcakes or crackers
- Plain biscuits

What the netmums say

Healthy snacks

Bananas – don't leave home without one! Also fruit pots, and rice cakes. I was lucky that mine would all eat food cold out of jars – a good habit to get them in to, so if desperate, you can crack open a jar anywhere! Also bread or toast, which they would chew on for ages. However, the best idea is just to breastfeed until they're one, then you're never without a meal or a snack!
Jayne from Harrogate, mum to Beth, six, Katie, four and Joe, one

I've always got packs of dried fruit in the bottom of the changing bag [see the note about dried fruit on p. 257]. And you can generally find rice cakes, breadsticks, dry cereals, fruit sticks and savoury biscuits or crackers in there, too! At home, for snacks, we might have flapjacks or cereal bars, fresh fruit, raw vegetable sticks, chocolate raisins, melba toasts, cheese . . . the list goes on!
Clair from Pontypridd, mum to Harrison, seven, Ewan, one and Lucas, one month

Max used to love things he could hold easily – carrot or cucumber sticks, breadsticks, toast soldiers – he would have one piece in each hand and munch away, so cute to watch. I used to buy dried fruit as well, which he loved, or a plain Rich Tea biscuit. I never panicked if we were out and I had nothing (although there was usually a little box of raisins lurking in my bag somewhere) as it's quite easy to find little snacks for them in most places. Even if I had to do a mad dash

into a newsagent's for some yoghurt raisins, or a cereal bar or something, to tide him over.
Rachel from Wallington, mum to Max, four

I tried to wean my son on to unusual tastes fairly early on so that he could sit in restaurants or in his pushchair quite happily sucking hummus off breadsticks or rice cakes. It's healthy and you can always find it in shops or on menus that don't cater for young babies. Another good one is avocado, which is soft enough for babies and available in most places.
Emily from Tunbridge Wells, mum to Henry, two

Leisure and Learning

Fun and games (again)

Now that she's nearly a year old, your little one will be looking around for toys, games and activities that tickle her fancy. There are hundreds of well-designed and stimulating products for babies on the market, and you don't necessarily need financial clout to get hold of them – ask your health visitor where your local toy library is, or see if there's one listed on the local boards at www.netmums.com. Boot sales and charity shops are a great source of second-hand toys in good condition. You could also try Freecycle (www.freecycle.org), a fantastic online community that allows people to offer and accept unwanted goods for free.

Meanwhile, as the cliché goes, babies and small children often get the most fun of all from cardboard boxes, pots and pans, or piles of cushions. Be prepared for some chaos – this sort of play can be noisy, messy or both. But your little one will love it – and she'll benefit, too, as imaginative, creative and physical play offers good developmental opportunities. Here are a few ideas:

Fun, fun, fun: Home-made games and activities your baby will love

Bang-on-the-drum: Give her some saucepans and a wooden spoon – but only if you can handle the noise! Alternatively, give her an item that will fit into the pans. She may spend ages putting it in and taking it out again.

Water play: Set her up outside with some plastic cups and a large bowl or sandpit full of water, and let her get splashing. Never leave her unsupervised with any amount of water, though, even for a moment.

Magazine shredding: Let her crumple and rip a magazine you've finished with – she'll love the noise it makes (but remove any staples first). She may try to put it in her mouth, in which case you will have to remove it gently before she attempts to swallow.

Paper and paint: It's early days for craft activities, but a baby of nearly one can have a surprising amount of fun with non-toxic finger paints and crayons. Cover clothing and the surrounding area!

Cushion relay: Set up an obstacle course made of cushions for your baby to negotiate. Give her a huge clap and a cheer when she reaches the finishing line.

Vroom-vrooms: Push her round the sitting room in a sturdy cardboard-box 'car'.

All About You

Planning your second

If you're thinking about trying for a second baby now, so that the age gap will be small, there are a few things worth bearing in mind. Ideally, your body needs about a year to recover completely from the physical effects of having a baby. It's also hard work looking after more than one little one – for instance, do you want to be changing two lots of nappies? Waiting until your first is a bit older means you'll be able to give her the benefit of your complete attention and devotion for longer – and she'll be better able to understand what's happening when she does have to deal with a new arrival in the family. The counter argument is that a small gap means the elder child won't really have any concept of sibling rivalry.

Other advantages of a small age gap are that it gets the really hard work out of the way early, and children who are closer in age are more likely to have shared interests and to play well together – although there's no guarantee of that, whatever the age gap! Practically, life can be easier with children of similar ages because they can share toys, enjoy the same entertainment, and, for a while at least, have the same or similar routines.

In truth, it's impossible to know when is the 'perfect' time to have your second baby. Practical factors, such as finance, space and careers, may have to be considered first. And let's face it, very often conception doesn't happen exactly when we'd like it to, anyway.

One thing's for sure. You'll have something the second-time round that you didn't have before – the benefit of experience.

What the netmums say

Planning a second baby

We planned to have our children 15 months apart – although admittedly we didn't think I'd get pregnant as quickly as I did the second time! The pros are that the elder one doesn't remember a time without the younger one, so there's no resentment, and they have similar development and sleep patterns – they share a bedroom and are the best of friends. The cons? Well, I'm shattered as I have two kids throwing toddler tantrums! Neither is mature enough to do what I say, so if they run in opposite directions, you're stuffed. And if they're both in the double buggy, it's hard work to push.

I'm glad I had two close together, in fact, although it was very hard work trying to do two things at once – breastfeeding one, while spoonfeeding the other, for example! I wouldn't change a thing, though.

Louise from Bournemouth, mum to Thomas, three and Oliver, one

My first two are 17 months apart and I have to admit I found it quite difficult. I was close in age to my sisters and I suppose my expectations of family life were based on that – also I was 35 when I had the first, so a bigger age gap was not really an option. Breastfeeding a tiny baby with a toddler at your side is not easy! I had a two-year gap before my third and I found that much easier as the elder two could entertain themselves while I fed the baby. For a long time, my house was full of baby stuff, nappies and plastic toys, plus various bouncy seats and highchairs. My children loved their cots and the eldest was reluctant to go into a bed, so at one time I had three cots in the house.

I had an enormous double buggy with a buggy board on the back to get around, and couldn't leave the house without a big change bag with two different sizes of cloth nappies in them! However, the advantages are that now I have no nappies and no buggies. In a few months' time the youngest will be at school – so I'm slowly regaining my life and body.

Julia from Tunbridge Wells, mum to Finn, seven, Rory, six and Aidan, four

The age gap between my two is 15 months, but I didn't plan it that way. I was breastfeeding at the time and I hadn't had a period since having my daughter, so I thought I was safe. I was shocked when the doctor told me I was pregnant. I just thought I was feeling knackered from being a mum to a six month old!

Anna from Herstmonceux, mum to Charlotte, four and Thomas, two

There are 16 months between mine. I was very worried about the gap initially, and felt guilty about my son losing out on being a baby, but to be honest, he was not bothered by Stella at all. In fact, he's only really started to take any notice of her now. I think having them so close meant he was too young for jealousy. Stella slotted nicely into his routine, which I stuck to rigidly, and it all flows OK most days. Bedtimes are a 'mare, though, as my other half is still at work until late. But it's getting easier. Some days I feel like I'm drowning in nappies, and I've actually fed Stella at the boob while cooking Seth's tea and singing 'wind the bobbin up', but you just have to get on with it. I no longer sweat the small stuff. I bath on alternate nights, I don't iron, and sometimes we watch CBeebies and eat fishfingers. I do what I have to do to stay sane!

Sheridan from Melbourn, mum to Seth, one and Stella, five months

I would say cost is the only real con of having children close together – apart from that I'd say it was the best thing we did. I got pregnant with my second six months after my first. They have so much in common now, they play with cars together, chase each other around, my elder son tries to feed my younger one! I'm now pregnant with our third, conceived six months after our younger son was born! I'm nervous about being a mum to three little ones, and it seems madness to have them close together in some ways, but I like the idea that I will get all the potty training and sleepless nights over with in one go!

Katie from Cambridge, mum to Ethan, two and Oliver, 11 months

Our daughter was two at the end of July and I'm just starting to feel broody again now. I would love to start trying, but we simply cannot afford it. We'll need to wait until our daughter starts school as we could not afford nursery fees for two. Roll on 2010! To be honest, I feel this will be a good gap – I'll have time in the day with the new baby and hopefully Abigail will be of an age where she can understand and feel included in it all. We'll see!

Helen from Newcastle upon Tyne, mum to Abigail, two

We decided we wanted our second child by the time our daughter was two, so we started trying when she was ten months old. However, she will be three in four months' time and we're still trying. I do sometimes feel sad that things didn't go to plan, but then I realise how lucky I am to have this special and wonderful time with my daughter.

Gemma from Norwich, mum to Caitlin, two

The Eleventh Month

Welcome to your eleventh month of motherhood

From the moment she was born, your baby's communication and language skills have been in development, and she may be close to speaking her first words by now. It's impossible to over-emphasise how important it is to talk to your baby – speech and language experts are concerned at what they see as an increasing lack of these skills in primary age children, and they believe that a simple lack of parent-to-child communication during the vital early years of life could be to blame. So now, more than ever, is the time to chat with – and listen to – your little one.

Perhaps just as exciting as the development of talking skills is the development of walking skills. A small number of babies have begun to take their first steps by ten or 11 months – you'll know if your baby's nearly there if she's already cruising and standing on her own, or taking steps while she holds on to your hands. It may be that she has the muscle strength to walk but not the confidence, in which case be sure to hold on tight!

If all the moving around and messy eating is getting to you, and your stress levels are bubbling upwards, don't worry – you'd have to be a saint not to get cross sometimes. While children can be held responsible for their actions, babies are just too little to know right from wrong. That doesn't mean they can't wind you up, though. When they do, it's time to stop, slow down . . . and take a long, slow, deep breath.

Health, Growth and Development

Baby milestones

Now that she is ten months old, your baby will typically:

- Respond to her name and understand some words, such as 'no', or simple instructions.
- Be able to bear her own weight when you hold her and bounce her on your knee.

And she might also:

- Cruise around the room, supporting herself on the furniture.
- Pull herself up to standing with support from you or a solid object such as a stable piece of furniture.
- Be able to stand unsupported for a while.
- Be attempting to feed herself with her own cutlery.
- Wave goodbye.
- Use a proper word, with the right meaning attached to it.
- Be taking her first steps alone.

Milestone focus: Walking

As with all developmental milestones, your baby will walk when she's ready. You can help and encourage her along the way, though, by buying her a sturdy push-along toy – carts particularly are a good idea because she can stop and put things in or take them out, which will encourage other physical skills. Don't forget to let her go barefoot indoors as much as possible. It's easier for her to walk without footwear, and safer because it allows her to grip better. Let her have lots of toddling time out of the playpen or pushchair. Do bear in mind that the use of baby walkers is discouraged by experts, because too much time spent in one of them may stunt developing walking skills – in any case, it should certainly be discarded once your baby is taking her first steps, or showing signs of doing so. (For more on baby walkers, see p. 137.)

Your baby will probably look rather ungainly as she perfects her balance and gets to grips with the fine art of putting one foot in front of the other. With time and practice, she'll become more confident, and a bit more graceful. Don't be surprised if she takes a step or two alone, then decides against trying again for a while – she may have scared herself with her boldness and temporarily lost confidence.

While it's true that walking is an especially exciting development in any parent's book, this is definitely the early end of this particular milestone spectrum – experts say that anything up to 18 months is a perfectly normal age for starting to walk. So it's quite possible that your baby seems nowhere near taking her first steps at this stage, even if some of her friends are. She's particularly likely to walk later if she sat up and crawled later – and, of course, if she was born prematurely. It can be hard when other, excessively proud mums are keen to trumpet their 'advanced' offspring's abilities. But the ability to walk is based on a mix of muscular development, confidence and motivation. The last factor explains why babies with an older sibling often take longer to learn to walk – if they have an older sister or brother prepared to fetch and carry for them, they may be less inclined to bother. In any case, it's a simple fact of life that some babies walk earlier than others – and, in most cases, it doesn't mean a thing!

Memory box

Your baby's first steps are a milestone you'll want to remember – don't forget to make a note in her baby book of when and where it happened. These things can be pretty spontaneous, so you might not get the chance to catch it on your camera or camcorder – but do try to get some footage of some of those wobbly early steps when you can!

The great dummy debate (part two)

If your baby has a dummy, you may want to think about beginning to wean her off it around now, or at least reducing its use if it's become a very frequent daytime habit. Health professionals tend to discourage dummy use after the age of one – mainly for the sake of speech and language development – and point out that it's easier to stop a dummy habit sooner, rather than later. Dental issues, which are frequently cited as a reason to avoid dummy use, aren't really such a concern (see below).

Why should we ditch the dummy?

From a dental point of view, there isn't really a strong argument against dummies as long as they are not used excessively – according to the British Orthodontic Society, a baby or child would have to be sucking a dummy (or her thumb) for more than six hours a day for it to have any effect on her teeth, and the long-term effects on the permanent teeth of dummy-users are likely to be 'negligible'. Added to that, modern varieties of dummy are designed with orthodontics in mind, anyway, as they come with flat heads, rather than rounded ones, which minimises the risk of damage to teeth still further.

The main concern over dummy use is that it could interfere with development of a baby's speech and language skills, which are, in fact, already in the making well before her first birthday. Babies need free mouths so they can practise making sounds and moving their lips, tongues and jaws – all good preparation for talking. So the worry is that, if she has a dummy in it for any significant length of time, those opportunities may be restricted.

One other, more practical reason for getting rid of the dummy is so that you won't have to keep getting up in the night to give it back to her when she wakes up looking for it!

How to ditch the dummy

If you want to ditch the dummy, you might find it best to bite the bullet and take it away altogether. At this early stage, you won't be able to reason with your baby in the same way that you could with an older toddler, so you'll simply have to spend a couple of days distracting her with extra attention, play or cuddles, instead. If you're trying to take it away at night, and she's always needed it to go to sleep, you may have to use some form of sleep training, such as controlled crying or gradual retreat, to get her to settle without it. (For more details about sleep training, see p. 200.)

However, you may find that an easier, if more long-winded, way to drop the dummy is to reduce its use gradually, so that eventually she just has it for sleep times, and occasional moments when she particularly needs comfort. You may then want to remove it entirely, or you may choose to let her carry on like that for a while – lots of mums give their baby a dummy on this basis, anyway, and that's fine. Some parents feel it's easier to stop dummy use when a child's a bit older and can be gently reminded that she's a 'big girl' now; or at least persuaded to give up her dummy to the care of the 'dummy fairy', or by way of a 'donation to needy orphan babies'!

Choose your timing carefully before removing a major source of comfort – don't attempt to do so if your baby's going through a clingy phase or is poorly, or if there's some other major upheaval or change going on in her life at the time, such as you going back to work, for example, or a house move. Wait for a more settled period.

What the netmums say

Dummies

Both my children had dummies. Joey was 18 months when I took his away from him and all I did was throw them all in the bin. He cried for a little bit but he soon forgot about them. Leo was 12 months and again, I just threw them all away and it didn't really seem to bother him too much.
Amy from Tamworth, mum to Joey, four and Leo, two

My older son still has his dummy at night, and my younger one has started having a dummy to settle him for naps. I think there's too much snobbery about dummies and for some babies they're a godsend. People often say they're proud not to have given a baby a dummy, and to me, that just continues the myth that giving a baby a dummy makes you a failure. I think responsible use of a dummy can help make for a happy baby.
Lucie from Leeds, mum to Joe, three and Oliver, three months

I used to be in the anti-dummy camp but once my first son was born he was very difficult to calm or get to sleep and I found that a dummy sometimes helped. He only used it sometimes to get to sleep and he wouldn't bother with it in the day. My second son is a much more 'sucky' baby, but he still doesn't spend huge amounts of time with a dummy in his mouth. He sometimes goes to sleep with one, and during the day he sometimes has short periods where he suddenly needs a comfort suck in between breastfeeds. (While I'm a huge advocate of breastfeeding, no one wants a baby on their breast virtually all day if it's not for milk.) My view now is that, as with many similar topics, parents should try to keep a reasonably open mind. It's absolutely fine to do a bit of research and have in mind parenting techniques that sound 'right' to you, but when your baby arrives, you sometimes find you have to be flexible.

Susan from Hatfield, mum to Adem, two and Raif, three months

My son was a big baby and was constantly sucking at the breast for comfort. After much soul-searching, I discussed it with my midwife, who reassured us that dummy-sucking was proven to be soothing for babies, and was easier to stop than thumb-sucking, because you could simply take the dummy away. I also discussed it with my orthodontist, who told me there was no evidence that dummies caused 'buck' teeth. So I gave Jamie a dummy. And what a relief it was! He slept better, he sucked at the breast less, and it really helped through the colic days. Now, at six months, he only gets his dummy if it's snoozy time – but even then, he doesn't always want it and I never force him to take it. So we're hopeful that 'coming off' the dummy will be easier than we originally thought. Other mums I know are ashamed their children have dummies, but I'm not in the slightest. I used to think that people gave their children dummies because they couldn't be bothered to soothe their kids themselves – but I've learned very quickly that you need an open mind to be a parent!

Wendy from Edinburgh, mum to Jamie, six months

I gave my son a dummy when he was a week old, just for sleep times, but at four months he began waking in the night 15 to 20 times because he kept losing it and would only settle if I put it back in! After a couple of nights of this I woke up one morning feeling absolutely shattered and threw them all in the bin! It was two days of hell while he learned to soothe himself to sleep, but after that he slept through the night, and still does now.

Leanne from Tamworth, mum to Joshua, seven months

Leisure and Learning

Talk to your baby

This is relevant and vital advice for every single month of your baby's first year (and far beyond it, too) – talking with and listening to your baby will boost development of speech and language skills, which will later play a vital social and educational role in her life. Chatting to your baby doesn't always come naturally to some mums, and you might feel a bit daft having what seems to be a one-way conversation with someone who cannot talk back. But babies can understand what you're saying long before they can start to express thoughts for themselves clearly, so even though she can't have a proper conversation with you yet, there's every reason for you to have one with her!

Don't talk so much that your baby can't get a word in, though. Allowing her to respond to you and listening to what she has to say is equally important. She might not be making much sense now, but she soon will be – so give her as many opportunities as you can to develop her speech by talking, and listening, to her.

Chatter matters: Top tips for talking, and listening, to your baby

- Be sure to stop talking sometimes and let her have a turn! Listen to what she's saying – and respond whenever she talks to you.
- Get down to her level, and aim to keep eye contact when you're talking to her.
- Use body language to help illustrate what you're saying –

actions, gestures and facial expressions will all help her to make sense of the accompanying words.

- There's nothing wrong with parentese – using short, simple words and phrases in a slow, sing-song tone – but there's no need to use babyspeak or make up words. If you mean dog, say dog, not woof-woof.

- You don't have to set aside time for talking to your baby. Just do it as you carry on about your business, chatting about everything you're doing with her, or anything that she can see. Ask her lots of questions – one day, she'll surprise you with an answer!

- Boost her vocabulary by giving everything a label. Don't just talk about objects, though – talk about actions, colours and simple concepts, too, such as hot and cold, up and down, in and out. Research has shown that toddlers with chatty mothers have a bigger-than-average vocabulary and that they're more likely to be intelligent, too.

- Don't make a big deal out of it when she says something wrong. Respond with encouragement, and repeat the correct word back to her.

- Keep on reading! Introduce new books, but don't worry if she has old favourites, because repetition is a good way to learn. When you look at books together, talk about the story and pictures.

- Play action games, sing songs and recite nursery rhymes together.

- Very short, occasional bursts of telly-watching, once she's able to sit still for long enough to appreciate it, are unlikely to have a negative effect on your baby. But little ones cannot learn language from the box in the same way that they can from interaction with another human being, so keep viewing times well restricted, and try to watch with them and encourage conversations that arise from her viewing. (For more on television for babies, see p. 287.)

- Just like adults, babies may not want to talk or listen much if they are hungry, tired or poorly. Respect her needs – if she seems to want a bit of peace and quiet, let her have it!

What the netmums say

The importance of talking to your baby

I talked to Daisy all the time, from reading the babycare books out loud, to explaining what I was doing all the time. I had her in a carrier a lot of the time when she was small, so together we watered the garden, planted seeds, fed the cats, went shopping, and all the time I talked to her, and sang to her. (I did give her a break from my incessant ramblings sometimes!) She's always had an incredible understanding of things. Her language is amazing, too, and I attribute this to so much talking and reading to her when she was very young.

Kath from Nottingham, mum to Daisy, three

When I first found out I was pregnant with my first child, I started talking to her, wittering away about what we would do together once she was born, what advice I would give her as she got older, etc. Once she was born, it was natural to continue chatting to her, responding to her smiles, coos and giggles, running a commentary on everything we were doing. If we were out walking, I'd chat about trees, dogs, anything we could see, and point them out to her. With my second daughter, I continued to chat, but now it was to both of them, and the attention was not so focused on her. Even now, she's not as naturally chatty as her older sister, but I am not sure if this is due to having less attention from me, or if she is just naturally this way. My son is now a very vocal 17 month old, so the noise level in our home has increased no end! I think it either comes naturally to chat to your baby, or it doesn't. Some mums find it harder, I know, and have to think more about what they say, or don't say. But in the long run, it's one of the best things you can do for your kids.

Chantelle from Christchurch, mum to Daisy, five, Ruby, four and Dylan, one

I always talked to Max – as soon as I knew I was pregnant with him I started telling him what I was doing, where I was going – poor boy probably had his hands over his ears! I remember his first word, at ten months, when he picked up his bowl after lunch and said 'gone'. Talk about proud mummy! So I carried on chatting to him about everything – when we were having a bath (empty, full, tap, bubbles) or driving (car, van, bike, etc). His vocabulary now is brilliant. He'll say things and I think where on earth did that come from? I really think that when you talk to your baby lots, it helps their development so much – their ability to speak, their interest in things and their social skills. For them to be able to carry and hold a conversation at a young age is a great achievement, and so encouraging for them, too.

Rachel from Wallington, mum to Max, four

I chatted all the time to Ruby from bump to now. I'd talk about how much housework there was to be done, and how annoying daytime telly is! I even made up songs so she could hear me if I wasn't in the room – something like 'mummy's on the loo, mummy's on the looooooo!' or 'I'm cooking in the kitchen, cooking in the kitchen!' I feel a bit silly admitting it, but it's fun. Funny thing is, she now talks more than I do! She babbles constantly, and has so many clear words. She's so chatty and I'm sure it's because I talk all the time to her.

Amanda from Bristol, mum to Ruby, one

All About You

Keeping your cool

For most of us, having children brings with it some pretty serious challenges to our tempers, and it doesn't always help to tell yourself that, at this age, they're too young to know any better! For a nearly one-year-old, life is a long series of clumsily executed experiments and explorations, driven by a fierce and ever-growing independence. Babies of this age are easily frustrated and easily tired – both of which can lead to much grizzling and grumbling on their part. But dealing with all these issues when you're also trying to cope with a continuing lack of sleep and/or an exhausting return to work, worries about money, relationships, childcare and tedious but necessary domestic chores, can be enough to try the patience of the saintliest parents. It's really not that surprising if tempers fray sometimes. Don't feel bad when it happens to you. It happens to the best of us. A few ploys to help you cope when anger threatens, and to help reduce the number of times it does, are outlined in the box below.

Just say 'no'

A child who's not yet reached her first birthday is too young to be labelled 'naughty' – curious and clumsy, yes; attention-seeking and boundary-pushing, perhaps; but naughty, no! So you cannot issue consequences or tick her off in the same way that you might with an older child, but you can begin to teach her right from wrong around now. This is especially important if she, or someone else, is likely to be hurt as a result of her actions. A little judicious use of the word 'no', issued in a stern tone of voice and accompanied by appropriate gestures or actions, may do the trick. By the age of 11 months, most babies understand exactly what 'no' means, and enough about body language and different voices to work out that whatever they're doing is not acceptable. Use the word 'no' sparingly, though – use it too frequently and it will cease to mean much.

Temper, temper: How to be a cooler, calmer parent

Breathe deeply, walk away: If you can feel your temperature rising, pause for a moment and take some deep breaths. And if it's gone beyond that and you're ready to let rip, leave the room for a little while, instead. Make sure the room is safe, or that your baby is safely strapped in her highchair or in a cot or playpen, before you go. If there's someone else around – your partner, mum or a friend, call on them to take over.

See the funny side: A good sense of humour is definitely required for motherhood. Try to laugh at yourself if you can, and don't be surprised if your baby laughs with you.

Empathise with your baby: Try to understand how it feels to be her. She's literally finding her feet as she negotiates the amazing maze of her first year.

Don't feel guilty: There's no benefit in feeling bad when you do lose your temper. You're only human. But be sure to make it up with your baby as soon as you possibly can.

Count your blessings: When the heat's on and the pressure's high, try to remind yourself how lucky you are to have your baby. Could you really imagine life without her?

Give yourself a break: It's hard work being a mum, physically and emotionally. Make sure you get some time to yourself – especially if you're at home all day with your little one. Take a few minutes break whenever you get the chance, and indulge yourself regularly with a treat – whether a glass of wine, a hot bath or an early night with clean sheets and a stack of glossy magazines.

Get a good night's sleep: Exhaustion always makes stressful situations worse. If you're still having broken nights, consider sleep training your baby – with commitment, you *can* get her to sleep through the night, if you want to. Failing that, try to get to bed early or snatch power naps whenever possible during the day, to make up for any shortfall in sleep.

Slow down, do less: Try not to have too much else on during your baby's first year. If finances allow, and the option's available, consider taking a long sabbatical from work, or a return to part-time hours. Avoid taking on any major projects, such as house renovation – now isn't the time! And when you are with your baby, make it count – slow down, relax, take life at her pace and wallow in each other's company.

Don't compete in the lifestyle Olympics: Set your own standard for living and ignore everyone else's – it's your baby, your home, your relationship. Life's too short to turn into a competition. If you're happy, your partner's happy and your baby's happy, nothing else really matters.

Seek help, if you need it: If you're struggling with any significant difficulties in life, and/or you're losing your temper regularly, or to a frightening extent, confide in someone – a close, sensible friend, or better still, a sympathetic professional, such as a health visitor, GP or someone working for an appropriate charity, such as Homestart. (Details for Homestart and other helpful organisations and phonelines are included in the appendix at the back of the book.)

What the netmums say

Keeping cool

I have had a few moments over the years where I've had to leave them somewhere safe (usually a pram or cot) and walk away to a different room for a few seconds' sanity. Deep breaths . . . pink fluffy clouds . . . I think knowing when you need to walk away is a very important skill to learn.

Clair from Pontypridd, mum to Harrison, seven, Ewan, one and Lucas, one month

Henry has insisted on feeding himself for a while now, which is fantastic, but messy! Recently, he's developed a new favourite game, which is standing up in his highchair and emptying his bowl of food on to the floor. It's extremely frustrating, and I have little or no patience for this behaviour. I do now strap him in, but despite telling him not to in a stern voice, I generally get ignored. My new technique has been to take him out of his chair and put him on the floor, but that just causes tears, or he wags his finger at me. I'm not sure what the answer is to this issue. I find the only thing that I can do to calm down is either walk away, or let him cry and ignore him. When he stops, I then start the meal again.

Amanda from London, mum to Henry, aged one

When Seth was little, he'd fight sleep all day and then be screaming mad all afternoon and evening. I often had to take myself off into the bathroom to have a weep or breathe slowly to calm down. Then I'd strap him in his sling and walk him round the fields where we could both have a good yell and the walk would help both of us! I was, and still am, the 'woman who walks', and if I'm having a mardy day and the babies are griping, we'll go out for a walk, anywhere – even when I'm on my knees with tiredness. They often either stop crying or fall asleep once you get going.

Sheridan from Melbourn, mum to Seth, one and Stella, five months

I've been blessed with a very happy, well-behaved little boy but even so, I used to find myself burning with anger and shouting at him sometimes. It got to the point where I had to face facts – perhaps the problem wasn't him, or the stresses of being a parent. Maybe the problem was me, and how stressful I'd made it? I'd taken on too much and life was hectic: I was planning a wedding, and trying to juggle two business ventures. Barely any time was spent solely with Archie. My weight dropped to seven stone, and I was getting only about five hours' sleep a night, if that (through no fault of my son's, who's a good sleeper). I was tired, short tempered and stressed – Archie only had to look in the wrong direction and I'd lose my temper. Life was just one big rush. Thankfully, reality finally came crashing down and I decided, on the advice of friends, to take a break from work. I couldn't believe what a difference it made, having quality time to spend with Archie. There were no more angry moments or raised voices, because we didn't have to rush any more. I was actually enjoying watching him dress himself, and relishing the 20 minutes it took to take a two-minute walk, stopping to look at every leaf or stone on the path! In short, I was enjoying being a parent again, because I was allocating enough time to do so. I now manage my time much more effectively, and work far less, and I'm so much happier. Obviously, in an ideal world we'd allocate all our time to our children. But life, work, household chores all need some of your time, too. But that's the key word – some, not all. I have a better relationship with my son and my husband now. I'm not trying to say that by slowing down you're never again going to feel at your wits' end. But it might help!

Jess from Huntingdon, mum to Archie, two

The Twelfth Month

Welcome to your twelfth month of motherhood

Congratulations! You're not far away from celebrating your first year of motherhood. There are plenty more parental challenges ahead – probably another two decades' worth! But once you've got through your first baby's first year, you've got through one of the hardest parts of all. If you had a particularly traumatic birth, you may find its anniversary brings back some difficult memories. This is quite normal. Talking about it, if you can, is a positive thing to do.

Your nearly one-year-old baby may be a walking, talking toddler by now, but many will be some way off those stages – always remember that the speed of developmental progress a child makes in her first year varies enormously. There are some things you can generally expect of her by now, though, and they are outlined over the page – do chat to a health professional if you have any concerns.

Don't forget to mark your little one's birthday in some small way. Perhaps you could invite a handful of close friends round to watch as she rips open the colourful paper on an interesting present – just don't be too surprised if she prefers to play with the box and the gift wrap, rather than the toy. While you're at it, why not pop the cork on a bottle of bubbly and raise a glass to your own achievements – your first year as parents. Here's to the next one!

Health, Growth and Development

Baby milestones

Now that she is 11 months old, your baby will typically:

- Have mastered the skill of letting go – deliberately releasing an object from her grasp, or handing something to you, if you ask for it.
- Be able to move around the room in some way, whether crawling, bottom-shuffling, wriggling, rolling or cruising.
- Be able to pick up small objects between thumb and finger, and enjoy putting objects in a container.
- Have a good understanding of some simple instructions or questions.
- Drink from a cup.

And she might also:

- Have taken her first steps.
- Use one or more proper words, in context, with the right meaning attached to them.
- Feed herself with her own cutlery.
- Attempt her first scribbles with a crayon.

Milestone focus: Talking

Around now, some babies will start to use one or two recognisable words with meaning, as opposed to churning them out, accidentally, while babbling, although anything between 12 and 18 months is normal for this milestone, and as with all others, there's wide variation. It's very likely her early words won't sound quite like they're supposed to, and she may well simplify what she's trying to say by dropping off consonants, which can sometimes prove tricky – 'doh' instead of 'dog', for example.

Even if she's not using proper words, she's likely to be making lots of speechlike sounds at this stage, babbling loudly in a conversational rhythm, and talking in a language of her very own. Alongside her own language development, her understanding of yours has grown – so by now, she will usually respond to her name, understand a number of familiar words, such as 'bye-bye' or 'milk', and have grasped the meaning of some simple instructions, such as 'give it to Daddy'.

To encourage your baby's talking skills, the very best thing you can to is to talk to her yourself, because it's by listening to how words sound and the way sentences are formed that she learns to do it for herself. (For more about this, see pp. 371–8.)

Memory box

Make a written note of your baby's first few words – it's amazing how easily important little memories such as this can be lost over time.

More on milestones

Now that your baby's approaching her first birthday, you may be worried if she hasn't reached the developmental milestones that some of her peers have. Milestones mean different things for different parents. It's undeniably thrilling, and reassuring, when your little one gets the hang of certain achievements, but it can add to life's worries, usually unnecessarily, if she isn't there yet.

The truth is that, with just under a year of life under her belt, it's early days for most things – she'll almost certainly walk, talk and acquire all those other significant skills of infancy in her own, sweet time. So take any milestone guidance you are offered – from this book, and elsewhere – as a very broad indication of what to expect and when. This is particularly important advice if your baby was born prematurely, because she may be some weeks or even months behind 'normal' guidelines.

Don't discount milestone guidelines completely, though, because significant delays can sometimes signal a problem that needs addressing. As a general rule, you should talk to your health visitor or GP about it if your one-year-old baby *isn't* doing one or more of the following things:

- Sitting up strongly for long periods on her own.
- Moving across the room under her own steam in some way.
- Responding to her name or other familiar words, or if she doesn't seem to hear loud everyday noises, such as the vacuum cleaner or telephone.
- Recognising people or objects she knows from across the room.
- Spotting and/or picking up very small objects, such as crumbs, between her thumb and finger.
- Manipulating larger objects and passing them easily from one hand to another.
- Babbling, or if she isn't babbling any more, having done so early on.
- Eating food with lumpy textures, or feeding herself a fairly broad range of finger foods.

What the netmums say

Milestones

All the milestones they reach are special, and they create such wonderful memories. Two spring to mind for me – my daughter saying Mama for the first time, as I put her to bed one night. (It reduced me to tears – especially as she kept repeating it.) And my son, aged about four months and recovering from a bone infection in hospital, lying on his back in the cot, then rocking from side to side before rolling over on to his tum with a big smile! He then spent the next hour rolling around the cot – much to my delight, and his!
Heather from Sheffield, mum to Jasmine, four and Jack, two

I think it's a shame when mothers compare their babies, and constantly ask what yours has or hasn't done yet. Mine have been relatively early or average in most things, but I've never bragged about it. I can't stand mums who do that. I think the milestones are handy in some ways, though – it can be helpful to know roughly what to expect. Even though all babies are different, you do need to know the point at which to be concerned. I compare my children to each other in terms of when they have done things, but only in a fun, curious way. It's interesting to watch how each develops at their own pace!

Chantelle from Christchurch, mum to Daisy, six, Ruby, four and Dylan, one

My gorgeous baby girl said her first word at nine months, but didn't walk until she was 18 months. I was convinced my baby was strange and would never walk, and fretted because everyone else I know with a baby was buying their second pair of proper walking shoes. But she did! Everyone's baby develops differently and I hate all those 'tick boxes' you're supposed to fill in. Fair enough if there are problems, but if not, then celebrate the fact that your baby can count to three at 14 months, and ignore the fact that they're still shuffling about on their bottoms at 18 months. I mean, it's all evened out by the time they are five, hasn't it?

Sally from Matfen, mum to Lily, one

Jayden has delayed gross motor skills, which meant he was late with everything regarding movement. He didn't roll over until nine months, sit up properly until he was 12 months, crawl until he was 14 months, pull up to stand until 17 months or walk unaided until he was just over two. He's seeing a consultant, but they have no idea what's causing this, as everything else seems fine. All they can come up with is his traumatic birth. I think it's natural to worry when your little one isn't doing something that all the others seem to do, but I think there is too much pressure on them to do something by a certain time nowadays. They will still do it, when they're ready. Just look at Jayden!

Emma from Radstock, mum to Jayden, three and Finley, one

Milestones have been the bane of my life since my second daughter was born. She had problems at birth and we were told all manner of things that might happen as a result, and consequently I've been obsessed with milestones – all of which she has been late with but because they are so rigid they do not allow for late development, which may eventually be normal. I have been through a lot of unnecessary stress, because despite my sleepness nights, my daughter is now crawling, cruising and starting to talk – all of which have been much later than 'normal'. I think it's really important for the sanity of us mums to stress that the range of development is vast. It's stressful being a mum and it makes matters so much worse by giving deadlines for development.

Abi from Wotton-under-Edge, mum to Laurie, four and Anya, one

Feeding

Eating like an adult

By the time your baby reaches the end of this month, in other words, when she turns one, she can eat more or less what you eat. However, you should continue to leave out salt when cooking for her, and keep an eye on her intake of very salty products – try to ration processed and pre-packaged foods, such as sausages and fishfingers, to no more than a couple of times a week, if you can, and cook from scratch as often as you're able. Continue to avoid adding sugar to foods, or offering sugary products too regularly, and keep an eye out for anything, such as whole nuts, that could be a choking hazard or cause an allergic reaction.

Now that she's eating the same foods as you are, it will make eating together as a family more natural. This is a habit to aim for as much as possible, because it will help to foster healthy attitudes towards food and eating that will stand her in good stead throughout her childhood and beyond.

Milky, milky

Once she reaches the end of this month and turns one, your baby can begin to drink ordinary full-fat cow's milk. Up until then, it's not an appropriate main drink alternative to breast or formula, because it doesn't contain the necessary nutrients required during her first year. Follow-on formula milks are available but they aren't necessary if your little one is eating a normal range of foods.

Milk and milk products continue to be a vital source of calcium as well as a number of important vitamins and minerals after the age of one, so it's recommended that she continues to consume between half a pint and one pint, daily, of milk products such as cheese and yoghurt, milk on cereal, and milky puddings and sauces are included in this, so if she's getting one or two portions of these things a day, she'll only need one to two milk drinks a day on top. And if she won't drink milk at all, around three portions of milk products should still be enough for her calcium needs

Some babies of this age still have a heavy milk habit, often based on 'comfort' associations rather than genuine hunger, but too much milk now can fill her up and spoil her appetite for the good mix of solids she needs. So if she's consuming more than a pint of milk a day, aim to cut down and when you do give her a milk drink, always do so after rather than before a main meal. Reduce her milk intake gradually by offering some of her feeds diluted with water, increasing the ratio of water to milk until she's happy with just water. Distraction in the form of play, a walk outside or a cuddle with Dad should help her forget that she's missing out on a customary fix.

If you and your baby are still enjoying breastfeeds, then carry on. However, too many breastfeeds can also affect appetite, so avoid offering the boob before mealtimes. If your breastfed baby doesn't drink cow's milk at all, you'll need to make sure she gets some other dairy products, such as cheese and yoghurt, as it's impossible to know if she's getting sufficient quantities of breast milk to get the same level of nutrients that these foods provide. And it's still important that she learns to drink from a cup, so be sure to offer her water in her beaker with meals and snacks.

Off the bottle

Health professionals are advised by the government 'actively to discourage' bottle use from the age of one. That's because excessive or extended bottlefeeding is linked to tooth decay (see p. 175) and the incidence of anaemia, caused because babies who prefer to drink from a bottle, at the expense of a good range of solid foods, risk iron deficiency. Some experts suspect that an out-of-control bottle habit may interfere with a baby's development, because if she's continually sucking from, or lugging around, a bottle, it will reduce her opportunities to talk and play. Although these may be the consequences of fairly extreme bottle habits, now's a good time to help your little one kick hers completely – or at the very least, to impose some limits.

Your baby should have got to grips with a cup of some kind by now. If she hasn't, try to replace her bottles with a beaker gradually – you may find that when you make the switch from formula to ordinary milk is a good time to try, because she may be more likely to accept a different taste in a different container. If it's tough trying to get shot of your baby's beloved bottle, bear in mind that it'll be easier to do it now than later. Often, though, babies will make the swap with surprisingly little fuss.

If your baby *does* still drink from a bottle, it's really important for the sake of her teeth that you only ever put milk or water in it. Another thing you can do to minimise the drawbacks of bottle use is to make sure she always sits down for feeds and isn't allowed to tote her bottle around with her, swigging from it at will. And if she clings steadfastly to her last bottle of the day for comfort, make sure she has it before she goes into her cot, and clean her teeth afterwards.

If she needs a bottle in order to settle to sleep at night, then that's not a good habit, as she may then also need one to settle if she wakes in the night (and the last thing you want to do is get up and go down to a cold kitchen to make her one). There's also a risk of tooth decay if traces of milk sit around in her mouth overnight. Cutting out this bedtime bottle may well be hard. You could try offering water in the bottle, instead, or diluting the milk with water, upping the water-milk ratio over a period of time. As for feeds in the middle of the night, your baby definitely doesn't need these now. Offering her one is simply encouraging a comfort habit that means a disturbed night for you.

What the netmums say

Kicking the bottle

Ruby was a bottle-loving baby, and as I couldn't breastfeed I just gave her one whenever she wanted one, thinking it was the right thing to do – so by seven months she was having a full bottle of formula six to seven times a day. The heath visitor urged me to cut out most of the bottles and replace with water from beakers. It was really hard trying to get her off the bottle, then we found a brand of beaker that worked! So within a few months I got the six to seven bottles a day down to two – one in the morning and one in the evening – then I cut out the morning one, and she's now having one beaker of milk with her breakfast, water or juice from a beaker throughout the day, and a bottle of cow's milk before bed. She's not going to let go of it just yet, and I'm not too worried. It's only one bottle a day, and it's part of her routine.

Amanda from Bristol, mum to Ruby, one

We dropped the morning bottle when our son was a few days from his first birthday. I ran out of formula and didn't have the money to buy more, and as I knew he would be going on to cow's milk in a few days I changed there and then, putting it in a beaker rather than the bottle. He didn't make a fuss about it – I think the bottle was merely a container to house the stuff he wanted, which was the milk! We changed his evening bottle when he was just over a year old to a beaker and, again, there were no problems and no fussing – he just got on with it.

Dyanne from Dunfermline, mum to Luke, two

Charlotte still has a bottle of milk – she calls it her 'bob-bob' – before bedtime. I don't let her take it to bed with her, though – she'll sit on the sofa with me and teddy while we read a story. And she drinks from a normal cup during the day. Since her baby brother was born, she's asked for a bottle a few times during the day. I then tell her that it's just for babies, but that she can have a cup of milk, which usually works. I'm not even going to try and take the evening bottle away from her at the moment. I'm sure she'll stop asking for one eventually.

Carmen from Catterick Garrison, mum to Charlotte, two and Leo, two months

Leisure and Learning

Babies and television

By now, your little one has probably discovered what that grey box in the corner of your living room is for and, unless you don't have one at all or have been very singleminded about keeping it off while she's around, chances are she's already discovered the joys of telly.

Debate about whether too much television is bad for children has rumbled for a long time, and you may well wonder whether it's all right to introduce your baby to it at this early stage. It's true that some recent studies have warned against letting babies develop a small-screen habit, mainly because of fears that it could have a negative impact on their speech and language skills, stifle imagination and play, and even contribute to major modern ills, such as attention deficit disorders, depression and obesity. For example, in his 2007 book *Remotely Controlled*, psychologist Aric Sigman recommended that children under three be stopped from watching television altogether; and the American Academy of Pediatrics has also published advice that it should be avoided for the under-twos.

However, as most mums will tell you, these aren't particularly realistic conclusions. Unless you're prepared to unplug your television set permanently and remove it from the house (and keep her from watching at other people's houses), you'd be setting yourself up for a hard task if you tried to achieve a totally telly-free zone. Besides, it can be argued that small doses of appropriate viewing are beneficial for babies – particularly as programming for little ones these days is carefully designed to be educational. It's also a good way to relax, which is something we all need to do from time to time. Then of course, there's the unavoidable fact that, sometimes, you simply need a reliable distraction for your baby in order to grab a few moments in which to get something done.

So don't feel bad if you let your baby watch a bit of television sometimes – but do make sure she's watching the right level for her age, and set careful limits on how often she watches. There's no official guideline to go by, so in the end it's down to you to impose your own rules. However, the National Literacy Trust recommends no more than half an hour of 'appropriate' viewing daily for tots under two.

Telly for tots: Helping your baby to get the most out of TV

- Watch with your child (whenever possible!) and talk about it while watching and afterwards, or base play around what she has seen, so her two-way communication skills get a boost from the experience.

- Don't have the television on in the background. Researchers have found that this can affect the quality and quantity of a child's play, and distract parents and children from listening and talking to one another.
- Make sure that what she's watching is age-appropriate. If you stick to channels such as Cbeebies, you can't go far wrong. Bear in mind that the pressures of advertising kick in early, if you're going to let her watch a commercial channel.
- Programmes with 'low stimulus' are best for babies – in other words, where there's not too much happening on screen. So something with a single adult presenter is ideal.
- Try not to get into the habit of daily viewing, or she'll soon come to expect it every day, and aim to switch off after half an hour. You can make it easier to enforce this by paying a little attention to TV schedules, so that you switch on as her favourite programme starts, and turn off once the credits roll. If you stick with favoured DVDs or videos, you can play them precisely when you want to.
- Don't worry if she wants to watch the same thing over and over again. In fact, it can be beneficial because repetition will help her to reinforce learning of words and phrases.

What the netmums say

Watching TV – good thing, bad thing?

Holly watches *In the Night Garden* with Daddy after tea and before bath, bottle and bed. She loves it, but we wouldn't encourage her to watch it on her own . . . it's something they do together. Gary knows all the words and songs!
Sarah from Ledbury, mum to Holly, nine months

I know it sounds awful, but my son *loves* Mickey Mouse Club House! I think it started because he just loved to look at all the contrasting colours. But now he gets excited whenever I put it on – and as soon at the 'Hot Dog Song' comes on at the end he goes crazy, laughing and kicking his legs! Don't get me wrong, I don't have him in front of the telly all day, but if he's grizzly and that show's on, it cheers him up instantly!

Daisy from Twickenham, mum to Freddie, seven months

My son fell in love with *Bear in the Big Blue House* when he was about six months old. I used to put it on for him while I got ready for work in the morning before our hike to the childminder. I think it contributed towards the fact that he could count to five before he was a year old, so no, I don't think TV is necessarily a bad thing for babies, and as long as it's monitored, I can't see the harm. I do think you've created a problem when they would rather stay indoors and watch television than go outside to have fun!

Dyanne from Dunfermline, mum to Luke, two

My stepmum has constantly told me that letting him watch TV as a baby would affect his speech and listening skills. But I've become quite relaxed about it now. I can see it's not great for them to sit in front of the television for long periods. But we get out and about lots during the day, and I don't think having the telly on for the odd half an hour will do him any harm. In fact, I actually believe the right programme can be very stimulating – and that's a good thing for young babies. Also it's great if you need a distraction for half an hour, to cook dinner or something.

Carly from Norwich, mum to Finley, seven months

Happy birthday, baby!

Hard to believe, but a year has gone by since you gave birth to your baby. Most parents are keen to mark the occasion in some way, but if you're planning to celebrate, aim to keep it a short, simple affair. Your baby won't appreciate, or even enjoy, too much excitement – and since birthday parties tend to require increasing levels of expense and imagination as the years go on, you may as well go for low-key while you can!

Keep the numbers down if possible – just a handful is ideal. Pick a good time – go for the morning if your baby generally naps in the afternoon. And keep your efforts minimal when it comes to catering – you'll probably have your hands full making sure your little one isn't crying or vomiting from the excitement of it all, so arrange a simple buffet, keeping crisps and sweet items to a minimum and steering clear of anything that could be a choking hazard and/or a common allergen, such as peanuts (which are both). A good rule at parties – for children of all ages – is that the sweets and treats only come out after some 'proper' food has been consumed.

A cake with a candle is a happy tradition, but you might want to keep the ceremony surrounding it short and sweet – a baby presented with a cake and the full attentions of an adoring crowd singing to her may be overwhelmed to the point of tears! Don't be tempted to give her more than a smallish slice, either, especially if she's not used to anything so rich. A bit of bunting or some brightly coloured streamers will add to the sense of celebration, but don't go over the top, as your efforts won't necessarily be appreciated. Avoid balloons, party poppers or anything else that could go off with a bang or make a loud noise (champagne corks excepted – pop out of her earshot!). She'll probably be feeling sensitive and maybe even a little scared with all the excitement, and won't need any unscheduled thrills or spills.

Don't expect too much from your baby if you do throw a bash and make her centre of attention – chances are she'll dissolve into tears, fall asleep or make a mess of her new party clothes at some point. After all – when it's your party, you can cry if you want to!

What the netmums say

First birthday celebrations

For Abi's first birthday we had a little celebration and a 'welcome to the family' party in her Grandad's big back garden – a bit like a naming ceremony, but not as formal, with lots of cake and lots of wine! We have family all over the country and it was nice for them to come together, especially as some had not met her yet. We said a few words, and her dad and I pledged to do our best by her, and chose some of our special friends to help give her guidance throughout life.

It was a wonderful day. There'll be plenty of opportunities for soft play, jelly and ice cream, party bags, etc, in the future!
Helen from Newcastle, mum to Abigail, two

My son's first birthday was more of a social gathering for friends and their babies. To make it a little more special I asked everyone to bring along a picture of themselves when they were one and had a 'guess who the baby is' competition. I also asked everyone to bring along something that I could put into a time capsule for my son to have when he reaches his 21st birthday.
Elaine from Ashford, mum to Matthew, eight and Katie, three

We didn't do anything particularly special for my elder daughter's first. Children that age don't really understand the concept of a party, so we just had the family round, gave her lots of presents, baked her a chocolate cake, and made a huge fuss of her. She loved it and it was a lot less stressful than having to make special arrangements. We'll be celebrating Jasmine's first birthday quietly, too, and relishing having her all to ourselves. No doubt parties will get bigger and more expensive as they get older!
Sara from Stafford, mum to Noor, three and Jasmine, 11 months

---

Memory box

Have your camera at the ready when your baby turns one. Save her birthday cards, and make a note of the presents she received. Her first-ever birthday has got to be something worth recording!

All About You

You've made it this far!

Well done, you. This must surely have been one of the most challenging years of your life so far, and you've reached the end of it in one piece. Most mums find their lives have changed beyond measure during the course of their first year of motherhood – for the better, of course!

What the netmums say

The first year of motherhood

Looking back, the first year changed my life more than I could have imagined. It was almost as though I was looking at the world through a mirror – everything was the same and yet completely different from before. I'd been through complete exhaustion and despair, then a surge of happiness and strength when I realised that I could cope. My relationship with my husband was tested to the extreme, but somehow we came through it. Most of all, everything had shifted. Things that I previously thought were important seemed less so, and I've become far calmer, less stressed and more able to cope with juggling and balancing my life.

Jen from Chorleywood, mum to Jack, four and Theo, one

It changed my life utterly, totally and completely – and definitely for the better! I had no idea I could be a mummy, but I could! I was never so tired or so happy in all my life and every second of lost sleep and pain was worth it a thousand times over (well, almost!). The love for my daughter was something I couldn't even have begun to imagine and no matter what else went on in my life, it didn't matter because my baby loved me and I loved her. Being a mummy is a true privilege and there aren't words to describe the excitement and love I feel when I look at my beautiful daughter. It opened up a whole new world for me, too. I now have friends (something I didn't have before she was born) because I've had to get out there and help her to find friends (thanks Netmums!). My only regret is that I didn't have a child earlier – I'm now a single parent, desperate for another child. The first year was brilliant and it's even better now. Just different. And a little more argumentative!

Kath from Nottingham, mum to Daisy, three

My first baby was difficult from the time he came out. What I have come to learn gradually – and still remind myself of – is that all babies are different and you cannot change that. My son is three years old now and his temperament has stayed with him. He's great fun and very bright, but still incredibly difficult at times. My advice is if you have a difficult child, acknowledge it and find the best support you can. And always ask for help. It took me a year to go and see my GP, who suspected PND. Find people who you can talk to and who may be in a similar situation. I found it much easier to confide in people who occasionally let rip about their child doing their head in. You need to be able to laugh about how bloody awful it can be! Comparing your child to others is the worst thing you can do and the thing you do most with your first born. Also, if you love your child, it will survive completely fine during its first year. What you need to concentrate on is making sure that you are OK.

Alix from Sheffield, mum to Dylan, three and Bevan, 11 months

I wish I hadn't even looked at any of those routine-obsessed baby books, and had the confidence to ignore them all from the word go! It was only when I started listening to Seth that things clicked. I also wish I'd been more aware of my health after he was born (I became hypothyroid after birth) and pushed for more help at the doctor's earlier. I also really wish I'd known how quickly time would go. When Seth was still waking four or five times a night at nine months I was frantic, but with my daughter I'm much calmer about sleepless nights, because I know now they are only for a relatively short while. I can't say I enjoyed the first six months. It was such a shock leaving work and being a stay-at-home mum. So much of my personality was invested in work that I felt lost. I was a teacher, and used to be able to see every day how well or badly I'd done. Results were measurable. So much of parenting a baby isn't measurable at all – it's only when they're NOT a serial killer at 20 that you see you did a good job. But now, 20 months in, I've relaxed into it, and allowed my pace of life to slow down to toddler speed.

Sheridan from Melbourn, mum to Seth, one and Stella, five months

The first year with my daughter was amazing. We were living away from our friends and family in a remote location and while this was hard, it made us very close. My other half worked long hours, and even when he was around, he struggled to come to terms with fatherhood and the extra demands made on him, and so it was all down to me. When I look back, I feel really pleased my daughter and I had that special time together and I'm proud of all I achieved. It was a lonely time, though, and I would say to any mum to think very carefully before moving away from your support network. What I did do, and what I think all new mums do, is worry over every little decision, and my advice would be not to worry too much. Try different things that YOU are happy with and find what works for you. And savour those times with your baby, because they are gone so fast!

I was shocked at how much love I felt for her, and at how much work it was – putting her first all the time, even if I was ill, tired, hungry or needed a rest. I sometimes wish I could go back to me then, and whisper in my ear to relax a bit, go with the flow more and to hold my baby girl again.

Heather from Sheffield, mum to Jasmine, four and Jack, two

It's been the hardest year of my life, in so many ways. The first three months were a blur, I didn't have a clue what I was doing. Then it started to get a bit better as I began to find my feet. The problem with babies, though, is that just when you think you've got it sussed, they change and it all goes out of the window! I wish I had been more confident at the beginning. I have far more faith in myself now than I did at the start and I believe I know what's best for my girl now. To be a happy mum, I think you need to have friends you can really talk to, and go out as much as possible. Sitting at home is the worst thing you can do!

Clare from Stockport, mum to Larissa, one

The first three months were incredibly hard. We had to deal with colic, and a lot of sickness after every feed. Then I had to go back into hospital for post-childbirth surgery at four weeks. We slowly got there, though, and things just kept getting easier. By six months, Bethany was constantly learning new ways to make us smile! The second half of the year went by so fast, I was trying to hang on to every moment, and I'm so glad I took so many photos and wrote so much in her baby books. There just wasn't time to treasure it all, but now I can look back whenever I want to.

It was definitely a year of ups and downs; the most exciting and scary and happy and challenging year of my life. I wouldn't have missed out on it for the world!

Beckie from Grimsby, mum to Bethany, one

We tried for 11 years before I finally got pregnant with Eve. I loved being pregnant, and had a reasonably easy labour – I thought, hey this is easy! But then came the constant breastfeeding, the colic, the lack of sleep. I can't remember much about Eve's first three months. And I really regret that. The irony isn't lost on me, that we tried for all those years and when I finally had Eve, it was completely different from how I had imagined it. It was also the most wonderful time of my life, watching this baby that I absolutely adored, growing and learning and laughing. Sometimes I did miss my old life of going out without a huge bag of supplies, and popping to the pub if we felt like it! But I wouldn't have missed it for the world – it was the hardest, yet most rewarding year of my life.

Mags from Bellshill, mum to Eve, two

When I think about my first year with my first daughter, I'm sure anyone else would think it was totally awful. I found out during pregnancy that she had Down's Syndrome, which was a big shock. It separates you from other new mums because all you can think is 'they have a normal baby, why don't I?' She had a huge hole in her heart and congenital cataracts. She had feeding difficulties. At eight weeks she had surgery on her eyes and soon after she went into heart failure, and had open heart surgery. My daughter was so brave throughout all of this. She smiled so much when she was in hospital, and loved to chatter to everyone. Her recovery following her operations has been amazing and I resolved to take her with me to lots of mums and toddlers groups, and not to hide her away as if I was embarrassed about her. She's such an outgoing little girl that she makes friends wherever we go. Looking back at that first year, things were initially difficult, but that's life. And mine has been transformed by this little bundle of fun. I've become a more thoughtful, caring person, more ready to see past people's 'shells' to what they're like on the inside.

My big tip for new mums is always to take a shower and get dressed first thing in the morning – perhaps when your baby has their first nap. It makes you feel much better, even if you're knackered, to be up and dressed. I think that doing this and making some time in the day to look after yourself (just brushing your teeth, applying moisturiser and make-up, etc) are essential. As is getting out as much as possible with your babies.

Lucy from Neston, mum to Ciara, two and twins Greg and Niamh, nine months

I loved being a mum so much that I was pregnant with my second baby when my first was six months old! The first year goes so fast and they learn so much, and grow, without you really realising it – one minute they're tiny, the next they are up to your knees! I'll never forget the first time my daughter ran into the kitchen, it was such a moment I had to sit down for a second. Now I'm into the second year and have another in tow and it just keeps getting better. You will never experience love, guilt, worry, happiness and sadness all at the same time as you do during the first year of parenthood!

Tracey from Liss, mum to Brooke, two and Gracie, eight months

The first year of motherhood was such a rollercoaster. But I loved it so much we'd already decided to try for number two by the time Noor was nine months! It seems to me that the first year is the biggest year of parenthood, with the most excitement and the most development and change. It's incredible to me that someone so tiny and helpless can turn into such a go-getting, fun, active, intelligent little person in such a short space of time. By the time they hit one, you have an idea of their personality and seeing that character emerging at such close quarters is such a privilege. It's when you start to fall in love with the person your child is rather than simply the idea of what she will become. And when it's your first baby, you just have so much time to focus on those amazing developments.

Sara from Stafford, mum to Noor, three and Jasmine, 11 months

The first year of our son's life was a huge learning curve for all of us. When he popped out into the world with no manual to tell me what to do or how to do it, I was pretty darn scared, to say the least! I wished they'd warned us in antenatal classes that it's hard bloomin' work caring for a new baby – the constant crying and feeding, as well as the lack of sleep! However, it all changes once they learn to communicate with you through smiles and laughs. Being a mother during the first year (and even now) is the hardest thing I've ever had to do – the best unpaid job, and the most rewarding! I cried on his first birthday. I couldn't believe how far we'd come in such a short space of time. He'd gone from this little bundle who didn't know what to do other than breathe, to this laughing, talking, crawling, walking, tantrumming little man! I was proud of all of us (still am!) and our journey. It didn't end there, of course, another new chapter opened.

Dyanne from Dunfermline, mum to Luke, two

Appendix 1:
Health and First Aid A–Z

The following A–Z is a basic guide to the main medical and first-aid issues likely to crop up during your baby's first year. For a proper diagnosis, and treatment of any symptoms that you are not sure about, you should always seek help from your GP. You can get medical advice over the telephone from NHS Direct (if you live in England and Wales) on 0845 4647 or NHS 24 (if you live in Scotland) on 08454 242424. *Don't forget to keep a note of your doctor's and health visitor's numbers, and the number for NHS Direct or equivalent pinned up by the telephone.*

In the event of a medical emergency or accident, if in any doubt at all, take your child to the nearest casualty unit, or dial 999.

Terms in bold print are referred to elsewhere in the A–Z.

A

Allergy: An immediate, adverse response caused when the body's immune system overreacts to a specific trigger substance, or allergen. Common allergens include certain foods, such as nuts, wheat and dairy products. Non-food allergens include pollen and animal hair. Symptoms of an allergic reaction may include an itchy rash, sneezing, red eyes, **vomiting**, **wheezing** and swelling around the mouth. The most severe, and thankfully very rare, form of allergic reaction (anaphylaxis) is most commonly caused by nuts. For more on allergies and advice on what to do in the event of an allergic attack, see pp. 133 and 166.

Antipyretics: Drugs that reduce fever (high temperature). There are two main forms that are suitable for babies under one: paracetamol (such as Calpol) and ibuprofen (such as Neurofen for Children), and both also work as analgesics, i.e. they give pain relief. Fever is a symptom of many different conditions, so one or both of these products are essential items for your medicine cabinet. However, it's vital always to read the label carefully before giving any medicine to your child. You need to be sure you give the right sort (only use one specifically marketed for babies), that your baby is an appropriate age and weight – paracetamol is suitable from two months, but only if your baby weighs more than 4kg (9lb); ibuprofen from three months, but only if your baby weighs more than 5kg (11lb) – and that you get the dose correct. These drugs *can* be given earlier but only under medical supervision, and, in any case, it's always wise to seek help from your doctor if a baby under three months has a fever.

Ibuprofen and paracetamol work in different ways, so it's safe to give both at the same time, or alternate them with short periods in between, for even more effective pain relief. For example, usually each drug can be given every six hours – by alternating them, you can give medicine every three hours. Do ask for medical advice before administering medicine this frequently, though, to rule out any potentially serious causes of fever. Occasionally, a high temperature can indicate a dangerous illness, such as **meningitis**, so you should always be alert to any other symptoms and seek help if the fever is persistent and not responding to the medicine. For more on controlling your baby's temperature, see Fever.

Apgar scale/score: Routine and speedy assessment of important health basics, such as skin colour, muscle tone, breathing and heart rate, carried out on a baby straight after birth by a health professional. Its purpose is to determine if a newborn needs urgent medical attention, not to make any long-term predictions about her health.

Aspirin: Commonly used drug given to adults for pain relief and to reduce high temperature. It should never be given to babies (or any child under 16) because it's been associated with the very rare but often fatal disease Reye's syndrome. Doctors may prescribe it to children for a few rare conditions, however, such as **Kawasaki disease**, or after cardiac surgery or a stroke.

Asthma: The most common chronic respiratory disorder in children, although it's fairly unusual for a diagnosis to be made before a child is a year old. One of the main symptoms is **wheezing**, which is common in babies when linked to viral infections, but rarely due to asthma.

Children are more at risk of developing asthma if they have **eczema** or allergies, or if a close relative has any of these conditions. Exposure to a trigger, such as exercise, animal hair, dust mites, cold air or cigarette smoke, results in narrowing of the airways in the lung, causing coughing, wheezing, breathlessness and chest tightness.

There's no cure for asthma, but treatment in the form of drugs, given via inhalers, can improve long-term prospects. For babies and children, a spacer – a plastic or metal container which the inhaler is fixed to, with a mouthpiece or mask at the other end – is often used to administer this medicine as it's easier and more effective. Avoiding specific triggers, such as cigarette smoke, can help. If tests reveal an allergy to house dust mites, some simple measures can be taken to alleviate the symptoms, such as using mattress covers and special pillows, hoovering when your child is not in the house and limiting her to one or two fluffy toys, which can be put in the freezer overnight regularly to kill any dust mites they may be harbouring. Severe asthma attacks can be dangerous and require emergency treatment.

B

Back pain: A common complaint for new mums, caused by pressure on the spine during pregnancy and the release of hormones that soften up the joints and ligaments for birth. Back pain is often made worse by poor posture while feeding, lifting or carrying the baby. Self-help is the most effective way to relieve it, in the form of regular, gentle exercise and careful attention to posture. There's more detail on these things on p. 245.

BCG vaccine: Injection that offers protection against tuberculosis (TB), an infectious disease that affects the lungs and other parts of the body and can cause a serious form of **meningitis**. Although still relatively unusual in the UK, cases are on the increase. Schoolchildren used to receive a routine BCG vaccination, but this has been replaced with a programme targeting those most likely to be at risk. Your baby may be offered a BCG vaccination if you live in an area where rates of tuberculosis are relatively high, or if you or your partner, or if any of your baby's grandparents, come from a country where TB is common. High risk areas are those where the incidence of TB is 40 or more cases per 100,000 people per year: your health visitor will let you know if you live in one.

Birthmarks: Coloured marks that develop on, or just below, the skin before, or soon after, birth. Known medically as naevi (naevus is the singular), birthmarks are common and come in many different forms. As many as one in three babies are born with a birthmark of some description. Some fade with time, others are permanent unless removed. Most birthmarks are harmless but some may require treatment for cosmetic reasons, or for a variety of medical ones (for instance, if a birth mark growing close to the eye is affecting vision, if one on the throat is affecting breathing, or one on the legs is rubbing and causing chafing. Birthmarks can also cause problems when they occur internally.)

Among the most common are the strawberry mark (capillary haemangioma), a raised red patch, which usually increases in size before gradually disappearing at some point over six to seven years; salmon patches (known as stork bites if they're on the nape of the neck), which are pink, flat and usually fade to nothing within a few years or even months; and Mongolian blue spots (congenital dermal melanocytosis), dark areas of skin usually found on the bottom or back and more common in babies of African or Asian birth.

Port-wine stains (naevi flammei) persist through childhood and tend to darken and thicken in adulthood. Effective treatments are available, and often it's better to treat early. You should seek medical advice if you suspect your child has one of these, especially if it's positioned on one side of the face because this may be a symptom of the rare Sturge-Weber syndrome, which is linked with epilepsy.

More information is available from the Birthmark Support Group (telephone 0845 045 4700; www.birthmarksupportgroup.org.uk).

Bronchiolitis: The most common serious respiratory infection of infancy. Bronchiolitis is caused by a virus, usually respiratory syncytial virus (RSV), which is at large during the winter months and is spread in saliva or mucus through coughs and sneezes, causing the smallest airways of the lungs (bronchioles) to become inflamed. Very young babies are at risk of bronchiolitis, especially if they were born prematurely, or have other medical problems.

A baby with bronchiolitis first develops a runny nose, which leads, after a few days, to a cough and increasing breathlessness and, usually, a high temperature (fever). There's often no real treatment and most cases can be managed at home, keeping fever down with **antipyretics** and giving regular small feeds. Saline nasal drops can aid breathing and help your baby to feed – these are available from the chemist, or your GP can prescribe them.

It's important to seek medical advice, because a baby with bronchiolitis may need to be admitted to hospital if she requires oxygen, or is drinking less than half of what she would normally take and is becoming dehydrated. Very rarely, the infection can be so serious that an infant will need to go into intensive care. Most recover after two weeks, but a small proportion are at risk of having recurrent episodes of coughing and wheezing over the next three to five years.

C

Chickenpox: Often mild but highly infectious disease, caused by the varicella zoster virus. Symptoms, including an itchy red rash of fluid-filled blisters that burst to form scabs, and a fever, take between ten and 21 days to appear after contact with the virus. A child is contagious for two days *before* the rash appears and then until all the blisters have crusted over. The disease is spread by breathing in droplets in the air that contain the virus. Generally, children with chickenpox are treated with fluids, **antipyretics** and creams to reduce the itch. Very few are admitted to hospital. However, chickenpox may lead to a number of rare or serious complications, including bacterial infection (when infection spreads into the body via one of the blisters) and encephalitis (infection spreading to the fluid surrounding the brain).

Chickenpox is fairly unusual in babies under one, who usually have some immunity if their mother has already had it. For the same reason, symptoms will usually be mild if a young baby *does* get chickenpox. However, if you know you have never had chickenpox and your baby comes into contact with someone with the disease (usually defined as close contact for more than 15 minutes), seek advice from your GP.

Cleft lip or palate: A split or opening in the top lip or palate (the roof of the mouth), or sometimes in both. This is the most common birth defect in the UK, affecting one in every 600–700 babies. Babies with clefts, particularly of the palate, may have problems with feeding at birth and then later on with speech, hearing and their teeth. Occasionally, babies have breathing problems from birth. Treatment is by surgery. A cleft lip is repaired early on, within the first three months, while the soft palate is operated on at around six months. If the problem is more severe, involving the hard palate and teeth, repair is usually by bone graft when the permanent teeth are through. A cleft palate is one of the things looked for at the routine baby check. If found, you may be seen by a specialist nurse, who will advise you on the common problems. More information is available from the Cleft Lip and Palate Association (020 7833 4883; www.clapa.com).

Club foot: See Talipes.

Coeliac disease: A condition that affects the lining of the small bowel, and is caused by sensitivity to gluten, the protein found in wheat, barley, and rye. It may lead to growth problems as well as abnormal stools and abdominal distension (a very swollen tummy) in young children, and appears after weaning when food products containing gluten are introduced. However, it's important to be aware that ordinary food intolerances can cause similar symptoms, and can often be confused with coeliac disease.

If coelic disease is suspected, your baby will need to undergo a screening test and, if the result is positive, a biopsy of the bowel to confirm the diagnosis. There's no cure and the only way to manage the condition, and to avoid the development of other more serious bowel diseases, such as cancer, is to stick to a gluten-free diet for life.

Colic: See Infant colic.

Common cold: Upper respiratory tract infection caused by one of several hundred viruses and usually spread through coughs and sneezes, or hand-o-hand contact. As the name suggests, these viruses are very common indeed – the average baby may catch up to ten of them in her first year. Symptoms include a cough, sore throat, blocked or runny nose, raised temperature and loss of appetite (and sleep!). There's no cure, although you can help by making sure your baby gets plenty of rest and ensuring her fluid intake is good, by giving regular, small feeds. If she's over six months and is refusing her usual solid foods, that's fine, as long as she's well hydrated – look for a moist mouth, and lots of wet nappies – and is taking her usual milk feeds. Treatment with infant paracetamol or ibuprofen may ease some symptoms but other over-the-counter oral medicines, such as cough mixtures, are often not appropriate for babies and are considered to have little benefit. You can ease blocked noses and aid feeding with the use of saline nasal drops – ask your GP or pharmacist about these. Sore noses can be soothed with a little Vaseline. It will also help if you keep her at the right temperature – warm, but not overheated.

You should see your GP if your baby's cold persists beyond ten days or if she develops other symptoms, such as an earache or breathing problems.

Congenital hypothyroidism: Disorder of the thyroid gland. This is one of the genetic diseases routinely screened for soon after birth with the **Guthrie or heel prick test.** The thyroid gland produces thyroxine, a hormone that has many important functions, especially its role in brain development. If congenital hypothyroidism is detected late, it may lead to permanent development abnormalities – one of the reasons why this test is so important.

Conjunctivitis: Inflammation of the conjunctiva, the whites of the eyes, caused either by an infection (viral or bacterial), irritant or allergy. Symptoms include red, sore, swollen, watery or itchy eyes, sometimes accompanied by a sticky discharge, which can usually be gently wiped away with some cooled boiled water and a clean piece of cotton wool for each wipe. The condition may clear up on its own but may need treatment in the form of antibiotic drops or ointment, so you should always seek advice from a GP. When a baby develops infective conjunctivitis within the first 28 days of birth it's known as neonatal conjunctivitis, and is usually the result of a bacterial infection picked up from the mother's vagina during birth.

Constipation: Condition that causes stools (poo) to be hard, making it difficult and painful for your baby to empty her bowels and leading to them being opened infrequently (less than twice a week). Symptoms to look out for are obvious tummy pain, a solid abdomen and hard or pellet-like stools or no sign of any stools at all. Constipation is rare in exclusively breastfed babies, because breast milk is so easy to digest, but can affect formula-fed babies if too much powder is used in their feeds, which is why it's vital to measure out and make up feeds as directed. However, it's normal for babies under six months to go a couple of days without a bowel movement and this may not necessarily mean they are constipated. It's common for babies going through the weaning process to become constipated while their digestive systems are getting used to the new composition of their food – and because their fluid intake often drops at the same time. Becoming constipated can be the start of a vicious circle for a baby, because if it hurts to try to poo, she will hold it in instead, compounding the problem.

You can ease constipation by lying your baby on her back and gently massaging her stomach, or pushing her legs gently in a cycling motion, to help get her digestive system moving. You can also give her water (boiled and cooled if she's not yet six months old) and if she's weaned, you can offer more fibre-rich solids, such as fruit and vegetables – prune purée or juice can be a great help. Your GP may also prescribe a laxative treatment, usually in the form of a syrup, or powder to be dissolved in liquid. These are also available over the counter, but do always seek advice from a doctor before giving your baby something like this, because it's vital to get the dose right. It's safe to give your baby laxative treatments for a prolonged period, but always see your GP if the constipation persists. Symptoms that may suggest your baby doesn't have simple constipation include vomiting, weight loss and – in the first 48 hours after birth – delayed passage of meconium (the sticky black poo that's passed in the first few days).

Contact dermatitis: Skin complaint that causes redness, soreness, itching and cracking of the skin. It occurs as a result of a sensitive reaction to an external irritant, such as a nappy, wee or diarrhoea, or allergen, such as a bath product or laundry detergent, often in the nappy area. It should be treated as **nappy rash**, but you will need to pinpoint the cause in order to avoid it in the future.

Cradle cap (seborrhoeic dermatitis or seborrhoeic eczema): A harmless, scaly, flaky covering of the scalp, very common in young babies. The cause is unknown, and it can persist for many months, but will usually clear up on its own before a child is two. Rarely, it may spread to other parts of the body in the form of a red rash, notably in the nappy area where it may be mistaken for **nappy rash** – if this occurs, an anti-fungal cream may be prescribed. The scalp should be kept clean, using very mild shampoos, or your doctor may be able to prescribe a special medicated formulation.

Massaging a little olive oil or aqueous cream (available on prescription from your GP, or over the counter) into the head at night can help to loosen the crust. Avoid nut-based oils, such as almond or peanut oil, because of the risk of **allergies**, and commercial baby oils, which aren't natural. Although tempting, it's important not to pick at the scales because this can lead to soreness and infection. If your baby's scalp does become infected, see your GP because it will require treatment.

Cranial osteopathy: Alternative treatment involving gentle manipulation of a baby's head, based on the theory that birth can put extreme pressure on the bones in the head causing tension and discomfort. Practioners apply light pressure with their hands to specific points of the head, in an attempt to help release tension. There's no real medical evidence that it works, although some parents report that it has helped with **infant colic**, sleeplessness and feeding problems. Do bear in mind that you will have to pay for this treatment – it's not offered on the NHS but do check with your GP first. It's always best to do so if you are considering any alternative therapies, particularly if you plan to stop any existing treatments your baby is receiving.

Croup: An infection, usually viral, that affects the larynx (voicebox) and trachea (the large airway to the lungs) in babies over six months old. Symptoms often become worse at night, especially on waking, and include a harsh, barking cough and, in more severe cases, a rasping sound when breathing in. This is known as inspiratory stridor. Other symptoms include a runny nose and high temperature. Croup usually gets better on its own and you can ease the symptoms at home by keeping your baby calm, and giving her **antipyretics**. Sometimes a little cold air can help, so it's worth opening the window or wrapping her up well and going outside for a little while.

You should seek medical advice promptly if your child has stridor with every breath, and dial 999 if she also appears to be drowsy, or her face or lips appear blue.

Cystic fibrosis (CF): An hereditary, life-limiting disease that predominantly affects the lungs, but also the digestive system. Currently there is no cure but medical advances mean a child born with CF today has a good chance of reaching mid-adulthood. This is one of the conditions routinely tested for soon after birth with the **Guthrie or heel prick test.** For more information, contact the Cystic Fibrosis Trust (telephone 0845 859 1000; www.cftrust.org.uk).

D

Deep vein thrombosis: See **Thrombosis.**

Dehydration: What happens when the body loses water, which is essential for good health, often as a result of **fever, vomiting** or **diarrhoea**, or from simple overheating, as in sunstroke. Babies are particularly at risk, and if left, dehydration can become dangerous. Symptoms include a pale appearance, sunken eyes or fontanelle (the soft spot on the top of your baby's head), few wet nappies, dry mouth and lips, irritability and a lack of energy. If you think your baby's dehydrated, try to give her plenty of fluids in the form of milk feeds and water. Your GP may also prescribe an oral rehydration solution, which can help to replace any fluid losses. These solutions are available over the counter, but it's always best to check with a doctor or other health professional first, before administering one of them. It's also important not to give a solution for too long. If your baby hasn't vomited for four hours, you can reintroduce milk feeds.

Diarrhoea: Frequent, very runny stools (poo), not to be confused with the occasional loose stools that are often seen in breastfed babies. Diarrhoea will usually be very runny and smelly, and may be streaked with mucus. It is often accompanied by other symptoms, such as a **fever.** The most common cause of diarrhoea is the **rotavirus**, although badly made up formula milk, food poisoning, allergies or food intolerance may also be to blame.

The main risk is **dehydration**, which can be dangerous, so it's important to seek advice from your GP if your baby is suffering from diarrhoea. It can persist for up to a few weeks, which is all right if your baby isn't vomiting and is taking fluids. If it persists for too long, or your child continues to lose weight, your GP may prescribe a special pre-digested milk (if she is formula fed) that allows her guts to recover. If breastfeeding, you'll be advised to carry on in most cases as it's naturally easy to digest.

Diastasis recti: Temporary condition that occurs naturally in the majority of women during pregnancy and can persist afterwards. The pressure of the growing baby stretches the connective tissues between the two bands of the main tummy muscle (rectus abdominus) causing them to separate from one another. This will right itself, but gentle exercise can boost repair. For more information, see p. 79.

Diphtheria: Life-threatening disease that can cause breathing problems and damage the heart and nervous system. It is one of the diseases that UK children are offered protection against through routine vaccinations at two, three and four months old, and is now very rare in this country. For more information on **immunisations**, see pp. 58 and 89.

E
Earache: Pain in one or both ears, often caused by an **ear infection** but sometimes due to a simple build-up of mucus in the middle ear, usually after a cold. It won't always be obvious if your baby is suffering, although if she's tugging at her ear, that can be an indication. Earache on its own can be treated at home with an appropriate painkiller, such as infant paracetamol or ibuprofen. Your baby may also get some relief from a well-covered hot-water bottle placed under her ear. The mucus will usually clear up on its own once the infection's gone – although some may remain, causing dulled hearing for a little while, and occasionally a continued build-up can lead to the development of **glue ear.**

Ear infection (acute otitis media): The most common cause of earache in children. Many babies have ear infections, especially during the winter months. They are caused by mucus building up in the middle ear and becoming infected. As well as painful earache, symptoms may include a **fever**

and a runny nose. Sometimes the eardrum will burst, letting out some of the infected mucus. This is nothing to be alarmed by, and will often relieve the pain. Ear infections are usually caused by viruses, so can often be treated at home (see **Earache**) but if symptoms are severe or persistent, your doctor may diagnose a bacterial infection and prescribe medication. After an ear infection, your baby's hearing may be affected for up to four weeks. Go back to your GP if this goes on for longer. Repeated bouts of ear infections can lead to glue ear. Very rarely, the infection can spread to the bone behind the ear causing a serious infection known as mastoiditis, and, more rarely still, to the inner ear and brain, so it's important to seek help if the problem persists or symptoms worsen. You can reduce your baby's chance of getting ear infections by breastfeeding, avoiding dummy use (or being scrupulous about hygiene if she does have a dummy) and not allowing anyone to smoke around her.

Eczema (atopic dermatitis): A chronic, inflammatory skin condition that usually develops in early childhood, quite commonly during the first year, affecting up to 20 per cent of children. It often has a genetic component that causes the skin to be more susceptible to certain trigger factors, including irritants and allergens, which make the eczema worse. The skin, especially in skin creases, becomes red, sore, itchy, dry and cracked in varying degrees. Children with eczema have a high chance of also suffering from asthma or hay fever. Fortunately, the majority grow out of it later in childhood or by their teens.

Effective treatment for eczema is vital as persistent scratching can make it worse, with areas becoming raw, weeping, crusted and infected. Regular use of an emollient (a special moisturising cream or ointment) can help to restore the natural skin barrier and ease symptoms. There are many types and your GP can help you find the right one. Sometimes stronger treatment in the form of topical steroids (which come in the form of creams or lotions) are needed. These are usually highly effective and aren't harmful if given for very short periods of less than two weeks. However, they vary in strength so should never be used without medical supervision. Avoid trigger factors, such as perfumed soaps and biological detergents, and make sure your baby wears pure cotton clothing next to her skin. Although many complementary therapies are available, there's no evidence to suggest they work better than conventional treatment. If you do try any, it's important to continue using emollients at the same time.

For more information, contact the National Eczema Society (telephone 0800 089 1122; www.eczema.org).

F

Febrile convulsions (febrile seizures): Fits that are fairly common in babies over six months and young children. They are triggered by a high temperature, which is often the result of an infection or other illness. Some babies and children are more prone to them than others, especially if they've had one before, or a family member has suffered from them.

A child having a febrile convulsion may shake, jerk, go floppy or stiffen, turn pale, stop breathing briefly or lose consciousness. Her eyes may roll upwards, and she may wet or soil herself. It can be very scary for a parent to watch. Most febrile convulsions are over within a few minutes, after which the child will often sleep deeply. No treatment is required, and the convulsions do not cause any long-term health problems. However, if your baby is having a fit for the first time, it's advisable to dial 999. If she has had a fit before and you are confident about coping with it, it's OK to wait for up to three minutes before dialling 999: in most cases, the fit will be over by then and if not, it's important to get help. A child who suffers from febrile convulsions will normally grow out of them by the time she is six.

Febrile convulsions are not to be confused with epilepsy, a serious condition characterised by seizures occurring when the child has a normal temperature. The likelihood of your child developing epilepsy if she's had a febrile convulsion is minimal, unless there are other risk factors, such as family history.

Fever (high temperature): In children, a temperature above 38°C (100.4°F). High temperature or fever is a common symptom of a number of illnesses, including minor infections, such as colds and flu (see **Influenza**). Fever is not in itself dangerous (it's the body's way of fighting an infection) but can sometimes be an indication of conditions that are, such as **meningitis**. In most cases, fever can be treated at home with an appropriate medicine to reduce it, such as infant paracetamol or ibuprofen (see **Antipyretics**). You can also help by keeping your child cool – remove her clothes if necessary, and sponge her with tepid water. Don't use cold water as this will make her blood vessels constrict, making matters worse.

The best way to check your baby's temperature is with a thermometer. A number of different sorts are available, suitable for babies, and many parents find them a reassuring piece of medical equipment to have in the cabinet.

It can be difficult to know what's causing a fever and, very occasionally, it can indicate a serious condition, so if you're worried, you should seek advice from your GP or nearest casualty unit. You should always seek advice if a fever persists for more than two days.

Flu: See **Influenza.**

G

Gastroenteritis: Infection of the gut, caused by a virus or food poisoning, which causes **vomiting** and **diarrhoea**, as well as tummy pains and **fever**. It usually lasts for several days and clears up on its own. The main risk is **dehydration** so it's important to keep offering your baby her normal breast or bottle feeds. If she's refusing these, or bringing them up, you may need to give her an oral rehydration solution, which your GP can prescribe, during the vomiting phase, but you should reintroduce milk feeds if she's stopped vomiting for four to six hours. The diarrhoea can persist for up to two weeks, although that condition should show signs of improving in the second week – it's nothing to be too concerned about, as long as your baby's feeding and putting on weight. Always see a doctor if you notice blood in your baby's poo. If she is unable to keep oral rehydration solution down, is becoming increasingly listless, has stopped passing urine or is vomiting green bile, you should get her to your nearest casualty unit, because it may mean she is dehydrated. Rehydration treatment in hospital usually involves giving fluid via a nasal tube, or occasionally via a drip, which administers fluid through the bloodstream.

Gastro-oesophageal reflux (acid reflux or reflux): Regurgitation of the acidic contents of the stomach back into the oesophagus (foodpipe), and sometimes up to the throat, causing vomiting or posseting. It occurs because the valve action of the lower oesophageal sphincter – the muscular ring at the lower end of the oesophagus – isn't yet fully developed, and is very common. Up to 65 per cent of young babies are affected to some extent.

Symptoms vary in severity. When a baby with reflux is otherwise well and gaining weight, no treatment is needed and in most cases she will grow out if it by the time she is 18 months, usually once she's well established on solids and starting to walk, and therefore spending more time upright. In more serious cases, reflux can prevent a baby from gaining weight if she is unable to keep enough milk down, or because the discomfort causes poor feeding. Giving small, frequent feeds can help, as can holding your baby upright during feeds and for a while afterwards – putting her down to sleep on a cot mattress that's been raised to a 45 degree angle with a cushion underneath the head end, for example. Your GP may prescribe medication, such as Infant Gaviscon, which can be added to a milk feed or mixed with a little cooled boiled water and given on a spoon if you are breastfeeding. It works by thickening the contents of the stomach, making them less likely to come back up again. There are also medications that can help to reduce the acid in your baby's stomach, so she suffers less discomfort. However, in most cases, reflux is something that your baby will grow out of. Some babies with other health issues, particularly neurological problems, may have more serious reflux that will not simply go away, and occasionally in these cases, surgery might be needed. For more information, visit www.livingwithreflux.org.

Glue ear (otitis media with effusion): Build-up of sticky fluids in the middle ear, often caused by repeated bouts of ear infections, which can dull a baby's hearing and may even affect her speech development. Your GP may send you and your baby to a specialist for an assessment, but in most cases you'll be advised against treatment because the fluid usually drains away on its own, and normal hearing resumes, although this can take up to a year. Later, if the problem persists and threatens to affect hearing and speech and language development, your baby may be referred for grommet insertion – a tiny tube is inserted in the eardrum to allow air to pass into the middle ear, helping it to drain any build-up.

Guthrie or heel prick test: Routine screening process carried out about five days after birth, involving a tiny sample of blood being taken from your baby's heel. For more information on the Guthrie test, see p. 10.

H

Heatstroke: Potentially serious consequence of exposure to sun (see **Sunburn**).

Hernia: See **Inguinal hernia** and **Umbilical hernia.**

Hib: Infection caused by Haemophilus influenzae type b bacteria, which can lead to a number of serious diseases, such as septicaemia, **pneumonia** and **meningitis**. UK children are offered protection against Hib with routine vaccinations given at two, three and four months old. For more information, see p. 58.

I

Immunisations (vaccinations): Series of injections given to your baby over the course of her early years. They give protection against a variety of serious diseases including tetanus, polio, diphtheria, meningitis C and measles, mumps and rubella (MMR). For more information about the immunisations your baby will be offered during her first year, see p. 58.

Impetigo: Skin condition caused by bacteria entering broken skin, through a cut, cold sore or patch of **eczema**, for instance. Symptoms include breakouts of blisters that burst and release a yellow fluid, leaving the skin underneath red and sore. This then dries out to form an itchy crust. Your GP will prescribe antibiotic cream or syrup, and the infection can be expected to clear up after a few days. It's highly contagious and spread by physical contact, so it's important to keep your baby away from other children until the spots stop crusting, and to pay careful attention to hygiene at home – wash your hands regularly, and keep your baby's sponge and towel away from any others. If the impetigo keeps coming back, the whole family may need to be tested and treated.

Infant colic: The term used to describe bouts of inconsolable and often inexplicable crying, typically occuring in the late afternoon and evening, which are common in babies during their first three months. Since its cause is unknown – although there are a number of theories – there's no cure, but it can be soothed and relieved in several different ways, usually applied on a trial and error basis. However, it's important to rule out any genuine medical causes for the crying, such as **gastro-oesophageal reflux**. For more on colic, see p. 60.

Infantile acne: Outbreaks of harmless, red, sometimes pus-filled spots on a baby's face, and a general roughening of her skin. Infantile acne, which is similar in appearance to adult acne, is thought to be due to the passing of hormones from mum to baby in the latter stages of pregnancy and may occur immediately after birth or a few weeks afterwards. It clears up on its own within a few weeks, but it's a good idea to keep the skin clean with a mild soap in the meantime. Don't be tempted to pick or squeeze the spots, because this may result in an infection.

Influenza (flu): Infectious upper respiratory tract disease caused by a virus and transmitted, like the common cold, through coughs and sneezes, and direct contact. Symptoms are similar to those of the **cold** and so the two are often confused, but with flu there may also be chills, **fever**, nausea and **vomiting**, aching muscles and exhaustion. Most babies will recover from flu within a week or so (it is not dangerous to healthy babies in the same way it is to elderly people, who will often have other health issues such as heart problems and lowered immunity), although a cough may linger for a while. Treatment is rest and plenty of fluids, while some infant paracetamol or ibuprofen may reduce a high temperature and ease aches. A vaccine is recommended for children with chronic respiratory disorders, but it is not given routinely.

Inguinal hernia: A protrusion (bulging) in the groin, caused by a weakness in the muscle of the abdominal wall, more common in boy babies and those born prematurely. This bulging contains part of the intestine and usually appears if your baby's been crying or straining. Your doctor will usually be able to pop it back in temporarily – and may even teach you how to do so. However, it will need surgery to repair permanently and, in the meantime, it's important to keep an eye on it as there's a risk of a potentially serious complication occurring if the hernia becomes strangulated (twisted). You should seek medical advice if your baby seems unwell, or you notice any skin changes around the lump. A baby with an inguinal hernia is usually referred to a specialist surgical team, but the procedure is routine and involves an overnight stay, unless carried out in an emergency. There's a chance a hernia will occur on the other side, so the surgeon usually repairs both sides.

J

Jaundice: A yellow tinge to the skin and whites of the eyes. This is a very common condition in newborns – around half are affected to one degree or another – and especially in those born prematurely. It's caused by a build-up of bilirubin – a yellow substance found in bile, which is usually removed from the body by the liver – and occurs because the liver is immature and not yet functioning properly. Jaundice develops on day two after birth and usually goes, without the need for treatment, within a couple of weeks. (Although some people advise putting babies with jaundice in sunlight, this shouldn't be necessary and may put them at risk of sunburn.) However, in more severe cases, a baby with jaundice may need some phototherapy, which involves her being put under an ultraviolet light for a while. Occasionally, a blood transfusion is necessary. Jaundice can be an indication of some serious conditions, and in rare cases a build-up of bilirubin can cause dangerous complications, so it's important to have any worrying signs checked by your midwife, health visitor or GP. You should be concerned if your baby seems to look more yellow and has become more tired, is missing feeds or is losing weight. She may then be referred for a test at the hospital to check her levels of bilirubin.

K

Kawasaki disease: Rare illness that affects up to 2000 under-fives a year, and causes a wide range of symptoms, including a prolonged fever, conjunctivitis, a rash, swollen and red hands and feet, and red, dry or swollen lips and tongue. Children from Asian or Afro-Caribbean backgrounds are more at risk. The cause is unknown and diagnosis is often difficult. With prompt hospital treatment, a full recovery is possible. However, there is a small risk of serious complications, including heart problems.

M

Mastitis: Painful inflammation of the breast. It affects up to 10 per cent of breastfeeding mums and may cause a red, hot, sore or swollen patch on the breast, or flu-like symptoms. Taking paracetamol may ease the symptoms and won't harm your baby. There are two forms of mastitis – infectious and non-infectious. There's more on both, including their treatment, on p. 22.

Measles: Highly infectious viral disease, which is unusual these days thanks to the routine MMR (measles, mumps, rubella) vaccine that was introduced in 1988 and is given to babies at around 13 months (although with the recent scare over a possible link between MMR and autism, and therefore an increase in children not being vaccinated, the number of cases has risen again. The research that lead to the scare has since been discredited). Symptoms include fever, cough, red eyes and a rash that starts at the head and spreads over the rest of the body over a few days. Treatment is not normally necessary other than giving fluids and **antipyretics** but, rarely, very serious complications can occur, including **pneumonia**, and encephalitis (inflammation of the brain), which can be fatal.

If a child over six months who hasn't had the MMR vaccine comes into contact with measles, she can be given the vaccine early, because this can kick start the immune system into combating the virus before the illness takes hold. If the child is under six months, and her mother has had measles in the past, she will usually have immunity to the disease because her mother will have passed on protective antibodies during pregnancy. Otherwise, where a baby or child is at risk she may be offered an injection of human normal immunoglobulin (HNIG), a special concentration of antibodies that can give immediate short-term protection against the disease.

The Department of Health strongly advises that all children have the MMR vaccine at 13 months of age and then again at around four years of age, to promote long-term protection. For more information on this and all other immunisation issues, visit www.immunisation.nhs.uk.

Medium Chain Acyl-CoA Dehydrogenase Deficiency (MCADD): Rare, inherited disorder that interrupts the breakdown of fats, leading to a toxic build-up which if not treated can cause serious symptoms and lead to coma and even death. MCADD is among those conditions screened for soon after birth during the **Guthrie or heel prick test.**

Meningitis: Inflammation of the lining of the brain and spinal cord (the meninges), usually resulting from infection caused by viruses or bacteria. Viral meningitis is usually much less severe than bacterial meningitis, and more commonly affects teenagers and young adults rather than babies. A full recovery can be expected. Bacterial meningitis is caused by different types of bacteria, including meningococcus and Hib, and is much more common in childhood than among adults. This is much more serious and can result in death or complications such as brain damage or deafness. Vaccination has effectively reduced the incidence of bacterial meningitis caused by meningococcus C and Hib, but there is no vaccine against meningococcus B.

The early signs and symptoms of meningitis are non-specific, which makes early diagnosis difficult. Infants and young children may show any combination of fever, poor feeding, **vomiting**, high-pitched crying, irritability and drowsiness. Later signs include a bulging fontanelle, neck stiffness and lying with an arched back. The characteristic rash that is often mentioned in connection with the glass test (see **meningococcal septicaemia**) is present only if the infection is also in the bloodstream. This means that children with meningitis don't necessarily have the rash, so you shouldn't delay in getting help for your child just because she doesn't have one.

Diagnosis is usually confirmed with a lumbar puncture – when the doctor removes some fluid from the spine with a fine needle placed between two spinal bones in the lower back. Prompt treatment with antibiotics can reduce the risk of complications. The most common one is hearing loss, which is why all babies and children are given a hearing test some time after treatment. More serious complications include brain abcesses and stroke, which can be fatal, so it's vital to seek urgent help if you are concerned.

Meningococcal septicaemia: Blood poisoning caused by the same bacteria that can cause **meningitis**. Septicaemia needs urgent treatment as it can develop into a very serious condition within hours. The main symptoms are fever, drowsiness, cold hands and feet, breathlessness, pain in the muscles and a spreading, purple, blotchy rash that doesn't fade under pressure. Check this with the glass test – press the side of a clear drinking glass against the skin. If the rash doesn't lose colour or fade, it could be meningococcal septicaemia, and you should get help immediately. Early symptoms, such as fever and **vomiting**, may be similar to a cold or flu, especially as the rash may not appear immediately. If you are concerned, whether the rash has appeared or not, you should seek immediate advice from your doctor, or take your baby to the nearest casualty unit. Meningococcal septicaemia can kill very quickly or result in amputations, but the earlier it's picked up, the better the chances of recovery. For more information, see www.meningitis.org.

Milk spots (milia): Very common, harmless rash of tiny white or yellow cysts on the face and neck, which may appear in the first few weeks, and usually clear up by about six weeks. They are caused by secretions of the skin glands.

Mumps: Contagious viral infection that causes fever, lethargy and infection of the parotid salivary glands, found just below and in front of the ears. Usually, one side of the face is swollen initially and both sides are affected after a few days. The swelling is uncomfortable and children may complain of earache or painful chewing and swallowing. The illness is generally mild and requires no treatment, although possible complications include hearing loss, viral meningitis, pancreatitis and (in older boys) inflamed testicles. Like **measles**, mumps has become rare in this country because of the routine MMR jab, but is on the increase once more.

N

Nappy rash: Very common irritation of the skin on a baby's bottom and/or genital area, usually resulting from prolonged contact with urine and/or poo. The ammonia generated by excreta causes the soreness and pink or red spots or blotches. Nappy rash can also be caused by a fungal infection, such as thrush, which can develop in warm, damp conditions. Most nappy rashes are mild and clear up with the aid of an over-the-counter healing cream. You should change your baby's nappy more frequently than normal, take extra care in keeping the area clean and dry and let the air get to it when possible. A nappy rash that refuses to clear up may possibly be a fungal infection, for which you'll need to see your GP. Other complications include the development of a bacterial infection in the region, which can become especially inflamed and sore. This may cause a fever and treatment with antibiotics may be required. Occasionally, nappy rash may be caused or exacerbated by an underlying skin condition, such as **eczema, cradle cap (seborrhoeic dermatitis)** or **contact dermatitis**. For more on nappy rash and how to deal with it, see p. 93.

O

Oral thrush (oral candidiasis): Fungal infection that causes sore, white, curd-like patches inside a baby's mouth or on the tongue, which can make feeding difficult and painful. Oral thrush occurs when levels of a naturally occurring fungus in the body become too high – probably because babies' immune systems are immature, and sometimes as a consequence of taking antibiotics, which reduce the healthy bacteria in the mouth. If you're breastfeeding, the infection can be passed from you to your baby, or from your baby to you, which may cause your nipples to become sore and itchy. It may clear up on its own, or your GP may prescribe treatment in the form of anti-fungal medication – for both of you, if necessary. Careful cleaning and sterilising of dummies and bottle teats, and keeping your nipples clean and dry can help to prevent the thrush occurring or recurring.

P

Phenylketonuria (PKU): Rare genetic disorder, one of the conditions tested for in the **Guthrie or heel-prick test**, carried out soon after birth. It causes a build-up of phenylalanine, a natural substance found in protein, which if left untreated can lead to problems with brain development and learning difficulties. Early detection greatly reduces the risk of long-term complications.

Pneumonia: Infection of the lungs caused by either a virus (most commonly) or bacteria. Symptoms include **fever**, a cough, lethargy, breathlessness and production of phlegm (thick mucus) from the throat. Sometimes infants and children also suffer from abdominal pain if the infection is at the base of the lungs. A doctor may detect signs of pneumonia by listening to your child's chest and consequently may request an x-ray or hospital examination.

If it's caught early and treated with oral antibiotics, most children recover without having to go to hospital. However, a baby or child with pneumonia might need to do so if she's vomiting, is breathless and needs oxygen, or if the fever persists despite being dosed with antibiotics for several days. Recurrent bouts of pneumonia may indicate an underlying problem.

Polio: Life-threatening virus that attacks the nervous system and can cause paralysis or death. Polio has been virtually eradicated in this country, thanks to vaccination. It is one of the diseases that UK children are offered protection against with routine vaccinations given at two, three and four months old (as well as a bit later in childhood, and during their teens). For more on **immunisations,** see p. 58.

Positional plagiocephaly: The most common cause of skull asymmetry in young babies, usually affecting the back of the head on one side. It's caused by pressure on the growing skull, resulting in the abnormal moulding and flattening of one side. Positional plagiocephaly has become more common in recent years, since the launch of the 'Back to Sleep' campaign – which recommends babies sleep on their backs to reduce the risk of sudden infant death syndrome (SIDS) – and also because babies tend to spend a lot of time in car seats these days. Once one side becomes flatter, the head will always tend to fall to that side when the baby sleeps, exacerbating the problem. It usually improves as the child grows and develops, and spends more time upright.

Simple measures you can take to combat it include encouraging supervised 'tummy time' from an early age, placing toys on the side of the cot to encourage your baby to turn her head away from the flattened side, and limiting the time she spends in a car seat. Doctors stress that no pain or discomfort is caused, and as most cases correct themselves with time, they generally advise against treatments that are available privately. These are controversial, involving the baby wearing a corrective helmet or head band for at least 23 hours a day, which can cause pressure sores and skin irritation.

Rarely the flattening can be caused by premature ageing of growth lines in the skull. Your GP may refer you to a specialist paediatrician who can arrange an x-ray.

Posseting: Harmless regurgitation of milk feeds, experienced by virtually all babies to some extent during the first year. Severe or repeated regurgitation after feeds may be caused by **gastro-oesophageal reflux** or **pyloric stenosis.**

Postnatal depression (PND): Form of depression that strikes after giving birth, thought to be triggered by a combination of factors including stress, exhaustion and changing hormones. Symptoms include anxiety, irritability, tearfulness and an inability to bond with your baby. Levels of severity vary and, if serious, counselling or antidepressants may be prescribed, while rest and support are vital in all cases. For more information, see p. 81.

Post-partum thyroiditis (silent thyroidism): Inflammation of the mother's thyroid gland, which is located in the neck and produces thyroid, a hormone that helps to regulate the body's metabolism and growth. Thyroiditis develops soon after giving birth and usually ceases within six months. Symptoms include a swollen and tender neck, palpitations, anxiety, loss of weight, fatigue and depression, which is why it is sometimes wrongly diagnosed as PND. However, it can be tested for and successfully treated.

Pyloric stenosis: Condition that causes a blockage in babies' stomachs, leading to vomiting, which may be projectile (very forceful), and eventually dehydration, weight loss and lethargy. It's caused by the enlargement of the pylorus, the muscle that controls the opening where food leaves the stomach to enter the small bowel, and usually develops when a baby is four to six weeks old. It's more common in boys, and if there is a family history of the condition. Diagnosis is either by examination or by ultrasound scan. Treatment is to stop oral feeds and give fluids by a drip into the blood, followed by surgery. Babies recover very quickly and usually go home after three days. They will rarely have problems in later life.

R

Reflux: See **Gastro-oesophageal reflux.**

Ringworm: Common fungal condition that affects children and adults of all ages, leaving an itchy, red, ring-like rash on the body or scalp. It's passed on by contact with either an infected person, animal or object. It can be cleared up with an anti-fungal treatment prescribed by a GP.

Roseola infantum: Viral infection, common in babies over six months, that results in a rash and high temperature. Caused by a strain of the herpes virus, it's spread by close contact with other children. Symptoms include a fever, sometimes accompanied by cold symptoms, diarrhoea and irritability. Then, once the fever's subsided, a rash of tiny pink spots appears on the face and trunk, spreads to the legs and disappears after a few days. Occasionally, the high temperature can lead to febrile convulsions. As roseola is viral there's no specific treatment, but appropriate measures for bringing down a fever can help.

Rotavirus: Highly contagious virus that infects the small intestine and is the main cause of gastroenteritis. Usually, a child will start to vomit and then develop diarrhoea, which can vary in severity – in some cases it lasts for a few days, in others for over a week, leading to dehydration and hospital admission.

Rubella (German measles): A very infectious viral illness, which is passed on through droplets in the air. Symptoms include a fever, a pink-red rash and swollen lymph glands. This is one of the three diseases protected against by the MMR vaccine (see Measles and Mumps), which is offered to babies routinely at 13 months. Nearly half of the children who contract rubella have no symptoms, and the other half are rarely very unwell. The reason immunisation is available is that if a woman contracts the infection for the first time during the first three months of pregnancy, there's a very high likelihood her baby will suffer birth defects. By immunising everyone and reducing its incidence in children, the risk to vulnerable pregnant women falls considerably.

S
Seborrhoeic dermatitis: See Cradle cap.

Sickle-cell disorder: An incurable genetic disease in which red blood cells change their shape and cause blockages in small blood vessels. Both parents must be carriers. Sickle-cell disorder is checked for during the routine Guthrie or heel prick test. It's most common in people of African and Caribbean descent, but also occurs in people from the Middle East and parts of India.

Slapped cheek disease/syndrome (fifth disease): A contagious infection that's caused by the parvovirus B19 virus. It's most common in school-aged children but can occasionally affect babies. Symptoms are red cheeks and a rash on the body and limbs as well as a fever and other cold or flu-like symptoms. Since it's viral in origin, there's no treatment, although you can offer antipyretics to bring down temperature and ease symptoms. The rash may come and go with temperature or exposure to sunlight, and this can go on for weeks. Women in the first 20 weeks of pregnancy should avoid contact with the infection, as there is a slightly increased risk of miscarriage if they catch it. It can also cause severe anaemia in people with weakened immune systems, or those who suffer from certain blood abnormalities such as sickle cell disease.

Sticky eye: A discharge of crusty pus that occurs when the tear ducts are blocked. It's common in very young babies, and often mistaken for conjunctivitis. The discharge can be gently removed with cooled boiled water and cotton wool (always use a clean piece for each wipe). If the white of the eye or surrounding skin show any redness, you should see your GP as this could indicate it's infected.

Sucking blisters (nursing blisters): Painless blisters that form on a baby's lips in the early days or weeks of breastfeeding. They're a harmless sign that your baby is feeding well, and they will soon fade.

Sunburn: The damaging effect of overexposure to the harmful ultraviolet (UV) rays of the sun. Sunburn can be very dangerous because it increases your baby's chances of developing skin cancers later in life. Children are more vulnerable to sunburn than adults because their skin is more delicate, and those with fair skin and fair or red hair are most at risk. Symptoms of sunburn include red, sore skin that's hot to the touch, blistering and fever. Avoidance is the best policy – babies are best kept out of direct sunlight altogether, particularly during the hottest part of the day between noon and 4p.m. If she's outside, keep her under shade and make sure she's wearing clothes that cover her totally, and a wide-brimmed hat. Always apply an appropriate high-factor (at least 20) sunscreen, and reapply frequently, especially after swimming. Even then, you should still keep exposure times to a minimum. If your baby is in her buggy, make sure she is comprehensively sheltered by a parasol or sunshade.

If your baby does suffer from sunburn, you should move her into the shade or a cool room as soon as possible, and cool the overheated skin by sponging with cold water or soaking the affected area in a tepid bath for ten minutes. Give her lots of fluids (breast milk alone if she is breastfed, or formula milk with extra cooled boiled water) and apply a suitable soothing cream, such as calamine lotion or aloe vera. Too much sun may also result in heatstroke, which can cause nausea and **vomiting**, a raised temperature, confusion and dizziness. If your baby has severe sunburn, or seems to be suffering from heatstroke, you should consult a GP.

Swollen glands: Usually the result of a viral infection, such as sore throat or **tonsillitis**. The lymph glands (lymph nodes) are found under the skin in the neck, behind the ear and in the groin. The swelling occurs because the glands are doing their job in fighting the infection, and they can remain swollen for some time once the infection has cleared. In very rare cases, swollen glands may be due to more severe infection or to a serious illness, such as **Kawasaki disease**, and cancer, so you should seek your GP's advice if you are worried, particularly if there are other symptoms, such as lethargy, rash and weight loss.

T

Talipes: Birth abnormality in which one or both of a baby's feet twist inwards. It's thought to affect one in a thousand babies. The full medical name is congenital talipes equinovarus, or CTEV, and it's sometimes known as **club foot**. The most common type is positional, which occurs when the foot is squashed as the baby grows inside the womb. Moving the foot regularly can help ease the problem and it corrects itself as the baby grows. The other form, structural talipes, is more complex and may be caused by genetic factors. Various corrective treatments, including the use of splints – devices that are closely fixed to the foot which can help to reposition it - and surgery, can be carried out, and are usually started a few weeks after birth.

Teething: Process during which a baby's first set of teeth cut through the gums. It can begin any time during the first year, but most commonly starts at around six months. A tooth coming through can cause varying levels of pain and discomfort, and a number of other symptoms are linked to teething, including fever, red and swollen cheeks, excessive dribbling, **diarrhoea** and **nappy rash**. It's important not to put a fever down to teething if other problems are present, and to seek advice. For more information about teething, see p. 113.

Tetanus: A life-threatening disease that affects the nervous system. Tetanus is caused by bacteria that live in spores found in soil and animal poo. It's one of the diseases that UK children are offered protection against with routine vaccinations given at two, three and four months old. For more information on **immunisations**, see p. 58.

Thrombosis (venous): A condition that affects one or two women in every thousand during pregnancy or in the immediate weeks after birth. It's also known as a blood clot, and a specific form of it is **deep vein thrombosis**, or DVT. Symptoms include pain, swelling, tenderness and discolouration in the leg. Serious complications can occur if part of the clot breaks away and travels through the bloodstream (this is known as an embolus, and is particularly dangerous if it reaches the lung – pulmonary embolism – which if left can be fatal) so if you suspect you're suffering from this condition, you should see your GP, who may refer you for diagnostic tests. There are a number of drugs that can help, and you may be advised to wear compression stockings and to keep your legs raised as much as possible.

Thrush: See **Oral thrush**.

Tongue tie (ankyloglossia): Restriction of movement in the tongue due to its being anchored down by a short frenulum (the piece of skin that joins the tongue to the floor of the mouth). It doesn't usually require treatment but in cases where it is preventing a baby from breastfeeding successfully, your doctor or health visitor may recommend it is corrected with a simple surgical procedure, a frenulotomy. In some cases, a tongue-tie will be torn naturally as a baby gets older and begins to put things in her mouth.

Tonsillitis: Infection of the tonsils, the small glands found at the back of the throat behind the tongue, causing a sore throat, fever, swollen glands and difficulty in swallowing. In most cases, it's caused by a virus so doesn't respond to antibiotics, but **antipyretics** will help to ease the discomfort. If symptoms persist, or a temperature doesn't settle after two or three days, it's worth seeing your GP in case the cause is bacterial and can be cleared up with antibiotics.

Tuberculosis: See BCG.

U

Umbilical granuloma: A red, unhealed belly button due to the umbilical cord stump taking longer than it should to drop off and preventing tissue overgrowth. Usually, the umbilical cord dries and is separated by eight days in most infants, with the belly button healing in 12 to 15 days. An umbilical granuloma occurs when there is a delay in this process. If left, a persistent discharge can develop. In some cases, it goes away by itself, but can take time. The granuloma can be treated simply at home by applying a little cooking salt to the area, covering with clean gauze, and holding it in place for 10-30 minutes; then cleaning the site with warm water and repeating twice a day for three days. Always ask your health visitor for advice before attempting this treatment, though. Or the area can be cauterised by your GP with a chemical compound called silver nitrate. Infection is a possibility, especially if the surrounding skin looks red and angry, so it's important to keep a close eye on it and consult a health professional if you're worried.

Umbilical hernia: A common type of hernia in babies (one in six are believed to be affected). It occurs when the umbilical cord leaves a weak spot where it passes through the baby's abdominal wall during pregnancy, allowing part of the intestine or tissue to push through. The result is a lump or protrusion by the navel. Around 90 per cent of umbilical hernias heal on their own by the time a child is three or four years old, which is why doctors advise waiting until then before referring a child for routine hernia repair surgery.

Undescended testicle(s): A condition where one or both of a baby boy's testicles do not drop down into the scrotum from the abdomen, which they usually do towards the end of pregnancy. A health professional will check your baby boy soon after birth to make sure both his testicles have come down, and if one (or both) has not done so, the situation will be monitored all through his first year. If it fails to descend during that time, surgery will be necessary, as if left untreated, an undescended testicle can become painfully twisted (testicular torsion) and, later on, may affect fertility and increase the risk of testicular cancer developing.

V

Vitamin K deficiency bleeding (VKDB): Rare condition that strikes babies born with insufficient vitamin K, which plays a vital role in helping blood to clot properly. It can result in dangerous internal bleeding and, in some cases, a brain haemorrhage (haemorrhagic disease of the newborn, or HDN). Health professionals recommend that all newborn babies are given vitamin K soon after birth, either in the form of a single injection or in two or three separate doses given by mouth. Breast milk is a poor source of vitamin K so it's especially important for breastfed babies to receive these extra doses.

Vomiting: Newborn babies vomit frequently during their early weeks and months, often for quite benign reasons, such as being overfed, or after a prolonged bout of crying. Vomiting is also a symptom of many different illnesses, in particular stomach upset, such as **gastroenteritis**, and feeding difficulties, such as **gastro-oesophageal reflux** and **pyloric stenosis**.

Generally speaking, you should contact your doctor if your baby's vomiting is projectile and persistent; there is blood or bile (a green substance) in the vomit; the vomiting continues for more than 24 hours, or is accompanied by a swollen or painful abdomen. If in doubt, make a call to your GP or NHS Direct.

Vomiting puts your baby at risk of **dehydration**, particularly if it occurs with **diarrhoea** – sometimes known as D and V – so you will need to replace the fluids by offering frequent small feeds afterwards, some cooled boiled water (if formula fed – she won't need extra water if she is breastfed), or a dose of an oral rehydration solution.

W

Wheezing: High-pitched whistling noise made while breathing. It occurs when the small airways in the lungs become constricted due to infection, inflammation caused by asthma or an allergy, or because your baby has swallowed something that's lodged in her lungs. Treatment depends on how serious it is. Some babies with this symptom – known as 'happy wheezers' – continue to feed normally and are not too breathless. If a wheezing baby does need treatment, it may be given via an inhaler through a spacer, as with **asthma**.

Rarely, wheezing may indicate a more serious condition such as **cystic fibrosis** or heart disease. In these cases, there would be other problems, such as weight loss or a chronic cough, which should be picked up by your health visitor, or during routine assessments by your GP.

Whooping cough (pertussis): Very contagious infection of the lining of the respiratory tract (the airway that carries air to and from the lungs). The main symptom is a hacking cough, often followed by a sharp intake of breath, which can sound like a 'whoop'. Whooping cough has been immunised against since the 1950s, and so has become rare in the UK. Babies are protected against it when they have their routine vaccinations at two, three and four months. For more information on **immunisations**, see p. 58.

First Aid

It's worth getting to grips with the basics of first aid when you become a mum, and the best way to do this is to take a course run by the British Red Cross (telephone 0844 871 8000 or vist their website at www.redcross.org.uk), St John Ambulance (telephone 08700 10 49 50 or visit their website at www.sja.org.uk) or, in Scotland, the St Andrew's Ambulance Association (0141 332 4031; www.firstaid.org.uk). (If your baby spent time in special care and had breathing problems, you may be offered some training by one of the nurses before going home, or you can ask for it.)

It's possible to bone up on the basics of first aid on your own with help from a reputable source of information – look at the first-aid pages on the Netmums website (www.netmums.com) and in *Birth to Five*, the free NHS guide to caring for your baby. If your health visitor hasn't given you a copy, you can access it online at www.dh.gov.uk. However, techniques such as resuscitation can cause internal damage if carried out incorrectly – which is why a course run by a trained tutor is your best bet. *If in any doubt during an emergency, dial 999 and wait for an ambulance to arrive.*

First-aid basics

Bleeding: To stop severe bleeding, press firmly on the wound (first checking to make sure nothing is embedded in it) using a pad of clean cloth, such as a tea towel or pillow case. If the wound is on an arm or leg, raise the injured limb. Then seek help from your GP or at the nearest casualty department.

Burns: If your baby is burned – the most common cause in babies under one is a spilled hot drink – cool the affected area as quickly as possible by placing it under cold slowly running water for at least ten minutes. Remove tight clothing before any swelling begins, but do not attempt to remove any material that may be sticking to the burn. Cover the injury using clean, non-fluffy material to help prevent the wound becoming infected and reduce the pain – a clean plastic bag is good for burns to the hand, while kitchen film is best for arms and legs. Never apply butter or margarine to a burn or scald, or any other substance, such as lotion or ointment. If blisters appear, don't be tempted to pop them because this will increase the risk of infection and delay the healing process.

Once the burn is cooled and covered, **seek medical advice or dial 999.** Bear in mind that burns and scalds to the mouth or throat can be potentially life-threatening because a swelling in this area can affect a child's breathing – always call an ambulance immediately.

Choking: In most cases of choking, whatever is causing an obstruction in your baby's airwaves will become dislodged as she coughs and there will be no need for intervention – if your baby is coughing, allow her to do so, as it's the most effective way to clear an obstruction. (An effective cough is one where your child is able to speak or cry and take in a breath between coughs.) However, if the object's not budging and your baby is unable to cry or take a proper breath, you'll need to act. Check for any obvious obstruction first, and remove it only if it's easy to get at – don't probe blindly in the mouth because you may push it further in. Never be tempted to hold your baby upside down and shake her to remove a blockage – this could do more harm than good. Dial 999 before you do anything, but don't leave your child alone. While waiting for help, you should start the basic life-support manoeuvres that are appropriate for a choking infant aged under one. *The following instructions give a basic guide, but proper training is still your best bet.*

Sit down and lay your baby face down, along your forearm, with her head low, and your hand supporting her jaw in such a way as to keep her mouth open so that the object can drop out. Position the heel of your other hand between the shoulder blades and give five, firm slaps or blows against the back. If the obstruction has not cleared, turn your baby over, lay her along your thigh, still in a head down position. Then give five chest thrusts: place two fingers just below the nipple line (imagine a line stretching across the chest linking the nipples) in the centre of her chest, and give five sharp downward thrusts on the middle chest bone. Repeat the cycle three times, checking the mouth quickly after each one. (Chest thrusts can be tricky if you have not had training for this technique. If in doubt, continue instead with back blows until help arrives. Stop if the object becomes dislodged and your baby begins to cough, and encourage her to do so.)

If your baby loses consciousness during this process, you should stop the slaps and, if trained to do so, start giving mouth-to-mouth resuscitation. If your baby loses consciousness and you are not trained in or confident about performing resuscitation techniques, you should wait for help to arrive.

Foreign object: If your baby has something lodged firmly in her nose or ear, don't attempt to remove it yourself or you risk pushing it further in. Take her to your nearest casualty department.

Head injuries: To treat small bumps and bruises on a baby's head, apply ice or a packet of frozen vegetables, wrapped in a tea towel, directly to the injury site. Seek medical advice if your baby has suffered any significant head injury, especially if she has been knocked unconscious, even briefly. You should take your baby straight to the nearest casualty unit if she's had a knock on the head and has vomited more then twice, seems drowsy, has a large swelling on her head, or if the fall was a significant one, for example, down the stairs or from out of her car seat.

Poisons: If your baby swallows a potentially dangerous substance, such as a medicine or a household chemical, dial 999 or get her to your nearest casualty unit as soon as possible – and try to take a container of whatever she's swallowed with you to show the doctors. If she seems in pain or there is any staining, soreness or blistering around the mouth, wipe away any excess substance from the skin, and give her sips of water or milk to drink. Do NOT attempt to make her vomit: this may cause her to aspirate, in other words, the substance may be drawn into her lungs, where it could prove even more harmful.

Appendix 2: Useful Addresses

Baby activities

Busy Little Ones
Online directory of baby activities available around the UK, including swimming,
yoga, signing and many others.
Web: www.busylittleones.co.uk

Baby massage

International Association of Infant Massage
Tel: 02089 899597
Web: www.iaim.org.uk

Baby signing

Baby Signers
Web: www.babysigners.co.uk

Sing and Sign
Web: www.singandsign.com

Tiny Talk
Web: www.tinytalk.co.uk

Bodies after birth

Association of Chartered Physiotherapists in Women's Health
Web: www.acpwh.org.uk

Guild of Pregnancy and Postnatal Exercise Instructors
Web: www.postnatalexercise.co.uk

Pushy Mothers
Postnatal fitness classes based on a 'buggy workout', which you can take your baby along to.
Web: www.pushymothers.com

Breastfeeding

Association of Breastfeeding Mothers
Tel (counselling helpline): 08444 122 949
Web: www.abm.me.uk

The Baby Café
Charitable trust that runs a network of local drop-in centres for breastfeeding mums.
Address: The Baby Café Charitable Trust, PO Box 640, Haywards Heath, RH17 5WS
Web: www.thebabycafe.co.uk

Breastfeeding Network
Tel (supporter line): 0844 412 4664
Web: www.breastfeedingnetwork.org.uk

Breastfeeding NHS
Tel (national breastfeeding helpline): 0844 20 909 20
Web: www.breastfeeding.nhs.uk

La Leche League
Tel (helpline): 0845 120 2918
Web: www.laleche.org.uk

Midwives online
Provides a free breastfeeding email advisory and information service.
Web: www.midwivesonline.com

National Childbirth Trust
Tel (breastfeeding helpline): 0300 33 00 771
Web: www.nct.org.uk

Colic and crying

Cry-sis
Support for families with excessively crying, sleepless and demanding babies.
Tel (helpline): 08451 228 669
Web: www.cry-sis.org.uk

First shoes

Children's Foot Health Register
Web: www.shoe-shop.org.uk

General advice and support for new mums

Bliss
UK charity offering support and advice for parents of premature babies.
Tel (free support helpline): 0500 618 140
Web: www.bliss.org.uk

Healthvisitors.com
An organisation offering information for parents of children aged 0–5, compiled
by health visitors.
Tel: 01274 427132
Web: www.healthvisitors.com

Healthy Start
Government scheme providing needy families with vouchers for free milk fruit & veg, formula feed and vitamin supplements.
Web: www.healthystart.nhs.uk

Home-Start
Nationwide charity that offers practical support and friendship to families in need through a network of parent volunteers. All volunteers have at least one child under five.
Tel (free information line): 0800 068 6368
Web: www.home-start.org.uk

National Childbirth Trust (NCT)
Offers support, advice and friendship during pregnancy, childbirth and early parenthood. Valley cushions (inflatable cushions which offer relief when sitting if you are sore after birth) and breast pumps for hire.
Tel (enquiry line): 0300 33 00 770
Web: www.nct.org.uk

Netmums
The largest parenting website in the UK, offering advice and support, information, online forums and local meet-up groups throughout the country.
Web: www.netmums.com

NHS Direct
Medical advice from qualified staff available over the telephone. NHS Direct serves England and Wales.
Tel: 0845 4647

NHS 24
Medical advice from qualified staff available over the telephone. Serves Scotland.
Tel: 08454 242424

Parentline Plus
Registered charity, offering support to anyone parenting a child.
Tel (free helpline): 0808 800 2222
Web: www.parentlineplus.org.uk

Sure Start
The government's programme aimed at supporting parents and helping
children. Information on childcare, education and health issues.
Tel (public enquiry unit): 0870 000 2288
Web: www.surestart.gov.uk

Going back to work

Care Commission
Regulates care services in Scotland.
Web: www.carecommission.com

Care and Social Services Inspectorate Wales (CSSIW)
Web: www.cssiw.org.uk

Children's Information Service
Local information on childcare provision, including links to your local
authority's children's information services.
Web: www.childrensinformationservice.org

Citizens Advice
Charity that aims to offer free advice on legal, financial and other matters,
through a network of local Citizens Advice Bureau. Advice, and details of
your local bureau, available online.
Web: www.citizensadvice.org.uk

Criminal Records Bureau
Web: www.crb.gov.uk

Daycare Trust
Charity working to promote high-quality, affordable childcare.
Tel (information line): 0845 872 6251
Web: www.daycaretrust.org.uk

Department of Education Northern Ireland (DENI)
Regulates pre-school institutions and all aspects of education in Northern
Ireland.
Web: www.deni.gov.uk

The National Childminding Association of England and Wales (NCMA)
Tel: 0800 169 4486
Web: www.ncma.org.uk

National Day Nurseries Association
Web: www.ndna.org.uk

Ofsted
Inspectors from the Office for Standards in Education, Children's Services and
Skills regularly visit nurseries, childminders and schools. Their latest reports
can be found online.
Web: www.ofsted.gov.uk

National firm of Russell Jones & Walker
Solicitors specialising in employment law. Their free online service allows
you to get an opinion on your case from an employment lawyer.
Web: www.rjw.co.uk

Working Families
Organisation offering advice and information on all aspects of working
families' lives, including tax credits, childcare and legal rights.
Tel (helpline): 0800 013 0313
Web: www.workingfamilies.org.uk

Multiple births

Karen Gromada
US expert on looking after and breastfeeding twins, or more. Her website is a good source of information.
Web: www.karengromada.com

The Multiple Births Foundation
Tel: 0208 383 3519
Web: www.multiplebirths.org.uk

Twins and Multiple Births Association (TAMBA)
Tel (freephone twinline 10a.m. to 1p.m. and 7p.m. to 10p.m.): 0800 138 0509; out of Twinline hours: 0870 770 3305.
Web: www.tamba.org.uk

Twins UK
Organisation offering information and support for families with twins, triplets or more.
Tel: 01670 856996
Web: www.twinsuk.co.uk

Postnatal depression

Association for Postnatal Illness (APNI)
Telephone helpline and information for sufferers and healthcare professionals as well as a network of volunteer supporters who have themselves experienced postnatal illness.
Tel (helpline): 020 7386 0868
Web: http://apni.org

Perinatal Illness UK
Charity offering support to anyone suffering from emotional or psychological difficulties during pregnancy or after birth.
Tel: 07925 144411
Web: www.pni-uk.com

Registering your baby's birth

General Register Office
By law, your baby's birth must be registered within 42 days (21 days in Scotland). This can often be done at the hospital, before you go home, or otherwise you will have to visit the local Register Office.
Web: www.gro.gov.uk; www.gro-scotland.gov.uk; www.groni.gov.uk

Relationships

The Parent Connection
Excellent website offering relationship advice to parents.
Web: www.theparentconnection.org.uk

Relate
Relationship advice and counselling, sex therapy, workshops, mediation, consultations and support offered face-to-face, by telephone and through the web.
Tel: 0300 100 1234
Web: http://relate.org.uk

Safe sleeping

Foundation for the Study of Infant Deaths (FSID)
Charity working to prevent cot death. The FSID offers safe sleeping advice and supports bereaved parents. Baby room thermometers are available through their website, at a cost of £2.75.
Tel (helpline): 020 7233 2090
Web: www.fsid.org.uk

Safety

Child Accident Prevention Trust (CAPT)
Tel (safety advice and information line): 020 7608 7364
Web: www.capt.org.uk

Royal Society for the Prevention of Accidents (RoSPA)
Tel: 0121 248 2000
Web: www.rospa.com

Talking to your baby

Talk to Your Baby
Campaign, run by the National Literacy Trust, which aims to encourage chat between parents and their little ones. Lots of information online.
Web: www.literacytrust.org.uk/talktoyourbaby

Weaning

Allergy UK
Support and information for people with allergies and intolerances.
Tel (helpline): 01322 619898
Web: www.allergyuk.org

Baby Led Weaning
Site devoted to providing information and ideas about baby-led weaning.
Web: www.babyledweaning.com

British Dietetic Association (BDA)
Professional association for registered dietitians in the UK. Its website is a useful source of information about weaning and other dietary matters.
Web: www.bda.uk.com

Food Standards Agency
Government organisation offering information about all aspects of food and eating, including weaning and children's nutrition.
Web: www.food.gov.uk

Kids' Allergies
Lots of useful information and advice about children and allergies.
Web: www.kidsallergies.co.uk

Appendix 3: Further Reading

Bodies after Birth

The Complete Guide to Postnatal Fitness, Judy DiFiore (A&C Black, 2003)

General

Birth to Five, published by the NHS, offers a handy basic guide for first-time parents and is available free. If you're not given a copy, ask your midwife or health visitor. It's also available online at www.dh.gov.uk. In Scotland, NHS Health Scotland produces *Ready Steady Baby!*, free to first-time parents. Again, if you're not given a copy ask your midwife or health visitor, or check the website, www.readysteadybaby.org.uk

Weaning

Feeding your baby, Judy More (Teach Yourself, 2007)

What your baby needs

What to Buy for Your Baby, Liat Hughes Joshi and Caroline Cosgrove (White Ladder Press, 2008)

Appendix 4:
Memories and Milestones

Index

You can buy any of these other titles in the **netmums** series from your bookshop or direct from the publisher.

FREE P&P AND UK DELIVERY
(Overseas and Ireland £3.50 per book)

FEEDING KIDS   *Netmums with Judith Wills*   £14.99

Feeding Kids includes 120 easy-to-prepare and delicious recipes provided by Netmums members that will fit perfectly into your busy family life.

HOW TO BE A HAPPY MUM   £12.99
Netmums with Siobhan Freegard

How to be a Happy Mum identifies the top ten stresses mothers have to cope with and offers sound advice on how to overcome them from other mothers who have been there, done it and lived to tell the tale.

TODDLING TO TEN   *Netmums with Hollie Smith*   £12.99

Toddling to Ten looks at fifty of the most common parenting problems – from ditching the dummy to beating bullying – and offers expert advice to help you combat them along with the personal stories from the Netmums themselves.

YOUR PREGNANCY   *Netmums with Hilary Pereira*   £12.99

Your Pregnancy is an invaluable source of mum-to-mum insights and practical know-how from Netmums members, which will make you feel as though you have your very own antenatal group in the comfort of your home.

To order, simply call 01235 400 414
visit our website: www.headline.co.uk
or email orders@bookpoint.co.uk

Prices and availability are subject to change without notice.

To become part of the Netmums community, log on to www.netmums.com.

netmums